The Seven Commandments
of the
Sacred Buffalo Calf Woman

The Biography of Martin High Bear (1919-1995)
Lakota Medicine Man and Spiritual Leader

Edited by R. High Bear, W. Two Feathers and K. Wilson

Published by:
Trine Day LLC
PO Box 577
Walterville, OR 97489
1-800-556-2012
www.TrineDay.com
trineday@icloud.com

Library of Congress Control Number: 2023952280

High Bear, Rose.
The Seven Commandments of the Sacred Buffalo Calf Woman—1st ed.
p. cm.

Epub (ISBN-13) 978-1-63424-461-9
Print (ISBN-13) 978-1-63424-460-2
1. Martin High Bear (1919-1995) 2. Native American Prophecies. 3. Indians of North America Rites and ceremonies. 4. Vision quests North America 5. Shamans. 6. Sun dance. 7. HISTORY/Native American. I. High Bear, Rose. II. Title

First Edition
10 9 8 7 6 5 4 3 2 1

Distribution to the Trade by:
Independent Publishers Group (IPG)
814 North Franklin Street
Chicago, Illinois 60610
312.337.0747
www.ipgbook.com

This biography is dedicated to the
Generations of family, extended family
and future generations of the
Lakȟóta Medicine Man and Spiritual Leader
Martin High Bear (1919-1995).
This acknowledgement includes the circles of ťhakȟólaku (friends)
who loved and respected him throughout his
decades of selfless service
to his worldwide community and all the colors of mankind.

CONTENTS

MARTIN
HIGH BEAR

C. Gray
5-13

To Ron,
Blessings for all your service
& support C. Gray 7-13

B/W portrait of Martin High Bear by artist Carolyn Gray.

ACKNOWLEDGEMENTS

The Martin High Bear biography would not be possible without the assistance and support of dozens of family and friends willing to share their personal reminiscences. For Martin's vision to be completed, the support of family, friends, and interpreters was essential.

Words cannot express our heartfelt gratitude and appreciation toward many generous family members and individuals, including Melda and Melvin Garreaux and extended family, Clifford, Eddie and Leonard High Bear and families, Rufus Charger, Harry Charger, Faye Long Break Dupree, Joe Flying Bye, Jerry Flute, Ed Red Owl, Jake Thompson, LaVera Rose, Helmina Makes Him First, Judy Trejo, Dean Barlese, Keith Pasche, Charles and Hazel Fast Horse, Leonard and Darlene Renville Pipeboy, Durwin White Lightning, Michael and Wohpe Two Feathers, Dr. Alfred Bird Bear Obes, Bobby LaBatte, Gordon Byrd, Eddie Crow, Katie Stirbeck, Dr. Jared Zeff, Clem Wilkes, Yuwach Gleisner, Jan Meyer, Chuck Benson, Linda Quinones, Lynn Page, Dawn Lowe, and Katherine K'iya Wilson.

In 1996 and 2000, the National Museum of Natural History Department of Anthropology awarded Community Fellowships to Rose. She conducted research at the Smithsonian Institution's National Museum of Natural History under guidance of Joallyn Archambault, PhD., Director of the American Indian program. She also completed research at the National Archives in Washington D.C. Anthropologist Ray DeMallie, PhD provided valuable guidance, while Kiowa author N. Scott Momaday provided encouragement.

It was essential to increase awareness and understanding of wisdom and perspectives of elders and peers from Martin's community at Cheyenne River Sioux Reservation and Standing Rock Indian Reservation. Numerous trips were made between 1996 and

2006 so oral histories and personal reminiscences could be recorded of dozens of individuals from the Northern Great Plains and beyond. Forty video recordings of Lakȟóta/Dakhóta/Nakȟóta Elders
were completed in 1998 and 1999. Partnerships with Cheyenne
River Elderly Protection Team, United Tribes Technical College,
CATV (Community Access Television of Bismarck/Mandan), and
Sitting Bull College to conduct these oral histories. Partial funding
was provided by the South Dakota Arts and Humanities Councils
and the North Dakota Humanities Council.

Standing Rock Sioux Tribe Elders included: Zona Loans Arrow,
Ada Red Horse, Agatha Fool Bear, Agatha Holy Bull, Emma Lam-
bert, Arlene Reddoor Benson, Evangeline Fast Horse, Felix Kidder,
Rose Goodleft, George Iron Shield, Helmina and Blanche Makes
Him First, Henry Lawrence, Joe Flying Bye, Leona Ryan, Lillian
Martinez, Madeline Little Eagle, Lillian Brown, Grace Jamerson,
Mary Louise Defender Wilson, Pete Looking Horse, Reginald Bird
Horse, Sybil Iron Archambault, Ben One Feather, Verna Cadotte,
and Theresa Martin.

Cheyenne River Indian Reservation Elders included: Leroy
Curley, Lorraine Leblanc, Reuben Ward, Keith Jewett, Florence
Arpan, Marcella Ryan Lebeau, Shirley Keith, Silvan Chuck Brown
Robe, Cecelia Frasier, Charles Fast Horse, Clementine Day, Dora
Bruguier, Dora Bruguier, Betty Crow, Dorothy Clark, Ione Lee,
Marie Elkhead Fiddler, Leonard Fiddler, Shirley Fiddler, Eddie
DuPris, Iyonne Garreau, Elsie Slides Off, and Ellen In The Woods.

We especially acknowledge two gifted photographers, Joe
Cantrell (Cherokee) and Keri Pickett who generously contributed
photographs of Martin for his biography, and two artists including
German artist Hermann Haindl and American artist Carolyn Gray
for their portraits of Martin. We are grateful to other unnamed
individuals who contributed photos and art for more than thirty
years.

After 36 years of recording trips, archival research, and writing,
plus the last year of editing support by Wohpe Two Feathers and
K'iya Wilson, the biography is completed so the ancient teachings
of respect and honor, as reflected in Martin's spiritual vision, can
be gifted to a world hungry for unity and harmony.

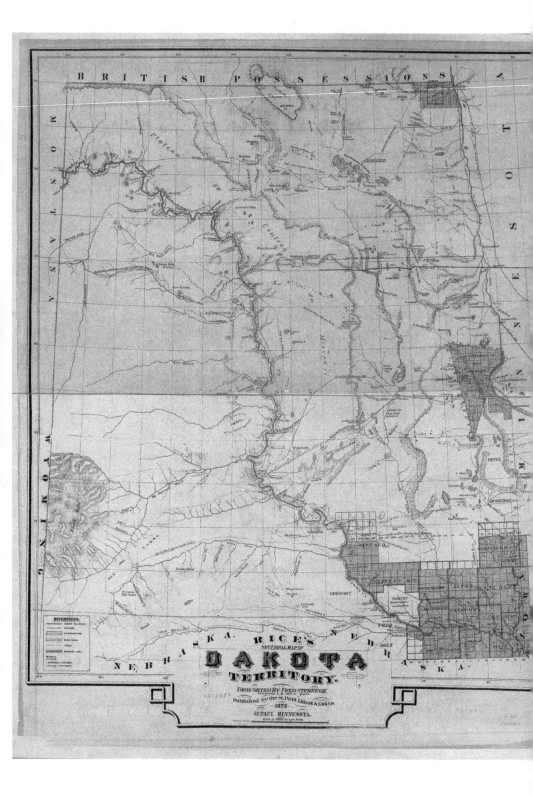

RICE'S
SECTIONAL MAP OF
DAKOTA
TERRITORY.

DRAUGHTED BY FRED STRUNEGK.

Published by the St. Paul Litho & Eng Co.
1872
ST PAUL MINNESOTA.

PREFACE

A uthor and Co-Editor Rose High Bear (Deg Hit'an Dine, Inupiaq) is Founding Director of the Native American nonprofit organization, Elderberry Wisdom Farm and Blue Elderberry Farm, LLC, located in rural Marion County, Oregon. Born in the remote subarctic Athabascan village of McGrath on Alaska's Kuskoquim River, she was separated from her biological family as a young child and raised in rural Coos County, Oregon. Following graduation from Oregon State University, Corvallis, OR, she made Portland her home where, in the 1980's she began to attend Lakȟóta ceremonies with members of the Mt. Hood Sun Dance community.

During Winter Solstice in 1987, Rose had a vision. When she sought guidance on its meaning from Lakȟóta Medicine Man and spiritual leader, Martin High Bear, he advised her to complete a Haŋbléčheya (Vision Quest ceremony). He said that if she could pray about it, she would be able to interpret and understand the meaning of the vision she had been gifted.

The next summer, Martin and his helpers put her into her Haŋbléčheya altar at Enola Hill, in the Cascade Mountain Range near Mt. Hood Sun Dance camp. Inside the altar, she prayed for three days and nights.

Her friendship with Martin eventually blossomed into a loving relationship and they exchanged marriage vows at the Mt. Hood Sun Dance camp. After the Sun Dance ceremony he headed back to South Dakota for more ceremonies. During that time, a Grandmother Spirit visited Rose, and advised her that she would be writing the story of Martin's life, stating that "...His teachings will have an impact on the peoples of the world."

When Martin returned, Rose shared the message with him. Silence filled the room as he reflected. "I don't think so..." he finally said. "It isn't the way of our people to write things down. Our way is oral tradition." He then mentioned that his nephew had purchased a video camera and was recording oral histories of Elders from his reservation in South Dakota.

She didn't regard herself as a writer so it was a relief to let it go. She'd felt sharing Lakȟóta cultural values and spiritual philosophy would require a depth of understanding she lacked. She told friends later, "There's probably a good reason why the Spirit World told me I'd be writing Martin's book. If it is meant to happen, it will happen in its own time, but it's a big obligation for someone who is not Lakȟóta or a writer." She put the Grandmother's message to the back of her mind. It took seven years before the vision of writing his biography would be mentioned again.

They were separated for a while when Rose went home to work on the Exxon Valdez Oil Spill for the State of Alaska. When Martin traveled to Anchorage the summer of 1990, he continued to mention his nephew's oral history recording work. Rose felt his hints had a deeper purpose, so she purchased a video camera and started recording him whenever he spoke to groups. They also began to record other Native Elders.

After they returned to Oregon, Martin and Rose began to plan a documentary production. By 1993, they had formed a Native American nonprofit in order to produce the documentary featuring Native American history and spiritual teachings. Martin continued to be interviewed for other publications and was also growing more comfortable with the role of book publishing for educating the public.

In the Spring of 1995, Martin's lead woman Sun Dancer, Barb Omaha, traveled to Portland from Minneapolis to attend the spring Sun Dance meeting. She mentioned recent book releases and the growing collection of biographies of Martin's peers, including Grampa Fools Crow, Noble Red Man, Archie Fire Lame Deer and Wallace Black Elk. Their biographies had been welcomed and the Elders weren't being criticized for sharing.

Barb suggested, "Uncle Martin, you should have the book of your life written too." Looking at Rose, he said: "Yes, I guess that would be okay."

Rose thought to herself, "I guess the spirits were right. It's actually going to happen." However, before she could record more of his teachings, he crossed over to the Spirit World. It would take more than three and a half decades from the time of the visitation of the ancestor until she could complete her obligation.

Martin had always emphasized in his messages that whatever Great Spirit created is never lost, that their teachings had only been forgotten, and he said it was up to today's people to restore them. He felt that if the old teachings, at risk for over a century, were restored, it would help to restore hope among his people and bring about the transformation they craved. This became an important part of his messages along with the Seven Commandments he shared.

He believed that it was the role of the Elders to demonstrate and shelter respect for Creation, generosity, commitment to help others, quietness, humility in resolving conflict, courage transcending hardship, humor, enjoyment of life, and other qualities. These traditional cultural values were reflected in the lives of Martin's ancestors and revealed in print in his great grandfather Martin Charger's biography.

Rose continued to video record oral history so she could fulfill the 1988 message from the Grandmother. In June 1999 and June 2000, forty respected Elders from the Standing Rock and Cheyenne River Reservations were video recorded and their memories preserved. They shared their memories of their "growing up" days, the importance of their traditional First Foods, and reminiscences of parents and grandparents. They especially included cultural values passed down within families from generation to generation. Messages for today's parents and children included the importance of restoring family cultural values and other teachings from their traditional roots.

The collection presented Northern Great Plains Elders as distinctive and exemplary role models for other Native Americans as well, and for people of all cultures. Throughout the recordings, Lakȟóta, Dakȟóta and Nakȟóta Elders were recognized as rapidly vanishing and irreplaceable keepers of Great Plains oral history and tradition; a society of philosophers who continued from generation to generation to probe deeply into life and preserve a balanced, harmonious and happy way of life for their descendants. The values they extolled have been entrusted orally for generations and represent an ancient legacy of knowledge that had become as endangered as the many disappearing species in today's fragile ecosystems.

The recording work that cemented the relationship between Martin and Rose continued to unfold over several decades, culminating in the release of his biography. It shares prophetic messages from Martin's vision of the Seven Teachings of the Sacred Buffalo Calf Woman, symbolizing the restoration of ancient cultural values and spiritual qualities of Martin's ancestors. It also includes decades of tributes from members of Martin's spiritual communities who learned from him as he spoke his native language. He had only completed the third grade at tribal school so his ability to express the full meaning of his teachings in the English language was limited, and his grammar was not always correct. Since the voices of his family and colleagues are included, readers will be able to recognize the deeper significance of Martin's life, his spiritual work, and his vision.

Photo of Martin's Father Paul High Bear.

Chapter 1

Martin's Lineage

In the winter of 1994, Martin introduced himself to a local church group who had invited him to speak to their congregation. In the traditional manner, he began by introducing his lineage. As a storyteller, he also shared the cultural values he had been gifted in his vision:

Well, my name is Martin High Bear. I'm a Medicine Man, spiritual advisor from Eagle Butte, South Dakota, from the Cheyenne River Reservation. I came from a line of Medicine People in my blood relations. I had a Great Grandfather, Chief High Bear. He was a chief with the Húŋkpapȟa and Sitting Bull at Standing Rock Reservation. He was a few years older than Sitting Bull.

I got this power through my great-great-grandparents. Four of my grandfathers were Medicine People, and I had some grandmothers and they, too, were Medicine Women – four grandmothers. And so this is why I was appointed to be what I am today.

My dad was to be a Medicine Man, but he didn't. So when I became a Medicine Man, I had to start from scratch. There was a generational gap from my great grandmothers and great grandfathers. But I took care of it and went up on the hill on Vision Quest, and so I kept up the tradition as a healer. Maybe later on, one of my grandchildren may pick it up from me and carry it on into the next generation. It is passed on like that.

When I was a young boy, I can't remember that part when my grandfather doctored me. I was told that he put out four little pieces of clay. Then he touched every one of them. They had a blue flame coming out of each one of them. He was praying. Then he said, 'Grandson, close your eyes. I'm not going to burn you. I'm going to doctor you. The flames are going to heal you.' He picked that flame up and put it in his mouth. He prayed to God. Then he blew and that flame came out of his mouth all over my body. Twice he done that. Then he took them flames and put them back in the clay where they came from. He made a sweeping motion and they all went out. He put them away and he said, 'My grandson is doctored.' And so that was the way they used to doctor back in the old days. In fact, I have the power that he used to have. It was given to me, so today I can heal people with fire. I use this fire in the Sweat Lodge.

Then, I had a great-great-grandfather. We say his name in our language – *Wawáphope*. It means "can't puncture me." It is his Indian name. I guess people used to shoot him and he would keep going. It was told to me about his power. One day, they had a gathering and the people wanted to know if he could still perform that. He didn't say anything. A while after that, they had a big gathering again. He said, "I came here to show the people that I still have my power." And so he got up in front; so far in front of them. The army was there so he told a group of army people who were there with rifles to shoot him.

Well, they all got up and pointed a gun at him. None of them had the nerve to pull the trigger, except just one. One soldier pulled the trigger. My grandfather kind of smiled back and pointed down. When they walked up where he was standing, the bullet was laying on the ground, flattened. It didn't go through him. And so, *Wawáphope* means *"never puncture."*

GREAT GRANDMOTHERS

My youngest great grandmother[1] works with a screech [burrowing] owl. It is a little owl that lives under Mother Earth. I don't know if any of you have been to a prairie dog town. Screech owls live with the prairie dogs.

I seen it with my own eyes when I was a young boy. She doctored my kidneys. This is one of the things that happened back in the old days. I always remember when my mother told me about it.

She was sitting on a little wooden chair that she had made. When I was lying on the floor on the blanket, she had me lay on my stomach. She untied her moccasins. She

---

1   Martin introduced his paternal great grandmother who could turn herself into a burrowing owl. They said she had a buckskin shawl that had owl feathers sewn all over it which helped her blend into her environment. She had doctored him when he was a young boy and again later in his life.

prayed with that moccasin and threw it on the floor. Here came that screech owl from that moccasin. When it landed on the ground, it turned into a screech owl and that screech owl started flying inside the room. I was lying there with my eyes looking toward my great gramma.

She told him, 'Go doctor my great grandson.'

It came down on my back and started walking all over my back, my legs and arms. It started flying and came back to her. He came up and I heard the same thing.

And as Mom tells it, "Gramma asked the screech owl, 'Are you through?'"

That screech owl started flying up in the air again and came up on top of me a second time, walked all over my back and picked where my kidneys are. She jumped up and down on each kidney, and then she came back and looked at my gramma.

She looked down at the screech owl. And my mother thought my grandmother was going to pick up that screech owl. She got within six inches of that screech owl and when she reached down, it turned back into her moccasin. She puts on her moccasin and you are healed. Maybe then she would give you a little herb or something to protect yourself.

MARTIN'S FATHER, PAUL HIGH BEAR

Martin's father, Paul High Bear, was born in Cannonball, North Dakota on the Standing Rock Indian Reservation to Barbara Brown Elk and Valentine Blue Earth.[2] Although he had no birth certificate, the date of his birth was shown as 1895, and sometimes as July 28, 1900.

Paul's parents passed away when he was very young, so he was raised by the High Bear side of the family which is why he is known as High Bear.[3]

---

2   Paul's mother, Barbara, was born 1/1/1833 and died 10/1/1916. Her father, Joseph High Bear, Sr., was born 1/01/1833 and died 10/26/1910.

3   High Bear ancestors were Iháŋkthuŋwaŋna, also known as Yanktonai (Dwellers of the End or Yankton) or Nakȟóta Oyate and Dakȟóta Oyate. The Iháŋkthuŋwaŋna homeland was in central North Dakota along the James River near today's Jamestown. They also traveled to different parts of the Great Plains of North and South Dakota as climate and food sources permitted, including parts of Nebraska, Iowa, Saskatchewan, Manitoba as well as the woodlands of Ontario, Minnesota and Wisconsin. They lived along the northern part of the Canšaša River, renamed the Dakota River and then the James River in the late 19th and early 20th century by European settlers who migrated into central North Dakota and formed the settlement of Jamestown.

Indian boys outside classroom at Ft. Yates Boarding School.

When young, Paul was in the first class held at Fort Yates Boarding School after it opened in 1900. He also attended boarding school in Bismarck, North Dakota. Paul would joke about being in the first classroom at Fort Yates. "It is all my fault," he said. "All the trouble our people got into going to school learning to speak English, learning all the White Man's ways and problems with alcohol.... I started it."

In 1976 Paul was recorded in the South Dakota Oral History Project at the University of South Dakota:

> I was born in 1900 on the Cannonball River and I had long braided hair, wore moccasins. At the time when I tend school, had a haircut. Clear back in my boyhood I went to school in Fort Yates. My grandfather says I got to know what the English language is and follow the footsteps of the White ... the White people ways. Then I went to school in Cannonball when I was eight to ten. And I walked two miles to school every day and there was no such thing as the automobile or anything at that time. The people were on wagon; in the winter, dogsled. And the nice, good people ... I used to tie my sled on the back of their sled sometimes. I then walked little ways to our home.
>
> And at that time in the year after, we came to the Cheyenne River Indian Reservation where my grandmother's sister, Mrs. Adam Swift Horse lived in White Horse. And

in 1910, when we went back in the fall, the schools were all filled up and I was sent to Martin School where I attended school in 1910. In 1911, I went to school back in Fort Yates.

In 1912, I signed up to Bismarck Indian School for three and a half years. In that year, in that fall, well, all schools were closed up and I don't know where to go, so I went back to Bismarck Indian School. They took me in and I took up vocational training as a carpenter and a painter, cement, dairy, and part of it boiler furnace.

And from there I came over here. And at the age of seventeen, I attend school at White Horse with the White kids, horseback ... and we lived about a mile from my grandmother's place.

And during that fall my grandmother died – the one that raised me – so I was without folks in this world. But my grandmother's sister took me over and kept me, which I attend school with the White kids.

I realized that I loved to go to school. The schools is where they made the most of our time ... but, you know at that time we worked half a day ... worked half a day and go to school half day. We didn't have much time for school in them days. And when I went to school at Fort Yates, and when I went to school in Martin School, I was an altar boy under Father Burnett and under the Father Martin. Well, them are the good days and the good Christian life and the people were more interesting ... where the Indian schools were fifty-fifty with the religion of God. So both times in this school, I was altar boy. It was more like a mission school. And the discipline, and everybody was nice people, I could say.... And that's why I understand what a "yes" or "no" is.[4]

Paul spoke of his grandfather, Chief Joseph High Bear, a nineteenth century Upper Yanktonai from the James River in central North Dakota and how he got his name Joseph. Historical reports from Indian agent Jim McLaughlin at Standing Rock Indian Reservation reported that: *"High Bear was the Fourth chief of Upper Yanktonai Sioux. Is progressive and well-disposed and of considerable force of character."*

The tribe was forced to move in the aftermath of the Dakota Wars of 1862, previously known as the Minnesota Uprising. They

---

4   From a recording of Paul in 1976 during the American Indian Research Project at the University of South Dakota, Vermillion, S.D.

settled on the eastern bank of the Missouri River across from Cannonball, North Dakota on the Standing Rock Indian Reservation. They were later forced to relocate west of the Missouri River onto the Standing Rock Indian Reservation. Some of their descendants still live in Cannonball to this day.

Paul shared about how his grandfather received the name Joseph:

> Now there's a story about my grandfather ... the band that first lived in Cannonball ... a Catholic priest was first ... and he landed ... right straight east of where the river is ... everything is new to them. The Tribes go down to the river and they see this boat. And this priest came there and he wanted to stop and stay with the Indian people; and he was the first missionary. My Grandfather took him, and showed where he lived along the banks of the Missouri River ... about four miles from the mouth of the Cannonball River ... and the community all got together and they built a squaw shed, closed in enough that he lived in there.
>
> And he goes out on horseback, no saddles, just horseback and used to tell the people to 'tend church, attend evening service.' That's how come one of the most big denominations are Catholics in that time amongst the Sioux Indians. So that's where the missionary start. But when he took this Catholic priest in, he gave him that name, Joseph. So he named my grandfather.
>
> So it says: "High Bear was one of the first Indians to encourage his fellow man to follow the ways of the White. He is good natured and a fine fellow. He was a delegate from the Standing Rock Sioux Tribe to the Indian Congress and while there, conducted himself in a most satisfactory manner."[5]

And it looks like T.A. Stephan, Indian Agent says:

> February 4, 1879: High Bear, bearer of this, requests me to give him a certificate about his character and standing. I do this with pleasure. He is a good, kind, well-meaning Indian and endeavors to do what is right. He works, sends his children to school, and gives a good example to the rest of the Indians. I recommend him to the white man who may meet him to treat him kindly and friendly, and he is a friend of the White.

5   During the interview, Paul's interviewer commented about Chief High Bear and statements from the United States Congress, signed by Captain Mercer of the United States Army and J.R. Wise, Indian Agent.

And then here's another one here:

> The bearer, Joseph High Bear, is a pretty good Indian and I think he deserves friendly treatment from the white people."[6]

Paul then continued:

> I never did even understand when I went to school, because I was raised by my grandfather that never seen ... maybe ... White people in his early days where he became the chief. And then when he went to Washington and all those places, I got his papers with me here in my house ... and it's stated in there that High Bear, when the White man meets him, they should give him some of the generous way of life that he has participated in with the Indians ... from the White people.
>
> And in 1879, he had two daughters, that's in the first year of their written history of the Yanktonai Sioux. There's two daughters. They went to Hampton, Virginia. And that's mixed with different nationalities and that's how come the Indian race of people became as so-called half breeds, or breeds, what you call nowadays. He was seventy-five years old when he died.

Paul married Louise Grey Bear Charger in 1918 and lived in White Horse and then LaPlant on the Cheyenne River Indian Reservation near the Charger homestead. At the time Martin was born (in 1919), they were living in a canvas tent near her parents' home. To support his family, Paul worked hard. He worked for the government at Cheyenne Agency as a night watchman. Paul also had a contract with the Bureau of Indian Affairs to haul coal to the reservation schools. He would unload coal from rail cars into his large delivery truck and travel to tribal schools on Cheyenne River and Standing Rock Indian reservations to make his coal deliveries. When Martin had grown a little older and his father became ill, he helped do his work.

Paul later married Amy Garter at Pierre on March 3, 1950. They made their home at the Old Cheyenne Agency and Marksville, South Dakota. He drove a school bus in the late 1950s. During the building of the Oahe Dam in Pierre, he worked as a heavy equipment operator. In 1973 they moved to Eagle Butte where he worked as a carpenter for the tribe's Housing Authority. He retired in 1978 and they lived near the reservation until his passing in May 1995.

6   Signed by P.F. Weis, Indian Physician, June 5, 1907

BLUE EARTH LINEAGE

Paul's biological father, Valentine Blue Earth, was descended from Chief Blue Earth. Prior to the Minnesota Uprising, Chief Blue Earth and his family lived along the Makhátho Wakpá (Blue Earth River) in west central Minnesota east of Pipestone, Minnesota. They were forced to move in the 1860s to the west of the Missouri River. Chief Blue Earth settled on the north side of Standing Rock Indian Reservation near the Cannonball River until his death later in the 1860s.[7]

A nineteenth century story was documented about a Blue Earth ("Mankato") warrior who engaged in a battle during the Sioux Wars (Minnesota Uprising) to protect their land from an incoming U.S. military unit. Here we see a Native American perspective that is rarely shared by a participant about this battle:

> Just as we were about to charge word came that a large number of mounted soldiers were coming up from the east toward Fort Ridgely. This stopped the charge and created some excitement. Mankato at once took some men from the coulee and went out to meet them. He told me he did not take more than fifty, but he scattered them out and they all yelled and made such a noise that the Whites must have thought there were a great many more, and they stopped on the prairie and began fighting. They had a cannon and used it, but it did no harm. If the Indians had any men killed in the fight I never heard of it. Mankato flourished his men around so, and all the Indians in the coulee kept up a noise, and at last the Whites began to fall back, and they retreated about two miles and began to dig breastworks. Mankato followed them and left about thirty men to watch them, and returned to the fight at the coulee with the rest. The Indians were laughing when they came back at the way they had deceived the white men, and we were all glad that the Whites had not pushed forward and driven us away. Mankato (Blue Earth) was killed here, and we lost a very good and brave war chief. He was killed by a cannon ball that was so nearly spent that he was not afraid of it, and it struck him in the

---

7   Martin's sister, Melda, shared that Chief Blue Earth's grave near Cannonball was submerged under water when the Missouri River was dammed in the 1950's; and that Uncle Richard Blue Earth, who died in World War I in the battlefield of France, received the Congressional medal of honor. His flag is flown every year at the Cannonball Flag Day Powwow.

back, as he lay on the ground, and killed him. He was a very brave man and a good leader.[8]

MOTHER'S SIDE OF THE FAMILY

Martin's mother was Louise Grey Bear Bagola.[9] Louise's father was Samuel Charger, who was born 15 May 1882 at Cheyenne River Agency, SD. He married Rosa Red Weasel[10] at LaPlant, SD and gave birth to Philip E. Charger, Martin's uncle on 27 October 1909. Samuel was the author of Chief Martin Charger's biography, which included a short bio of Samuel.[11]

Louise Gray Bear's Dakhóta father, Solomon Gray Bear (CRA–299) was born in 1865 and was murdered on July 5, 1905 by cattle rustlers outside of his ranch in LaPlant, Cheyenne River Agency. His lineage showed that he was a descendant of Lightning Blanket, a Dakhóta warrior from Shakopee, Minnesota who fought in the Battle of Fort Ridgely, Minnesota in 1862 during the Dakota War.[12] After he was imprisoned and released, he shared the Dakhóta side of the story, which was translated into English by Joseph Coursolle and published in multiple prairie newspapers in Minnesota between 1897 and 1908.[13]

8   *A Sioux Story of the War: Chief Big Eagle's Story of the Sioux Outbreak of 1862* by Wamditanka, Holcombe, R. I., Minnesota Historical Society 1845-1916, 1894, pp 399.
9   Martin's mother, Louise Grey Bear Bagola (CRA 0301) was born 12/31/1899 and died 10/16/1982.
10   Louise's mother Rosa Red Weasel married Samuel Charger at LaPlant, South Dakota. They had one son, Philip E. Charger, born October 27, 1909. Louise was raised by Grandfather Samuel Charger. Her other siblings included Sophie Left Handed Bear, Jane Grey Bear, and Martin's cousins, Harry Charger and Rufus Charger. Agency reports show that Rosa completed fifth grade at the Agency Boarding School and Pierre Boarding School.
11   It stated: "Samuel Charger was born May 15, 1882 in the Cheyenne River Agency, South Dakota. His father's Indian name is Waanataŋ, or Martin Charger. His mother's name is Wasumaniwin or Eliza Charger. He was married at LaPlant, South Dakota to Rosa Red Weasel. They have one son, Philip E. Charger, born October 27, 1909. Samuel Charger attended Day School from 1888 to 1894 and also Government Boarding School at the Cheyenne Agency, and graduated from the eighth grade. He has held the following positions: Tribal Council Chairman for thirteen years, Government Employee for twelve years, County Constable and Justice of the Peace, Field Representative for the law firm of Case and Calhoun for twenty-one years, and other minor positions, also takes an active part in matters affecting the tribe. At the present time he is a rancher. Member of the Episcopal church, and a staunch Republican since 1924."
12   Solomon Gray Bear's mother was MánikhiyA hé wiŋ, or Moves Her. His father, Wičháŋhpi dúta, or Red Star, was also known as Ak'íŋ wakháŋhdi, or Lightning Blanket. His English name was David Wells from Shakopee, Minnesota. Lightning Blanket narrated an account in Dakota of the "Story of the Battle of Fort Ridgely, Minn., August 20 and 22, 1862."
13   *St. Paul Pioneer Press*, October 17, 1897, p. 12; *Morton Enterprise*, Morton, Minn.;

Martin's birth must have held great significance to his grand-parents. A letter to the Secretary of the Interior, showed that the government allotted land parcels to tribal members at Cheyenne Agency shortly after their grandson's birth, including 36-year old Samuel Charger's allotment #327 for 320 acres on Cheyenne River Indian Reservation.[14] His correspondence to and from the Department of the Interior was prolific over decades.

LEGACY OF *WAÁNATAŊ*, OR CHIEF MARTIN CHARGER

Martin said of his great grandfather, Chief Martin Charger: "It is on my mother's side where I got my Indian name. My mother is from Cheyenne River Reservation, another band of the Teton Sioux Nation, the *Mnikȟówožu* (Plants by the Water). My grandfather Sam Charger raised me. He was a son of Martin Charger, the Chief. *Waánataŋ* was his Indian name, "He Charges You."

Martin continued:

> The government took his last name and translated it into En-glish. He became *"Charger."* After you've been baptized, they give you a first name, so they gave him that first name, Mar-tin.[15] My Indian name is from my great grandfather. Chief Martin Charger's Indian name was passed on to me. That's why I got two Indian names: One from the spirits that come

O. S. Smith, August 28, 1908, p. 1.; Allen R. Woolworth Papers, Minnesota Historical Soci-ety; *Through Dakota Eyes*, Anderson and Woolworth, Minnesota Historical Society Press, 1988, pp. 153-7.

14   1919 records of Agent Swensson about Sam Charger showed that he completed the eighth grade at the Cheyenne Agency Boarding School. He inherited a half section of his mother's land, 106-acres of his sister's estate, and some small shares on the old Yankton and Crow Creek reservations. Samuel Charger's allotment letter declared: "We have the honor to transmit herewith ninety-three (93) applications of Indian Allottees for patents in fee to their respective allotments ... The Allottees listed on this schedule, most of whom are full-blood Indians, are of a very promising class, practically all of them being English speaking, fairly well educated, and of desirable ages to assume the responsibilities of full citizenship, whose present status is set forth in our report on each individual recommended."

15   Martin Charger (born 1833), Siksicela (šikší-šilyéla) Band of Sans Arcs, was a leading man in the formation of Charger's Camp, a co-founder of the Fool Soldiers, a pro-U.S. *akíčhita* force drawn from the "friendly" contingent of the Sans Arc and Two Kettle bands of the Teton Sioux Nation. Martin shared further about Chief Charger ... that he had a brother whose Indian name was "Promise" when they translated it into En-glish. They were full brothers, but one brother went by the name Promise and the other went by the name Charger.... One was a chief and the other one was younger, an Epis-copal minister. There were four full-blood brothers. Each one had a different last name. "Back in the days of our ancestors, each one was given a name, given an Indian name and some of those Indian names were passed on for generations. The grandmothers, the grandfathers passed them on to the kids to keep that name alive."

work with me and the other one was the name of my great grandfather which was given to me by my grandparents.

I know back in our ancestors' days, some of them had to earn that name. The spirits gave me a name after I'd been up on the hill, Vision Quest and came back down to be a Medicine Man. The spirits called me another name in the prayer they give me, and they used my Indian name in that prayer.

I had two chiefs from my great-great-grandpas so I can say I'm a *"half breed"* – half Húŋkpapȟa and half Minikonju [*Mnikȟówožu*] from my mother's side [he chuckles]. But like I say, this is some of the things we have to study on. I respect and honor, but I don't go around bragging about it.

Martin's maternal great grandfather, Chief Martin Charger, belonged to the Siksicela [šikší -šilyéla] Band of Sans Arc or *Without Bows*, also called *the Keeper of the Pipe Band*,[16] one of the seven bands of Teton Sioux Nation. In the mid-nineteenth century, their hunting range was to the north and east of the Black Hills, extending east to the Missouri River near the Mnikȟówožu. They also enjoyed a close link to the Húŋkphapȟa, often hunting with them north of the Grand River.[17]

Martin Charger's history and rich cultural values were documented by Samuel Charger and published by the South Dakota State Historical Society in 1946.[18] Samuel Charger's role of sharing and preserving these stories for future generations provides a glimpse of history rarely available to the public. Expanding upon Samuel's earlier unpublished 1922 version, it revealed his peoples' tribal history from the mid-nineteenth century at the time of the Dakota Wars of 1856-65. Chief Charger's band, called the Fool Soldiers Society, became caught between anti- and pro-U.S. factions during a major transition in the life of the Sioux.

Perhaps more important, Samuel's document is a source of inspiration to today's descendants because it reveals his father's rich legacy of traditional Native American cultural values which guided his father and the Fool Soldiers Band. Chief Martin Charger demonstrated humility, patience, integrity and generosity, plus a desire for peaceful resolution of conflict. These spiritual qualities

16   Joyzelle Gingway Godfrey, Preface to *The Dakota Way of Life*, vii.
17   Sans Arc *History: The Sans Arcs, 1850-1870*, Kingsley M. Bray
18   *The Biography of Martin Charger*, South Dakota Historical Collections, Vol XXII, 1946 p. 1-30.

17

are reflected in the vision of the Band and provide a dramatic contrast to images of savage violence previously portrayed.

He Was Named Dependable

Chief Martin Charger was born in 1834 in what is now known as the Black Hills, and belonged to the band of Indians known as the Sansarc, (or Sans Arc) his mother (Her Good Ground) being a member of the Sansarc Band.[19]

The childhood days of Martin Charger were of a roving nature, as the band moved from place to place. They went south as far as where the city of Yankton now stands and north as far as the Little Missouri, Powder and Tongue rivers, Montana, and west as far as the Black Hills. As meat was their chief article of food, they were in search of buffalo; they followed them up north in the spring season, and in winter followed them south as the great herds generally drifted south during the winter months.

When Charger was small, his father noticed that the boy was not easily discouraged, had a lot of patience and wanted to stay at home and help his mother around the thípi (tipi), being at all times obedient to his parents. He never gave up until he finished a job and was never known to lie to his parents. Thus, he earned his name, Dependable.

Generosity

At the age of ten, Charger knew a Chief, One Feather, a member of his band, who had a relative killed by the Crows in a War party. One Feather, so the story goes, took his relative's death so hard that he made a feast and laid his hands on the heads of all the braves and warriors in the band, swearing to retaliate for the killing, as was the custom at that time. Charger saw this ceremony. It left such a memorable impression on him, that young as he was, he wanted to go on the war party.

Shortly after this, Charger's father called his two sons into the tipi and told them that he had observed the customs and habits of the Indians during his lifetime and there were many things they did with which he did not agree. He told them that the life of an Indian is full of pride, that the four degrees in a war party consisted of honor, such as striking the enemy with a lance, to be wounded, or to steal the en-

---

19   The four bands of the Cheyenne River Sioux Tribe numbered 2,766 in 1922 and included Mnikȟówožu or Sansarc, meaning "Planting near Water," the Itázipčho or "Hunting Without Bows," the Oóhenuŋpa or "Two Kettle," and Sihásapa or "Blackfeet."

emies' ponies. But fame, he said, did not come with these alone. The fourth was Generosity to fellow tribesmen, which was something far more important. He impressed upon the young Charger that an Indian might be wounded a hundred times, but if he could not offer food to less fortunate Indians, he was "of no account," a saying among the Indians for many generations. Even though the Indian loses his life in battle, all was in vain if he did not also have a generous soul.

Spirituality

At the age of fifteen Charger saw what the Indians called mysterious powers used by the Medicine Man who was in the Black Hills camp. He performed his ceremony for the purpose of luring the buffalo nearby so all could get their supply without moving camp. He repeated this ceremony in the Indian camps during the winters of 1844 and 1845 when the famine raged in that country.

Bravery

Remembering his father's advice on the war party and the honor of an Indian to include generosity, Charger and his brother Little Hawk (who was said to be daring and not easily frightened) ran away from their home to join a war party when Charger was eighteen. The warrior uncles of his mother's family had influenced him and when the war party reached Crow Camp, the Sioux party was large and formidable.

The attack was made in the daytime and although Charger had never been in a fight before, he was able to take care of himself and his brother as well as defend some of the others during the fight – without a scratch!

When the victorious party came home, Charger's name was heralded throughout the camp and his father was proud of his son. From this first war party, Charger received honorable recognition and became a member of the Grass Society. The Grass Society and its members are picked from the tribe for their deeds of daring and bravery in battle.

Responsible to Family and Thiyóšpaye

At the age of nineteen, Charger married a Yankton Sioux girl named Walking Hail. It was in the same year the treaty was signed at Fort Laramie 1851. Walking Hail, with her parents, were going to the Fort. They had to turn back on account of sickness in the family and after they reached the Sioux Camp, Walking Hail's mother died.

According to the Indian custom Walking Hail was given to Charger when she became an orphan. The young Indian was so impressed with the new responsibility given him that he recalled his father's lecture on generosity and became noted for giving feasts. After he had been married a year the Crow Indians joined with the Sioux for the first time in history. He made great feasts and invited the Crows while they were in the Sioux Camp and all the older Indians sang praises of Charger. He not only gave feasts for the Indians but gave horses also.[20/21]

FOUR BEAR'S ORAL HISTORY ACCOUNT

Stories from Albert Four Bear, Jr., who as a young boy and after the death of his parents, had lived with Martin Charger. His story was preserved in a 1972 oral history interview by the Institute of American Indian Studies, University of South Dakota and summarized by interviewer Stephen Plummer.

The oral history account from Four Bear included a story about Charger in his younger days, "Martin Charger was very famous among the people in that area because of his ability as a hunter."

Mr. Four Bear said that Martin Charger could ride his horse off the side of a buffalo and shoot an arrow right through the buffalo and kill it...

He said, "You can't do that today, the people just aren't strong enough. But my grandfather could do that. He could shoot that arrow right through, into one side of the buffalo and have it fall out on the ground on the other side, which I think we'd all admit it's, ah, is a rather remarkable feat.

Martin Charger used to get in trouble all the time when he was young because Indians from other parts of the country would come in there, come into the Crow Creek area, and kill the buffalo. And he said that would mean that there wasn't good hunting for the people at Crow Creek. So Martin Charger and some of the other young men used to go on raiding parties to, ah, scare off Indians

20   *Biography of Martin Charger* by Charger, Samuel, 1882-; South Dakota State Historical Society. Pierre, S.D. : State Historical Society, 1946 South Dakota historical collections. Vol. 22.; yr:1946 no:22, pp.15.
21   Charger was nineteen at the time of the Fort Laramie Treaty of 1851. According to his biography, he was planning to attend the treaty council but family obligations became a higher priority.

coming in from other parts of different reservations and so forth, killing off the buffalo that belonged to the people at Crow Creek."

LEADERSHIP

Martin's cousin, Rufus Charger told of his great grandfather Charger's involvement in the Fool Soldiers Band. He expressed how this peaceful band formed in 1860 "as the atmosphere of distrust and resentment replaced the relative calm that had once prevailed in the Plains before the White Man came." Recorded at his home outside Eagle Butte, South Dakota, his message was preserved in an audio recording in the fall of 1996. Rufus said:

> Martin was named Martin Rufus, and my dad was named Rufus Martin, and I was named after Rufus Martin and my son is Rufus Martin III. Grandfather Martin Charger is a member of the Fool Soldier Band. These are all young men who were warriors, great warriors, great people. Among their people, there was a time that there were hostilities between Whites. They were supposed to see good, even with the White people. These young people called Fool Soldiers, they were outcasts. They were ridiculed. They were really great men, so even though they were ridiculed, they had a lot of respect because they were great warriors and outstanding men. That was the society he was a part of.
>
> I guess they were known for one thing, the release of captives, but there were a lot of things they did. There is a group being started here at Eagle Butte, the Fool Soldier Band. Some of them are dead, but the names are still here: Swift Bird, Four Bear, Charger. They are the survivors of that and they are forming a group and trying to get recognized for more than just that one thing they did. They did a lot of other fine things that are unknown.

DOING GOOD DEEDS

The tradition of doing good deeds was important to Charger and was reflected in other documented accounts of the formation of the Fool Soldiers Band. "...the [Fool Soldiers] Society was organized, rulings made and thus five became members. The rules were: When the Society is to do some good deed, one member shall go from tipi to tipi and take anything that is needed, and their wives shall cooperate with their husbands to the fullest extent. They (the women) will do all *the cooking; Property and food will be generously given at all times; the old and indigent will be cared for and in the buffalo chase, one member will go and bring in the meat to the less fortunate Indians so they shall not go hungry. It was 1860 when this society was organized..."[22] [23]*

MARCELLA LABEAU SPEAKS OF HER GREAT GRANDFATHER

The late Lakȟóta war heroine who served as a nurse in the battlefields of WWII, Marcella LaBeau, spoke of her great grandfather, Chief Four Bear, a member of the Fool Soldiers Band. Her oral history was video recorded in the summer of 1999 which shed light on the group of warriors and the importance of doing good deeds:

> I would like to share a story about my great grandfather. His name was Joseph Four Bear and he was a chief of the Two Kettle Band. When he was young, the story is told that he was a member of the Fool Soldier Band. And as young men, they organized themselves to do good and noble deeds. It is told that even their own people were opposed to doing that because of the environment at that time.
>
> That was back in 1862 and these warriors, these young men, they organized themselves. They had Martin Charger as their leader. And when the Minnesota Uprising happened in 1862, the Santee Sioux, White Lodge being their chief, took captive some White women and children from the Lake Shetak area in Minnesota. They took them to a place up by Mobridge near the Grand River. And they were holding them there as captives.
>
> When my grandfather and Martin Charger heard about this, they organized themselves and decided that this was one thing they could do, that it would be a good thing to rescue these White women and children and return them to their relatives. They began by gathering together their horses and blankets and other things. And the story says they crossed the Missouri River someplace around what is now Ft. Pierre. And the Missouri River is a treacherous river, but they swam their horses and their goods and swam the river and crossed to the other side. And they shown a

---

22   *Biography of Martin Charger*, p. 7.
23   *Four Bear Oral History*, South Dakota Oral History Project, University of South Dakota 1976

mirror to their people to the other side to let them know they had made it across and were on their way.

They went up the river on the east side to Chief White Lodge's camp and they negotiated the return of these White women and children. The story says they negotiated for the return of each one and then they would offer goods. And when the exchange was made, that person would go over to their side of the tent. And this continued until there was one person left and that was Mrs. Dooley.

And apparently White Lodge was not willing to part with her. And so White Lodge's son came into the picture and he spoke to his dad, telling him to turn her over to the Fool Soldier's Band. And it came to be that he did part with Mrs. Dooley. And they began their trip back down the east side of the Missouri River. And apparently on the way, a storm broke out, a winter storm.

The women and children were dressed very scantily. The story says that Martin Charger took off his moccasins and gave them to one of the women and he wrapped his own feet in cloth. Pretty Bear carried one of the children on his own back, so they made their way through the storm.

One night they found a place to stay, and they marched around the tent, or wherever they were housed, all night long so that White Lodge would not catch up with them. In that way they protected the women and children. So they stayed awake all night long and walked around the tent to protect these women and children. So they returned them down at Ft. Pierre to a man named Dupree and LaPlant, so eventually the women and children were returned to their relatives.

I found a letter over at the Cheyenne River Tribal Office and it was written by my mother. My mother said in the letter that her grandfather was Chief Joseph Four Bear and he was one of the Fool Soldier's Band and that was my connection with the story. I hadn't heard the story before until I found this letter my mother had written."[24]

---

24   After the interview was recorded, Marcella mentioned with sadness the letter from her mother, Four Bear's granddaughter. It had revealed how her grandfather, after he signed the peace treaty, lived out his life at Four Bear's camp until he passed away in 1909. "He didn't so much as dance Indian until the day he died" she said. "That really affected me to read that sentence. Because to me, if you can't be who you are, then who are you? It is like cultural genocide if you can't live your life the way you are and who you are."

PEACEFUL RESOLUTION OF CONFLICT

Charger's biography refers to how he encouraged peaceful resolution of conflict. After band members were murdered by a neighboring band, he discouraged the tradition of mourning their loss by seeking retribution for their deaths. Charger convinced his band to settle down according to the 1868 Sioux Treaty of Fort Laramie near the Cheyenne River Indian Agency which had been established near the confluence of the Cheyenne and Missouri Rivers.

> In 1869 when the hostile band stole some horses from the non-hostile bands, Charger once more established his reputation for good deeds and went in quest of the stolen horses. He found them in a camp on the Little Missouri and with the assistance of his uncles, the horses were delivered to their owners.
>
> Charger went north to the hostile bands and learned, much to his disappointment, that the Sans Arc band had gone to war against the Crow Indians. In this battle 15 of his fellow tribesmen were slain. There was sorrow and grief among his relatives and while he heard them singing and crying, he talked with them about moving back to the reservation which had been set aside for them. He convinced some of the tribe that it was the thing to do.[25]

STRENGTHENING RESILIENCE AND DISCERNMENT DURING HARDSHIP

Indian agent J.R. Hanson reported in 1868 that some bands had established farm operations but suffered crop failures and starvation due to the lack of game for hunting.[26] Despite this, and despite inadequate funding to operate their ranches and farms, Charger still encouraged his band to continue to try to settle down and establish their community.

Among other signs Charger observed over two decades as a chief, was the rapid decline of buffalo. The buffalo had flourished for thousands of years in the Northern Plains. However, in one year he witnessed the excessive slaughtering of buffalo and wild game that had once been so plentiful in the Northern Great Plains. It gave him much grief to see hunters (funded by the U.S. Govern-

---

25   *Biography of Martin Charger* by Charger, Samuel, 1882-; South Dakota State Historical Society. Pierre, S.D. : State Historical Society, 1946 South Dakota historical collections. Vol. 22.; yr:1946 no:22, pp.16
26   Correspondence from J.R. Hanson, Indian agent for Upper Missouri Sioux from Crow Creek Agency, Sep 16, 1868

ment) kill the buffalo for the bounty (or the hide only) and leave the dead carcasses on the ground to rot.

The buffalo were their chief sustenance and as they became hunted to extinction, Charger realized that tribes which had based their lifestyle on the buffalo were approaching a time of serious physical and cultural crisis. The Indians would be subdued and it seemed nothing could be done about it. It was for this and other reasons that later in life he reluctantly accepted the ways of the White Man, knowing that if he didn't, his family and his extended families might not survive. Small parties were making their raids on each other as usual, but Charger did not encourage retaliation.

The Rees (Arikara) were still making raids on the Sioux and two Ree warriors were slain that year. Charger, being busy making contacts with officers in charge of Fort Bennett Agency and interceding for his fellow tribesmen, knew that more perplexing problems were yet to confront them. He knew that in time, all would stop.[27]

According to Four Bear, Charger and other members of the Fool Soldiers Band attempted to settle down at Fort Thompson despite opposition to his progressive ways. It was told that log cabins were built for Chief Charger. According to Four Bear:

> It was said: And so they built some, some really nice log cabins there in Fort Thompson, and, and just wanted to settle down and do some gardening and raise some cattle and, and get back to life as they had known it before this whole thing took place. But one night while Martin Charger was sleeping some, ah, some of the old men in town got some white paint, ah, white paint or, or whitewash or something, and painted Martin, Martin Charger's cabin all white because they said they had become more White than Indian so why he shouldn't live in a white cabin.
>
> And they went to the houses of some of the other men and, and stole their horses and cattle and, and, ah, went through with, with big knives and, and chopped up their gardens and, and did all kinds of things to those old Fool Soldiers. And he said pretty soon Martin Charger and his friends decided that they had to leave the Fort Thompson area.... The people in Fort Thompson just didn't accept the Fool Soldiers coming back into the camp.

27   From *A History of Cheyenne River Indian Agency and Its Military Post, Fort Bennett 1868-1891*

They, they wouldn't leave them alone; they wouldn't let them settle down. And so Martin Charger and all his friends, ah, went elsewhere to settle, and his grandfather finally settled ... on the Cheyenne River Reservation."[28]

Fort Bennett was becoming established around that time on the banks of the Missouri River near Cheyenne River Agency[29] So Charger moved across the Missouri River with his band and established a camp at Little Bend where they began to build homes.[30] Others gradually followed his example, scattering 50-70 miles along the Missouri and helping each other build a total of eighty log houses with chimneys.

They were among the first to cultivate the soil. They began to till the land; raising corn and vegetables. The principal crops produced were sweet corn and other garden vegetables with mixed results and challenges as revealed in agency reports.[31]

This new camp at Little Bend was one of the first Indian communities in the plains attempting to learn the ways of the White Man. Despite condemnation from some of their own people (and crop failures), their community became resigned to the stipulations of the 1868 Treaty in the course of time.

Martin's great grandfather was offered opportunities to ranch at Charger's Camp. The introduction of cattle ranching as a means of economic development to the Cheyenne River Sioux took a while to be accepted. Native people had always hunted animals but the concept of ownership by individuals rather than the group had never occurred.

Cattle ranching became a strategy to confront the changing times of life without the buffalo. After having starved for sever-

---

28   Four Bear, oral history recording from South Dakota Oral History Project, University of South Dakota (1976).

29   On May 17, 1870, units of the 17th U.S. Infantry established a military station adjacent to the Cheyenne River Agency on the west river bottoms of the Missouri, eight miles above Fort Sully. Later known as the Fort Bennett Agency, it was built near the Cheyenne River Agency to assist in governing the Blackfeet, Minneconjou, Sans Arc, and Two Kettle bands of the Teton Sioux.

30   The military buildings at Fort Bennett were described as: "quarters for two companies, with necessary outbuildings, officers' quarters, hospital, guard house, block houses, two; storehouses, three, capacity inadequate; bake house, stable, workshops, laundress' quarters, etc. All the buildings are constructed of cottonwood logs, with the exception of a frame storehouse." South Dakota historical collections, Volume 8, South Dakota State Historical Society, South Dakota Dept. of History, 1916.

31   Samuel Charger Bio, p. 17

al generations, the people were initially less interested in raising cattle than they were in consuming them. Raising beef was less of a means of economic exchange, but more so represented a way to feed one's family and share with neighbors. Sharing beef at special gatherings and ceremonies became an integral and necessary part of life and brought new meaning to the communities.[32]

NEGOTIATING FOR PEACE

Along with the other bands of Sioux, the treaties they had been forced to sign eventually restricted them to the confines of their new reservations as reservation land became more like prison camps than land. To protest this, Charger and several other tribal leaders went to Washington DC starting in 1867. He also served as a delegate in 1870, 1875, 1888 and 1892.

Chief Martin Charger (row two, third from left) in Lakota delegation to Washington DC, (1875).
www.American-Tribes.com

In 1875, attempts by the government to coax the chiefs into an agreement to give up the Black Hills proved unsuccessful. According to the Charger biography:

> In 1875, Charger was one of the delegates sent to Washington for the purpose of negotiation for cession of the Black Hills. While in Washington, every bluff was used to intimidate the Chiefs. They were taken out in the sea at times and held until they signed the treaty. But they would not give up. It was Charger who thought of a scheme. He told the Commission that they were not the only head men of the Sioux nation, but that the majority of the tribe

---

32   *When Indians Became Cowboys: Native Peoples and Cattle Ranching in the American West*, Peter Iverson, U of OK Press, 1994)

was still in the buffalo country and when they had returned to the Reservation the question of the Treaty would be discussed upon a basis of a three fourths majority. The plan was considered by the authorities and it was finally agreed that Charger was right.[33]

On February 7, 1876, the War Department authorized General Sheridan to move onto Indian lands and force the Sioux at gunpoint to sign agreements confining them to their reservation boundaries. The first attack of the military happened on March 17, 1876. At the height of the conflict, forty per cent of the entire U. S. Army was deployed on the Northern Plains.[34]

In May of the next year, 1876, Charger was informed that General George Custer was stationed at Ft. Lincoln and the purpose was to launch a campaign against the Sioux nation. The Indians heard this with much distress and Charger called a meeting of a group of Indians composed of the Headmen and Chiefs who were requested to intercede on behalf of the hostile bands who were roaming in the Buffalo country.

This group met with Custer, a feast was made and the Indians discussed their mission. Custer told them that his mission was to discourage the War parties going on into the Sioux country. After the discussion was over Custer and the Indians danced. The different tribes took part in the dance and the Peace Pipe was smoked. Short Leg performed the ceremony and Custer smoked the Pipe. The Sioux delegation returned to their reservation, glad that they had accomplished their mission. However, within a month the Sioux tribe heard that Custer did not keep his pledge and they [General Custer and the Seventh Cavalry] were "wiped out."[35]

Following this Pipe ceremony, Lt. Col. George A. Custer and the U. S. Army's Seventh Cavalry, encountered an encampment of Sioux, Cheyenne and Arapaho at the Little Bighorn River. Before sunset on the evening of June 26, 1876, his detachment had been annihilated, the largest defeat ever of a U.S. force by Native

---

33   *Biography of Martin Charger* by Charger, Samuel, 1882-; South Dakota State Historical Society. Pierre, S.D. : State Historical Society, 1946 South Dakota historical collections. Vol. 22.; yr:1946 no:22, pp.17

34   Report of the Secretary of War, 1875 p 56, and 1876, pp. 24-25, and 48-49; Fort Laramie and the Sioux War of 1876, SD History Vol 17 (1987) pp. 238

35   *Biography of Martin Charger* by Charger, Samuel, 1882-; South Dakota State Historical Society. Pierre, S.D. : State Historical Society, 1946 South Dakota historical collections. Vol. 22.; yr:1946 no:22, pp.18

Americans.[36] Those who knew of the Pipe ceremony with General Custer understood why he was defeated in battle. He had violated the agreement during the Pipe ceremony for a peaceful settlement of the conflict.

Chief Charger witnessed multiple changes while guiding his family through hardships and successes during much of the nineteenth century, including his service as a judge at Fort Bennett between 1880 to 1900 until his passing on August 16, 1900.

---

36   This battle, originally known as Custer's Last Stand was renamed as The Battle at Little Bighorn in 1991. Battles are not usually named after the defeated.

Martin High Bear (photo taken in the late 1970s).

CHAPTER 2

THE THREE SPIRITUAL WORLDS
OF MARTIN HIGH BEAR

WALKING IN THREE SPIRITUAL WORLDS

When Martin Rufus High Bear was born, his grandparents knew he had inherited the gift to become a Medicine Man. Samuel and Rosa Charger foretold at the time of his birth that he would someday help to relieve more than a century of suffering his people had endured since first contact.

During his sun-setting years, Martin spoke of walking in three spiritual worlds during his lifetime. He explained that his first spiritual world began at the time of his birth on September 11, 1919 and continued through his childhood in the 1920s and into the 1930s.

A MEMORY FROM THE 1920S

The Charger household practiced Christianity, but they still believed in the ways of wonder and mystery of the Great Spirit. They privately practiced some spiritual traditions, so young Martin learned about his ancestors' spirituality from them[37] and other elders who gathered at their camp.

Martin remembered a council of elders who gathered in the mid-1920's and the messages they shared. Many guests who gathered one afternoon at the Charger's log cabin were elders. Children were not usually permitted to sit in council so most of the time his grandmother would let him go outside. Sometimes he preferred to be outside, but sometimes he would ask permission to come inside and listen.

This particular time, his grandmother wanted him to join them. She told him that if he was quiet, he could wrap a blanket around himself and sit down by her feet. As he stepped in the door, Mar-

---

37   Editor's Note: It was common for the oldest son to live with the Grandparents to learn their ways.

tin could smell the čheyáka tea, made from dried wild peppermint leaves, brewing on his grandmother's wood stove. "I cannot speak. I can only listen," he said, describing his memory of the council that day and how it painted an indelible picture in his memory.

The cabin was small, but it was large enough to hold a dozen or more guests. The elders sat in a circle on the floor, speaking in the Lakȟóta dialect about the old ways. They seemed so wise. He listened to them speak about prophecy and what they might do to help their people so their lives could be happier and the future brighter for the grandchildren.

An older man sitting across the room spoke about the warriors and how they had fought so hard to keep their land. The old man had become bitter and angry, especially after the government had forced them to lease their parcels to White ranchers in 1909. He felt the only way the people would survive was to fight for their rights. Reminding the other elders that the White Man had always broken the treaties, and that their words and writings on paper meant nothing, he proposed they train all the men on the reservation to fight so they could get their land back and restore their way of life. He spoke of how they now had to hide to keep their old ways alive and protect their people from the punishment of the Indian agent and tribal police.

Martin's grandmother spoke: "Fighting them again we would lose too many. The Whites living on our reservation, we have to learn to live with them and still protect our people. We can't go on fighting forever. It's a losing battle."

Another grandfather said: "If there are not enough of us, then we should get the tribes of all nations united and then go back to war against them."

A grandmother from the other side of the room said: "Going to war wouldn't work. It would kill our people off. Our people are too poisoned today. They are weak. We need to strengthen their spirits."

Another elder wanted to speak to the Father of the whole country and to have it recognized by the cameras and have their speeches recorded to document the injustices that were happening to them.

Someone else felt the only way they would be able to survive was for everyone else to know what they were fighting for. They were not going to be able to fight this battle alone, so they would need to get people of all nations and colors to understand and agree with what they were trying to do in light of the prophecies.

They spoke about prophecy and the return of the White Buffalo Calf Maiden. Before She was to come back again, their ancestors had prophesied that there were certain things the people had to fulfill. Some said that before She could return, the people would have to stand up and claim their spirits back. They would have to become warriors and Indians again.

One grandfather reminded the group about the words of Red Cloud and the prophecies that the people would dance again and be in harmony with the spirit. He felt that one day the Ghost Dance and other ceremonies would come back.

Another grandfather was doubtful. He spoke of how many of their people had become soft and had forgotten the prophecies and who they were as a nation. He expressed that their people had allowed the Whites to kill their spirits and take their women. "We have to stand up and stop it!" he said. "The prophecies say we have to stop this and then we will get it all back again."

Another elder, feeling the land was Great Spirit's and that nobody should own it, wanted them to restore their rights to use the land to hunt and harvest their wild foods again. He spoke of the starvation they faced on an almost daily basis since the buffalo had been killed off. He also lamented the loss of their traditions. "Warriors don't know how to be warriors anymore," he said. "How can we teach our young warriors to hunt when there's nothing to hunt anymore? Our language and our ways have to come back to our people. We have to stop speaking this new language."

Someone defended their use of the new language. "We got beaten so hard for speaking our language. We had to learn to speak English," he said, "and our children need to learn to speak English if they are going to survive in the White Man's world."

Another elder suggested they get help from a lawyer, an Indian man who had been shipped off to the boarding schools when he was young and had become a lawyer. He had come back seeking some of his relatives, his aunts and uncles on the reservation. He had given them his card and told them to contact him if they needed help with anything, and he would help them if he could. He felt this Native attorney would understand because he was mostly of their people. So they decided to contact him and see if he could help. Some who were still doing ceremony suggested they bring the Native attorney back to the ways of Sweat Lodges and ceremonies, but some of the others didn't want to speak of ceremonies, knowing that if they got caught, someone would be put in jail for 30 days to a year and their family's food provisions would be withheld.

Some of the grandmothers believed that the Catholic way was connected in some ways to their old ways, yet different. They had picked up the new way of spirituality by gathering in the Christian way. Some even felt the ways of their ancestors were no longer needed. But not everyone was convinced that Christianity was what their people needed. It had become a weapon that was used in multiple ways against them.

Another old man wanted to smoke the Pipe with everyone there, but some grandmothers and grandfathers who had become Christians felt that was no longer needed. Others felt it was needed. "It is the old people that send the prayers to get the spirits to come and help. We will not be able to resolve our problems without Pipe prayers."

Then Martin's grandmother spoke to him, "It is going to fall on you younger ones to save your people. You will have the strength to bring our culture and traditional ways back. You can help them go back to preparing the hides for clothing and providing traditional foods for the children. You can help to bring the language back to the people. It is you that will give the people the hope to live again."

Someone else spoke up: "The other responsibility of the younger ones is taking the alcohol away from where they sell those things and from the bars on the reservation."

Another spoke up saying that was not the problem.

Someone else felt this was a heavy burden to be putting on the younger ones.

Everybody had a different perspective of what was needed to help the people, so they ended the meeting, deciding they couldn't smoke the Pipe and pray because of the unresolved differences.

A variety of opinions were expressed that afternoon. It was clear that they wanted to do something to help the people, but they couldn't reach a consensus so the grandmothers got up to serve what they had from the kitchen. The inviting smell of soup was in the air from gramma's big kettle simmering on the wood stove with *pápa* (dried beef), *thíŋpsiŋla* (prairie turnips) and *waštúŋkala* (dried corn).

After the meal, Martin's grandfather spoke again: "They cannot kill our spirits! We are going to thrive again. We will become great people again and our spirits will be even stronger."

The council disturbed young Martin. Each speaker had been specific about what they felt was best for the people and what should be done to help. He agreed with some who spoke about fighting for their rights and that they could still be warriors, but that they now needed to do it in a peaceful way. He also understood the common sense and spiritual perspectives of some of his grandmothers. He felt everyone was right, but to him it felt chaotic. He was confused.

At that point, his grandmother told him he could go outside to play. As he stepped outside into the early evening sunset, he pondered the prophecies and the differing views and perceptions. They said these things were going to happen but he didn't see how it was possible.

The elders expressed that their *hokšíla* (boy) was going to grow up and "save" his people. His grandmother saw in him great healing for the people. They said he was a special child and that he had to be strong, but he didn't really feel special. He felt that was a big responsibility for him.

There wasn't always time for Martin to be a kid. Sometimes, he just wanted to be like the rest of the children that he would sometimes see in town or in church. Living out in the country with his grandparents secluded from other children, he didn't often get to see them or play with them. He knew he had more responsibilities than they did and it seemed that they didn't have to work as hard either.

Martin felt that the other children didn't understand him, plus he didn't like some of the things that they did. Living with his grandparents, Martin was always treated with respect, so in contrast, some of the behavior of the children seemed insensitive and cruel.

However, from what Martin had seen and what his grandmothers and the old people had talked about, he knew he wanted to help change things. He wanted to help partly because they had said he would be helping his people.

In his young spiritual mind, he was already being put on his path of service. Sometimes when his chores were done, he would take off walking to the beaver pond. He would skip rocks, and then he would grow very still and speak with the Spirit World. The winds surrounded him, whispering. He would ask them the secret ways of his ancestors, and for knowledge and understanding so he could be the great warrior that his grandmother and grandfather had predicted he would become.

Martin's grandparents, Sam and Rosa Charger.

CHAPTER 3

HIS FIRST SPIRITUAL WORLD

MARTIN'S BIRTH

Infant Martin was born in LaPlant, South Dakota on September 11, 1919 to Louise Grey Bear and Paul High Bear.[38] During his first year, he lived with his parents in their canvas tent outside the small cabin of maternal grandparents, Samuel Charger and Rosa Grey Bear Charger.

It was not an easy year to survive in a tent, according to weather reported in Ziebach County History the first month of his birth: *"On October 12, 1919, a snowstorm began and by morning the entire range country was covered with a white blanket about four feet deep. The snow lay on the ground all winter. On the fifteenth of March rain began falling. By morning, a full-fledged blizzard was raging, the worst storm that had been witnessed in this section to the memory of all. The storm let up, only to be renewed on the 18th. After the storm had subsided, cattle and sheep by the hundreds were found dead in the draws and creek bottoms where the winds had driven them to shelter and their deaths. Dead sheep lay all over the prairie country between Cherry Creek and the Cheyenne River."*[39]

Martin was treated with great respect throughout his growing up days. In Lakȟóta tradition, *Tȟakóža* – the oldest grandson, and *Winona* – the oldest granddaughter, were raised by grandparents. The family knew when he was born that Martin would someday become a Medicine Man. Therefore, it was no surprise that when he was a year old, the Chargers took him into their cabin to raise him. They may have also felt that his parents' canvas tent would not be adequate protection during unexpected cold winter blizzards.

---

38   Sam and Rosa were married at Cheyenne River Agency in August 1908. She moved from her settlement at Bad River and in 1919, they settled on their allotment where they began raising horses and a small herd of cattle.

39   "South Dakota's Ziebach County, History of the Prairie," Ziebach County Historical Society, Dupree, SD 1982.

The Charger settlement was down an eight-mile trail five miles outside of LaPlant. It included their four-room home, an older three-room log house, plus a barn, garage and chicken coop. There was no water on their property so they traveled by horse and wagon three miles twice a week to haul water from the LaPlant reservoir.

Martin's sister Melda remembered a story that had been told by her mother about Martin when he became ill as an infant:

> Our paternal grandfather High Bear was a Medicine Man. He lived away from the village on Standing Rock Indian Reservation.
>
> When he was a baby, Mom took Martin to see him because he couldn't urinate. The spirits had told old man High Bear they were coming to see him so he was expecting them. When mom looked at him, she got scared of him. He instructed her to lay the baby down and unwrap him. He was chewing on something. So here she took off his diaper off.
>
> Martin had been crying and couldn't lay still before, but when he looked at Grampa, he just cooperated.
>
> Grampa blew at his penis and he just started going to the bathroom. He said, 'Huh! He is well. Wrap him up and take him home.

Martin loved to tell stories of his years with his grandparents. Many times when he was asked to speak he would reminisce about his younger years living with them.

> And so today, I am happy to be here and to talk a little about myself, of my growing up days. I will tell you a little story of how I grew up in my little days, like you. I was raised with old parents way out in the country. When I was a baby, my grandmother and my grandfather wanted to raise me. My mother and dad wanted me to be the way my grandparents wanted me to be, so when I started walking, they took me. I was their oldest grandchild, so they was really honoring me. We call them *Čhaské*,[40] the oldest of the boys.
>
> My grandparents knew what I was going to be in the future. So when I was a little baby, my grandparents didn't want me to be baptized. So to this day, I was never baptized in no church. I have no birth certificate to show. I never

---

40   *Čhaské*, in the Lakȟóta language, means "oldest son." Special responsibilities were placed upon the oldest grandchildren. They were expected to learn the traditional ways and be role models for younger siblings.

forgot my language. In fact, I was ten years of age before I started learning how to speak English, because I spoke my language all the time. I grew up in the traditional Indian way and I remember how they lived back in them days. When I started realizing, when I started looking around, I recognize a lot of things.

My grandparents raised my uncle, Uncle Phillip ... he's the one who took care of me a lot when they'd go to church. Grampa was telling important things to my uncle.

And I had another uncle, Rufus Charger. They was still single yet. They both stayed with my grandparents.

So I lived out in the country. I had nobody to play with, but I had a lot of grandmothers and grandfathers. My grampa said, "Anybody comes, even you don't know 'em, call 'em granma and granpa, 'cause they're somebody's grampa and they're somebody's granma. Maybe not you, but some other girl or boy your age, it's their grandparents."

People gather. They all come out and camp around, because he was a Chief's son. They'd come over with a team of horses and they'd pitch up a tent and camp out one or two weeks at a time and then go back. Then maybe another, some more came. They were all related. So between my grandmother, she had a lot of relatives, and Chief Martin Charger had a lot of relatives.

They all come to meet the Chief's son and live with him a while. At nights, they'd have a little campfire going. When it was nice out, they'd sit outside and talk, talk about the old, talk about what's going to be happening.

I used to watch all the old men sit in a circle and talk about the old ones, what this guy did, and all. Once in a while, someone would pick up his pipe bag, put his Pipe together, fill the Pipe up, and give it to the next guy. Each one smoked it. Then he'd blow it out, plug it, put it back in the bag.

They'd visit awhile, maybe a half-hour or hour, and someone else would pull his bag out next. Each one would carry his pipe bag like that, smoke it with kinnikinnik, [čhaŋšáša in Lakhóta], the inner bark of red willow. That's the way they got along.

PETS FOR TOYS

There were very few children living near his grandparents' isolated homestead. Whenever young Martin had a chance to play, he would play out on the prairie with the birds and animals. He would sometimes pretend that his grandfather's herd of cattle were buffalo. Using a rock, he sharpened a stick and made special markings on it to create his own warrior hunting stick. When he used it to poke the cows pretending to kill them, his grandmother would threaten to burn his stick.

Young Martin also liked to play "Cowboys and Indians." He would try to kill the "cowboys"... played by the family dog. He used his special stick which he would pretend was a gun and sneak up behind the dog. He would grab him around the neck and say "t'Á! t'Á! t'Á!" ("Die! Die! Die!" in English).

Sometimes he shared his memories in even greater detail:

> So that's the way I grew up. I didn't have no toys like you have today to play with. I didn't have nobody to play with in my growing up days, but I had a lot of grandmothers and grandfathers.
>
> Each time they came over they would bring a little animal for me to play with. So in my younger days, I used to have wild animals that my Grandparents raised. I played with them. Them were my toys. I had a skunk for a couple, three years that I played with. I always remember that. And a raccoon that one of my grandparents brought me. I'd study them.
>
> I always say that the raccoon was one of the cleanest animals. You give him some food, he always reminds me of little Chief (Martin's Shih Tzu). He come up to me, kinda wobble-like, look up at me and squeal.
>
> Gramma said to me, 'Go feed him. He's hungry.' I'd go over and give him milk in a nursing bottle. Set him up against the wall, give him that nursing milk. They never milked a cow. They'd buy canned milk. He trailed me everywhere I went.
>
> Now one you don't want to have is a fox. They're tame, but you turn a fox loose in here and he'd tear up one of these cushions, digging to see what's in there. Really curious. They'll have everything scattered when they tear into it. They keep digging, just like they keep looking for something. Couldn't find it. They'd ransack everything. The raccoon will do that too.
>
> Then I had a wild cat that I played with. I also had a coyote that my uncle caught. He used to be a trapper. He caught this little pup and gave it to me. He built a cage for it. I was

warned not to stick my finger in the cage so I wouldn't get bit. But as I was playing outside, that little coyote got to know me and understand me, and he got to be a real close friend of mine. I had it tied outside in chains. So every day I'm playing with it. Evenings, I'd take a stroll with the coyote. We'd walk up on top of the mountain and I'd tell him to holler, 'See if your parents, your relatives, can hear you!' And he'd sit back and howl.

So I studied the animals when I was a little boy, grew up with them. You see, we can communicate with the four leggeds. And so, at that time they taught me how to study these animals. And to this day, I still remember. What the spirits told me, I was thankful.

Martin shared stories told him by a neighboring grampa when he was a young boy. One was about an ancient four legged which he described as a dog, a wolf, or coyote, although the markings didn't look coyote (the hair was too long to be a dog, plus it had unusual spots).

The creature was chasing this man around the world, chasing him all the places he needed to go. Whenever the spirit animal smelled him, he would rub his nose into the dirt showing the dirt smell was better than the man. The spirit animal chased him to the river and he tricked him into jumping into the water to clean himself. The man feared the animal because he would show his big teeth and try to bite him. So the man ran from fear and the dog chased him into the water until the water had taken the smell from the man. Any negative energy would be lifted from him and taken down the river with the water. The dog chased him to where he could find food. He was always tricking him into getting and learning the things he had to learn.

When the man became an old man, he was sitting under a tree reflecting. He had traveled all these places; and all these years, the dog had chased him. He was still sitting under the tree when the dog sat down next to him and gave a root to him. Although his teeth were old and yellow, the old man washed the root and chewed it up and ate it.

He turned to the dog and he said, "Okay, I am too old. If you want me, you can eat me." He says, "Go ahead and eat me."

The dog, instead of showing his teeth, he grins and looks down. He lays down next to the old man. The old man looks at the dog and says, "Aren't you going to eat me?"

The dog says, "I never intended to eat you. I just wanted to be loved." And the old man starts to pet the dog.

Martin then told of a close relationship he had with a beaver when he was young. The beaver lived in the pond. Young Martin would stand on the shore and when the beaver would appear on top of his den, he would try to communicate with it. He wanted to play with the beaver and swim with him, so he would wade out into the water and try to get him to come out to play, but the beaver would disappear under the water.

One time, Martin had gone out to the pond and was sitting on the edge of the water looking across at the horizon. The beaver started to squeal and beat his tail on his den. Martin turned at that point and saw a wild dog stalking him from behind. When he stood up and faced the dog, the dog ran away.

He realized that the beaver had saved his life, so soon after he began to take some of his lunch out to the beaver and put it down on the edge of the pond. Everyone spoke of the hard times during the 1920's and he thought maybe the beaver needed assistance too. Whenever Martin returned, the food would be gone. He knew it probably wasn't the kind of food the beaver was used to eating, but it was always gone. He wasn't sure if the beaver ate the food he left. He thought maybe he may have come and smelled it and realized it wasn't what he ate and left it for other relations.

The beaver dam sometimes held too much water back. The families needed it to irrigate their garden, so Martin's grandfather would pay someone in town to go out to the pond and dynamite it to free up the water. After it was dynamited, the beaver got busy rebuilding his home.

Martin gave encouragement to the beaver as he worked and he tried to help the beaver. He would break off sticks from branches that were long enough for the beaver to use in his den. They seemed to be able to see mind to mind. The beaver probably didn't understand why he was helping, but it seemed he was grateful.

When they blew up the dam, he admired the beaver because it didn't deter him from making a new one. He knew what he needed to do for his family. Martin as an adult reflected that people can learn from the beavers. No matter how much our space is torn down, we keep building the protection back up.

To Martin, the beaver was very sacred. The beaver had taught him that he was capable of loving things that are much like our own relations, sometimes even more than two-legged relations.

He also realized the beaver was a little selfish and self-centered because he liked the water to be built up so he could have his pond year-round. The water couldn't get down steam where it was needed. The dam starved the gardens, but still, some water got through there.

One time, after the dam had been dynamited again, Martin walked out to the pond and the beaver was no longer there. He looked and looked and waited a long time for him to return. Then he became very sad. He left the pond and didn't return for a long time.

When he was getting ready to be sent off to boarding school, he realized he wouldn't be able to go to the pond whenever he wanted to, so he went out one last time. He cut off a part of his hair. He said some prayers and gifted his hair to the water, asking help from the spirits of the place. He knew that no matter where he went in the world, he would be able to return there in his prayers.

STORIES SHARED BY ELDERS

The grampa also told him a story of the old days long ago as he spoke of "the glory and the honor of the old people":

> A child was born who was different from the others. She was born with no arms. As she was growing up, the other children would run and play stick games. They would use their bows and arrows, or collect herbs, but because she was born with no arms, she could not join them. Some of them looked at her as being not right because she was not like them. But the grandmother and the mother and the Medicine Man always knew she was special. Grandmother spent much time teaching her to weave roots and grasses into baskets with her toes.
>
> The ancestors would come and wake her in the middle of the night and call her outside and she would dance in the meadows with the spirits. When she would tell the others

what she had done, the children would laugh at her, thinking something was wrong with her. They didn't realize she was special and had been given great gifts.

The spirits were kind to her so she continued to get up with them in the middle of the night. They began to honor her with many gifts. They showed her patterns, and so she would weave them into the baskets she made, and then tell the stories to her grandmother. They started to show her visions and tell her what they meant. She was taught how to go into the lodges of her people and purify them.

She was given a vision of each and every girl who also had special gifts. She was told what they would learn, and who they should sit with to learn. One child had the gift to talk with the herbs and could hear them. So she brought her people food which fed and healed the people. Another child had a special relationship with the star nation. She knew which way the wind was going to blow and she brought the wind forth. She knew when winter was going to come and if the fall would come early or late.

Another of the children could talk with the spirit animals. The animals came and ate out of her hands. The birds sat on her and talked to her in their spirit animal form. Her ancestors gifted her with the ability to know where it was safe to travel. If there was trouble, they would go to the girl and tell her so she could warn her people.

One had the gift of water. She helped the people to go down to water to purify and heal themselves with the spirit of the water and helped the women birth the babies. And the water, which gave the life force form within, had gifts for the babies of all the elements. These gifts were given to the tribe through the newborns so they would be shared with all.

As she grew older, the girl with no arms became greatly honored and loved among her people. And when it came time, she was married to the chief's son. When their children were born, she taught them many gifts and they eventually became great spiritual people held in high regard within the tribe.

Each of them, in time, had children of their own who had gifts that were passed on to them. Each one, when born, were not born with the gifts of the one they were born from. Instead they received the gifts of the sister or the aunt or the uncle. So they learned more about their gifts from other members of the family. This confused some of the people. "If I am not of water, why did I birth someone gifted with water?"

And the ancestors said, 'The spirit that comes through each of you is an element that is one of its own, and that is what you are to gift to the *thiyóšpaye*. It will carry and share its gifts among all of the people. And so then the children became the gifts to the extended family, and all members of the oyáte helped to raise the children so they would know who they were.

Another story that Martin carried with him for years was about a sacred *Čhaŋnúŋpa* (Pipe) told by a LaPlant elder, another neighbor to his grandparents. He spoke about early contact with incoming fur traders and how alcohol was first introduced to his people:

Long ago, traders traveled the Northern Great Plains from place to place in horse-driven wagons. They would set up camp, trading for furs and selling pots and pans and other household items. They also had alcohol in big barrels on their wagons. A band of Indian people saw the traders camped along the Missouri River. One man, the keeper of a sacred Pipe, had furs to trade. He wanted to go down and trade with them. In past times, he had traded for items that benefitted his thiyóšpaye. The women liked the cooking pots and beads and fabric. The men liked the guns and ammunition and other things the traders offered.

Others wanted to bypass the camp. One of the men had been shown in a dream that it would not be a good thing. He told his relative that he was shown they should not take their sacred Pipe there. The keeper of the Pipe said that even if they all shared his Pipe for prayers, he was still the keeper of the Pipe and he was going to take it with him. Their group would trade with the traders and then catch up with the others later.

The people continued on while the man and some of his family members went down to the camp of the traders to look for things to trade for their furs. The language barrier between the French Man and the Indian was difficult. The light-skinned man offered them something to drink. The Pipe carrier refused.

The trader said "No, you must sit down and drink with me first before we trade." The man thought his spirit was strong enough to handle the alcohol. He wouldn't let the women drink

47

but two of the men drank with the trader, and then they passed out. The women became agitated and threw water on the men trying to get them to wake up. When they woke up, they tried to continue the trade with the light- skinned traders. The traders told them they had nothing left to trade with because they had drank all their furs away.

The men felt betrayed and angry. The man carrying the Pipe knew there was to be no anger or conflict around the Pipe. There was to be no violence or death around the sacred Pipe because it was a spiritual item that represented peace and harmony. But he was confused from his alcohol use, and so he fought with the fur trader. In the process, his Pipe dropped to the ground.

Another band had stopped at the trader's wagon and witnessed this incident. They had smoked with this band in the past and they knew how sacred the Pipe was. While the Pipe carrier was in a drunken state, the sacred Pipe changed nations. That's when the drunkenness and trouble started within this band. It became their downfall when the Pipe went into the hands of the other band.

The old man had said to young Martin after sharing his story, "That still needs to be corrected."

Young Martin sat in church praying about it. He thought to himself, "Yes, it will be corrected."

This was an important teaching for Martin to reflect upon. He preferred listening to the elders over going to school. The elder's story of the coming of the European traders with their alcohol and the beginning of his peoples' losses would linger in his memory throughout his lifetime. It would motivate him to make essential changes in his lifestyle, including giving up alcohol himself later in his life.

MARTIN'S SPIRITUALITY WAS GROWING

Martin was very young when his spiritual awakening began. His First Spiritual World started him on his lifelong path of service. He was in connection with the Spirit World during his early years.

By the time he was 10 or 12 years old, he continued to be guided on the *Čhaŋkú Wakȟáŋ*, the Holy Trail. The spirits were talking to him, working with him and training his mind. He became increasingly aware of spirituality growing inside of him, and he was also able to differentiate between the visions he was having and when they were just fantasies.

Sometimes his feelings disturbed him. They would overwhelm him, and he didn't always know what to do about them. So after church when his chores were done, he would take off walking. He would walk down to the pond and skip rocks. Then he would grow really still and talk to the prairie surrounding him. The winds would whisper to him and he would ask them the secrets and hidden things of his ancestors. He would ask them for the knowledge and understanding to become the great warrior like his grandmother and uncles had said he would become. The Spirit World continued to show him why it was so important that he honor his elders, listen to their instructions and learn to do his part.

As he grew older, he was being led to his own *Haŋblééheya* (Vision Quest). An incident he experienced when he was still a young boy frightened him. He was not yet a teenager when he put himself out on his own Vision Quest ceremony. Nobody put him up. He was alone and he didn't have much with him, but he had a vision.

In his vision, he witnessed the power of the Thunders. He saw large stones moving and crashing against each other across the sky. Everything was shaking. The Thunders were striking the earth and the sky. When they hit, the stones around him on the earth started glowing.

He thought the spirits were punishing him for doing something that he wasn't supposed to do, but they weren't. They were just showing him the gift he would have at a later age and what it looked like energy wise.

He got scolded for doing it, plus the experience created a fear of the power inside of him. It helped him realize that one can be fearful of their own power. He didn't feel he was worthy of the power, but he always listened for that sound. He was always looking to see where that light would flash, but whenever he got to see it, it came with a lingering fear.

Later in life, he would advise others not to be so foolish as he had been. He would caution others who had similar ideas, explaining that they might not have the protection they needed. He would say, "Just because you think you are called to be a Medicine

Man doesn't mean you are a Medicine Man. You have to grow into it and be trained. The power and medicine is already there, but people need to be able to look at their own life struggles, think about their mistakes and learn from them."

Respecting Both Christianity and Spirituality

Throughout his boyhood in the 1920's, young Martin continued listening to stories and historical accounts of elders who came to visit at their homestead. They spoke of past threats and violence from government policies forced upon them when they were caught practicing their cultural and spiritual traditions.

One event occurred twenty-nine years before his birth when more than three hundred elders, women and men and their children fled Standing Rock Indian Reservation following the murder of Sitting Bull. As they traveled south through Cheyenne Agency settlements, some Cheyenne River members joined them. They traveled through the bitter cold of winter to their deaths at the hands of the US Cavalry in the December 29, 1890 Massacre at Wounded Knee.

One grandfather told how their family had conducted traditional funerals and burial ceremonies of their ancestors for centuries. These ceremonies were now prohibited and they were forced to rely on the local priest or minister to conduct a Christian funeral. Unsettled, he told how his family's spiritual items, including his grandfather's *Čhaŋnúŋpa* (Sacred Pipe) and *Čháŋčheǧa* (drum); his grandmother's *Wagmúha* (rattle), and other ceremonial Medicine Bundles were confiscated. He didn't know what happened to them and whether they had been destroyed or put into a museum.

A grandmother shared how they were forced to give up their traditional Lakȟóta wedding ceremony and accept church wedding ceremonies. She cried saying how their hearts were also shattered as children and grandchildren were forcibly removed from their homes to attend church-run boarding schools.

Martin was troubled to hear their stories. It seemed the traumas had exacerbated their suffering. He would sit in church reflecting on them, daydreaming about the Indians of his ancestry and how he would someday help to save his people like the elders had predicted.

Families at Cheyenne Agency had learned to weather hard times since the 1880's when the reservation was first established.

Martin's grandparents relied on family, community networks and their spirituality in order to survive the poverty and other hardships. They maintained an optimistic attitude, sharing what they had with one another and providing encouragement and support when needed.

For the sake of unity, they joined two local churches in compliance with government officials at Cheyenne Agency. His grandfather Samuel, was a member of the Episcopal Church at LaPlant and also joined the Brotherhood of St. Andrew. His grandmother Rosa, was a member of LaPlant's Catholic Church and was active in the St. Joseph's Women's Society.

Sometimes, young Martin would travel to church with his grandparents. Sitting in the pew at church, he would think about what the elders had said about the old ways. He would remember the stories told to him, what they said was coming in the future.

In his prayers he would ask the ancestors to come and help him. From all that was said, he had moments of confusion. The people said that he would play a part in bringing the people back, but he didn't know how he was going to do that.

Sometimes, he would pretend he was on a mountain praying to *Tȟuŋkášila* – the grandfathers, for a vision of what he could do to save his people. He would daydream of riding up on horseback and rounding the people up and saving them, but somehow, he knew that wasn't the real vision. Then his grandmother would elbow him to sing and it would bring him back to attention.

Martin had been taught in the Catholic religion about saints his grandmother prayed to for different reasons. When he was sitting in church, he remembered what an elder had told him.

The old man had said, "Men like Jesus, women like Mary, and all the saints and prophets, all those they learned about at church and in the Bible, were our ancestors over across. But we have great ones that our old people talk about, saints and prophets among our own ancestors. Our ancestors, we can pray to them too. Ancestors like Red Cloud, the Buffalo Calf Pipe Woman, and others like Singing Eagle, and Blue Earth."

Martin began looking for those ancestors within his own lineage, so when he prayed to Virgin Mary, he would also pray to the Buffalo Calf Pipe Woman.

His grandmother didn't tell him, but others told him he needed to go on the mountain, walk the land and feel the connection with Mother Earth, just like their ancestors had done. He listened and so when he was not needed at home, he walked the foothills from place to place in nature to find his ancestors. The spirits were waiting to be called upon. He knew they were out there and would show themselves.

His grandmother had said that Mary would show herself to the people, so he was looking for his own, like the Sacred Buffalo Calf Woman. Mary was like an ancestor, but he really preferred to talk to his closest Indian ancestors. He felt they would be unconditional in their love for him and they would accept him as a direct descendant. It wasn't that Mary wouldn't accept him. It's just that she wasn't his direct family and that seemed important to him.

His search was at the beginning of his awakening. Even as a child, he had that spiritual longing in him, that spiritual seeking, wanting to find the real connection, not just what somebody else told him. Sitting in church, he would think of the stories his elders had told and ask for guidance so he would know what to do.

CELEBRATING CHRISTMAS

Martin's family celebrated Christmas and he liked to share his memories of them when gatherings were held around winter holiday time. He spoke from his home in Portland one Christmas:

> As long as I was growing up, I never hear my Grandparents ever argued about the religion. They respected and honored, I presume, because it was created from God. They believe in God. Every Sunday, my Uncle used to hitch up the team and buggy. They had a little light buggy. They'd go in town five miles to church on Sunday. My uncle used to stay home and take care of me. When they'd get in town, Gramma would go to the Catholic, and my Grampa would go to the Episcopal Church. When they'd come back, they'd probably stop at my folks' place, have coffee and head on back.
>
> It's just like I say. It's pretty near Christmas, right around the corner. I had a mother who really believed in Christmas. She believed in everything. I still hear a lot of things my mother said. She said, "You ought to be thinking about

Christmas." She worked hard in her church. She was one of their leaders. At the same time, she believed and honored all the kids. Come Christmas time, she used to make candy bags and pass it out to all the kids. That was the way she lived.

So today when Christmas comes, I think about my mother. My mother passed away, so when I came out here [to Portland, Oregon], I started doing that. One of my sisters was doing that until she passed away. We had a bunch of candy bags made and they were passed out. I wanted to take up where my mother left off. So this is why I honor Christmas.

This is why I've always talked about respect and honor of one another. This was the way the old people lived. That was one of their main goals. The old. The old traditional way about the Seven Ways. Everybody lived that way. And that's the reason I always talk about it, because it means a lot to the people.

They believed in Christmas. As long as they lived the traditional Indian way, they honored and respected Christ because they all believed in Him who was sent down and born to be a Medicine Man and spiritual advisor to the White people.

About the same time Christ came, they had the White Buffalo Calf Pipe brought to us. The Maiden brought it, and so this is why they celebrated Christmas. All hear them sing church hymns in the Lakȟóta language. Seems like everybody knew them songs. Some were Catholics, some Episcopal, Congregation. Them were the three important churches Indian people used to go to, but they also had their traditional ways to gather together.

I used to tell the people up here, "Come Christmas day or Christmas eve, you people should start the fire and have a good Sweat and honor this Medicine Man's birthday. Have respect for Him." I presume there were different places that started doing that. We honor that Man that was born, then nailed to a cross. I know that some of the old people say, "They should've given us Christ. We would have still had ... not him, but his lineage, as our leader." That's how much respect they had.

I just wanted to tell a little of my story of how I spent Christmas and New Year's. At Christmas time, my uncle used to hitch the horses up to the sled. Back in them days, we had a double-box and he would fill that up with hay, and my

Grampa and Uncle – they'd sit up on the seat of the wagon, and I and my Gramma, they fixed it so we dug into the hay with the blankets covered up. Thirty or forty below zero, and we had to go about ten or twelve miles to a church where they had Christmas.

When we'd get there, there was a lot of teams. Nobody traveled by cars. Horseback or in a wagon or bobsleds. They all meet at that church. It was a lot of snow and the winter was cold. The horses, I always remember, had icicles on their noses. Them are the days that people were pretty strong. They were healthy. They had a lot to live for.

They had a Christmas tree like the one we have here. People bring presents, but not presents like we have today. They were things that they made. Everybody had clothing or something for Christmas presents. They'd wrap them up, kind of like a giveaway to each other. They didn't have Christmas wrapping like we do today.

They used to stay up all night Christmas night at the guild hall. Some talked. Some would pray, and then they sing the songs, and they'd have a feast about midnight. My gramma, she fixed a bed underneath her bench where she was sitting, and that's where I slept. They'd stay up all night, until morning. About three in the morning, when everybody'd start breaking up, leaving, my Uncle would hitch the horses up. We still had enough hay, so we'd bundle ourselves and get inside the hay again and ride home.

They had a lot of respect for one another in them days. They'd drive a long way to share. Share each other's honor. Share each other's speech. Them were the ways they used to live back in the old days.

NEW YEAR CELEBRATION

Martin's family embraced the Indian way of life, but because of criticism of Indian religion, they practiced it privately at home while celebrating Christian traditions with the community. Martin told a story from his younger years when his grandparents prepared to travel several miles into LaPlant to bring in the New Year at the church.

His grandmother brushed his long black hair and pull it back into a pony tail at the bottom of his neck. She had a buckskin shirt that she had made for him, but he didn't like to wear it, so he resisted getting dressed. He didn't like wearing a lot of clothes and the buckskin made him too warm. She informed him that maybe he would need to go spend time chopping wood for the elders because they needed their wood supplies to make it through the hard winter, so then he got dressed.

One New Year's Eve, there was no snow and the ground was very dry from the drought. His uncle hitched up the horse and prepared the wagon. It was cold outside, so he packed the bed of the wagon with hay. To provide extra protection for Martin and his grandmother from the cold, he brought out hot rocks that had been heated in the wood stove along with the pots of food. Draped in blankets and warmed by the hot stones, they climbed into the hay pile and made the journey into town.

As they approached the church, a number of people were standing outside talking. Women were bringing pots of food tied up in cloth into the church. Everybody was dressed up. The men were dressed in pants, shirts and hats. Some were wearing chimney hats. It was nearly sunset and the sky was vibrant with yellows and pinks as everyone started to go inside the building. The elders called the children to come inside. Several children were standing outside the door of the church, but Martin felt uncomfortable around them.

At that point, a bird caught his interest. The bird was flying low like a grouse or maybe a burrowing owl so he wandered away following it around the side of the building. Fascinated, he followed it into the grass to watch it closer. At that point, his uncle came out and told him he needed to come in, so he dropped his head down, turned around and walked back to the door of the church.

Inside the gathering hall, about 20 adults and a handful of children were sitting down. Someone was in the front speaking in the Lakȟóta language. Martin had learned to speak English at boarding school by now, but he still spoke fluent Lakȟóta. He listened as the man shared stories about the past year and about the year coming up. Others spoke of the old ways and their traditional spirituality and about the importance of now going to church. They were gradually adjusting to the new religious beliefs and spiritual practices. Someone was saying that going backwards to do warrior stuff wasn't going to help the people anymore. Others spoke of how they had begun to worship inside because the people were getting older and could no longer do ceremonies outside in the cold. It seemed that some of the Christian beliefs had been accepted by some of the people in that circle who expressed that just believing in God was going to help.

Martin continued to listen but he wasn't comfortable inside the building. He felt really tired and didn't feel like he belonged. He just didn't feel that God was in there; he felt God outside with the colors of the sunset, the birds and the wind. He looked toward the window, watching the color of the lights reflecting beautiful sunset colors into the room. His mind skipped and he began to daydream, thinking about the bird he had been following. He thought about what was said earlier in the circle, about the things his grandmother said to him, and about all the work he had to do tomorrow morning.

When everybody stood up to sing Christian hymns, Martin did not rise to his feet. Then he got bumped on the shoulder by his uncle. He stood and blurted out a couple of words and moved his lips. Still looking out the window, he wished he could be outside. He could tell that this was going to be a very long night.

Then someone began to use their drum. When the people began to dance and sing the old ceremony songs, it lifted his spirits. He started to dance with them. He loved the rhythmic sound of the elk's teeth sewn on the front of his grandmother's dress. They hit together as she swayed back and forth. She wore her dark blue buckskin dress that she had died with the berries that are too bitter to eat. Martin remembered when she first made it. He had watched her rub the berries onto the front of the leather with a stone.

At midnight they enjoyed their old traditional foods, bowls of *pápa* (dried beef) soup made with *thíŋpsiŋla* (prairie turnips) and *waštúŋkala* (dried corn), plus *wasná* (pemmican) made by combining dried, pounded beef with dried chokecherry patties. Their dessert was chokecherry *wóžapi* (fruit soup) on Indian fry-bread.

Later on, the grandmothers put blankets and coats down in the corner of the building for the children to lay on. They were going to be there most of the night and as the children grew weary, they were told they could lay down. Martin's grandmother put blankets on Martin and he closed his eyes like he was going to sleep. When she walked away, he opened his eyes and stared out the window. Martin recounted:

Then come New Year's, they do the same thing. They all go back to the same little church again. They have a big feast at midnight, where they have the old traditional way. New Year comes in and they run the Old Year out. Different ones make a speech. The ones making the speech are the elderly predicting what's going to be. It seemed like they never missed it. Pretty accurate. What's New Year's going to be like? They talk about it. People listened. Them were the good old days!

I remember one New Year's when some of the menfolk were outside tending the horses. The church was just a little away, like from here to the road behind the guild hall. And in the church, there was somebody played the organ, played the hymn. They said, 'Somebody's in the church playing the organ.'

Everybody went out and listened. Didn't hear no voices, but you could hear the organ playing a hymn. Everybody came in and some of the menfolk went over to the church. Nobody'd put a padlock on the church, but there was about a foot of snow on the steps of the church. No tracks, but somebody was playing the organ. I always remember that as a little boy.

Martin once shared another story about himself that he had heard his parents tell. As a young boy, his grandparents' church gatherings frequently continued long into the night. One of his grandmas would fix a bed underneath her bench so when Martin grew tired, he always crawled underneath her seat and fell asleep.

He was still a young boy when his grandmother died. During her wake at the church, they laid her in her casket (which was on a pair of sawhorses) while friends and family came to mourn. After a while, young Martin disappeared and they couldn't find him anywhere. They finally found him where he had always gone when he was tired. He'd crawled underneath his gramma's casket to take a nap.

ABUNDANCE AT THE CHARGER RANCH

History refers to the years following World War One as a time of optimism.[41] It was widely reported how things were "looking up" for Indian families. Yet, on the Cheyenne River Indian Reservation, life continued to be challenging. Native families

41   In 1917, for the first time in 50 years since 1867, Indian births exceed deaths. In 1921, the Department of Interior became responsible for Indian education, medical and social services, instead of the War Department. In 1924, the U.S. Government awarded citizenship to all Native-born Indians.

faced significant hardships. Illnesses including tuberculosis and trachoma were prevalent, partially because the people had no immunity to settlers' diseases and because insufficient food supplies affected their health. Humble cabins lacked insulation, plumbing and electricity. Most people were still on horseback in those days, using horse drawn wagons.

The 1925 reports from Cheyenne River showed that families had to contend with hot summer winds, drought, grasshoppers, thunderstorms and hailstorms that frequently destroyed crops. However, they had successes during the US Government's Five-Year Program. Despite these obstacles, tribal members, including Martin's grandfather – Sam Charger, overcame bad weather, poor market conditions, credit limits, and increased leasing and ceding of tribal lands.

Indian families formed 25 farm chapters on 200-400 acres resulting in more productive gardens than ever before. Most land was semi-arid and more suitable for ranching, but some parts along stream bottoms, where fine clay soil or gumbo mixed with sandy loam, was fertile.[42] Each family raised hundreds of bushels of barley, oats, wheat, corn and flax in 1926, plus they had productive gardens, made root cellars and saved seeds for planting the next year or two. Reports showed that every family raised potatoes, turnips, onions, pumpkins, beans, and melons.[43]

FARM CHAPTERS FLOURISH ON CHEYENNE RIVER

In 1927, Samuel, serving as Secretary of the LaPlant Farm Chapter, reported that 40 families were keeping gardens, 12 were milking cows, 25 were keeping poultry and 4 tended pigs.[44] The Yellow Hawk Chapter formed a Women's Auxiliary on the Cheyenne River Reservation in 1928.

The women, including Grandmother Rosa and Martin's mother Louise High Bear, dried and canned garden crops; wild fruits and vegetables for winter and giveaway.[45] The Chapter was signed by: Rosa Charger; Jennie Medicine Body; Sophia Roan Bear; Eliz-

---

42   Report of Division of Industries District Superintendent O. O. Upchurch, 3 October 1926

43   In a letter to the Commissioner of Indian Affairs from Indian Agent RC Craige, January 19, 1926

44   Letter to the Commissioner of Indian Affairs from Sam Charger regarding Farm Chapter organizations, 2 June 1927

45   Letter from Chas Burke to Wm Roberts, about the weekly report of LaPlant's Yellow Hawk Chapter

abeth Garreau; Ida White Eye; Josephine Yellow Hawk; Annie Shaving; Lizzie Summers; Agnes Crow Feather; Margaret Spotted Rabbit; Elizabeth Crow Feather; Mrs. Cecelia Bowker; Mrs. Lucy Lee; Louise High Bear and Annie Eagle Boy.[46]

A 1928 newspaper article reported that: *"Prize winning vegetables grown 'in gumbo' by Indians at Cheyenne River Reservation's Indian Fair was one of the best ever held there. Poultry and corn exhibits included some ears of corn 14 inches long. Pumpkin, squash and melons included a pumpkin measuring 56 inches in circumference and 19 inches long."*

In 1929, when the Great Depression hit, Martin was ten years old. Thousands of farmers and ranchers in the Plains states went bankrupt and abandoned their allotments. Although White ranchers secured more land by purchasing or leasing it from the struggling Indian families,[47]

Ranching seemed to represent the only permanent economy possible to Indians in the region who overcame bad weather, poor market conditions, credit limits, and checker-boarded lands brought about by increased leasing and ceding of tribal lands. Martin's grandfather and other Indian ranchers were able to continue operating their ranches. Some gained employment from cowboying, rodeos, horse races and other celebrations helping to honor and acknowledge talents of Indian cowboys.

Despite the economic depression, Agency reports and other correspondence reflected signs of resilience among Cheyenne Agency families. The summer of 1930 was the second driest in the recorded history of the state. Reports described "baked-hardpan fields that were impenetrable by the little moisture that managed to reach the ground."[48] Despite that, the list of entries and prizes listed 29 Indians who entered and won 115 different exhibits at the August 1930 County Fair in Faith, South Dakota. The tribe's Home Demonstration Agent reported: *"The Indians received so many first and second prizes in competition with Whites. We realize that it requires hard work and determination to achieve such success and we wish to extend our congratulations to the prize winners and to those who advised and assisted the Indians in making their exhibits."*

46   Letter from Chas Burke to Wm Roberts, about report and positive progress of Yellow Hawk Chapter, 16 July 1928

47   *A New History of South Dakota, Ranching: East to West*, Bob Lee, Ch. 14, p. 255.

48   *History of Agriculture in South Dakota: A Historic Context*, SWCA Environmental Consultants, July 2013 21-22

While the mass exodus of White farmers out of South Dakota was occurring, Indian families continued to strengthen their efforts to grow, harvest and preserve food for the winter. 1930 Reports from Home Demonstration Agents documented extensive Cheyenne Agency Indians' exhibits at County Fairs which included: jelly (wild grape, cherry, buffalo berry, plum jelly and preserves), junior corn, yellow dent corn, white dent corn, flour corn, potatoes, watermelons, muskmelons, turmeric pickles, beet pickles, watermelon pickles. Dried displays included dried corn, hominy, buffalo berries, chokecherries, grapes, plums and June berries. Vegetables included turnips and corn on the cob, potatoes (Early Ohio and other), carrots, rutabaga, onions, cabbage, cucumbers, tomatoes, muskmelon and watermelon, plus wheat, oats, chickens, turkeys, and geese. Award-Winning Fancy included moccasins, quilts, pillow cases, dresser scarves, card table covers, crocheted work, and bead work.

Despite these successes, it was reported: *"The shortage of crops and gardens will make it necessary to help the Indians tide over the winter months. Even the wild fruit will not yield more than a half crop, or average more than a 60% yield in crops, garden, farm or fruit."*[49]

Again, during the summer of 1931, Indian agent reports showed that the drought and intense heat damaged corn, potatoes, and small grains crops. Grasshoppers, blister beetles, cucumber beetles and other garden insects caused severe damage to cucumbers, squash, pumpkin and melons.[50]

Correspondence from Charger and other farm chapter secretaries documented an unwavering commitment by Cheyenne River Sioux for improving prosperity in their communities. While they enjoyed another good year in 1931 with abundant harvests of wheat, corn, potatoes, turnips, onions, pumpkins, beans, and melons, the reports also documented difficulties: "... gardens, corn, potatoes, small grains have all suffered severely from the drought and intense heat. In many cases, grasshoppers have done untold damage. Garden insects have been especially severe on all garden stuff. The blister beetle on potatoes, and cucumber beetle on cucumbers, squash, pumpkin and melons were especially bad. Paris Green has given control of these in-

---

49   Letter from Commissioner C. J. Rhoads, to Miss Alice B. Hancock, Home Demonstration Agent, National Archives, Washington DC., 11 Sep 1930
50   USDA Extension Narrative Report for Dewey County, South Dakota, July 1931

sects in some places. There is still a chance of a small amount of their crops maturing with additional rain and cooler weather. There is sufficient evidence to show that the average Indian family has really tried to raise stuff this year by taking pains in keeping fields clean and fighting insects."[51]

Martin's grandparents spoke very little of the suffering around them. They had learned from their elders and ancestors never to complain about difficulties. Grandmother Rosa would tell him that their people were blessed with the strength to survive. She said the stronger and more fortunate ones helped their other relatives who might be lacking food or supplies. She would say, "We are the lucky ones. We have much compared to many of our people." She emphasized that the people were strong as long as they remained close to *Tȟuŋkášila*, Great Spirit, in their prayers.

However, what Martin saw troubled him. He questioned his grandparents. Martin said, "Gramma said we were rich, but I did not feel rich. I saw too much suffering during my growing up years." His grandmother continued to remind him that if they didn't let difficulties bother them, the challenges would make them even stronger.

This is why young Martin didn't have a lot of time to play. There was a lot of work to do. At 12 years of age, he helped his uncle in the garden. He helped his grandmother gather and dry foods. He helped deliver groceries, gather and chop wood, and carried water for his grandparents and other elders.

Recordings of Martin reflected this resilience:

> My grandparents, Charger, had a few head of cattle, 30 or 40. He raised them for eating purposes. We had calves. I never seen my grandfather sell any of them calves. I never seen him wean his calves. I never seen him take a needle and put medicine in these calves. They were healthy.
>
> And so, in the fall of the year, he'd look at the moon. And at a certain time, my grandfather said 'We're going to butcher, grandson. When the spider webs start floating around all over, that's when the flies are gone.' He'd tell my uncle to run in the cows and pick a nice cow out, not too fat. So they butchered two cows.

---

51   Narrative report, Dewey County, South Dakota, July 1931

They had no refrigerators, no electricity out there in the country, so they'd dry all the meat. We'd jerk all that dry meat, dry it and put it in great big old grub boxes, like suitcases or trunks that my uncle made. Then they'd put it away. They don't waste nothing.

Our ancestors didn't have kitchen utensils. Often people wondered how they warmed the water up to make soup. They build a fire and take these rocks and put water in the stomach of a dried out buffalo. They put meat and a hot rock in there and that's the way they boiled the water. Today, we just turn the faucet on to get hot water. In them days, that was the quickest way, to put a hot rock in water. That's how you cook it.

And so this is the way I grew up in my younger days. There sure is a lot of difference today from the way our ancestors lived – how people communicated, how they used to live. A lot of good things – living in tipis. Drinking from the water hole. Gunny sacks of dried meat, wild turnips and corn.

I don't think we can live that life today and have it come back again that way. Today, you have insulated coveralls and all that, and still we're cold. In them days, that's the way God created them to live. They enjoyed it. Like my grandfather said, 'Them are the good old days.'

During the summer, I used to go out with my grandmother. I'll always remember, we hitched up little white Indian ponies they called 'em ... to a wagon, to a little buggy. And we used to go out and dig the wild roots. Here we have wild turnips. So this time of the year, in June, we used to go out and dig wild turnips. Put them in a braid and leave them out somewhere to dry. Everything they dried. And that's all put away. Winter food. Then comes the fruit in June. We picked June berries and currants and she, she'd can all this. And we had a pantry, they called it, down in the basement, a little room. And gramma had them all stacked in shelves. Everything they need is already canned and put away, the wild fruit.

And in the fall, we picked chokecherries. Gramma used to come out with those chokecherries and she'd sit there all day pounding cherries. She'd dry them out just like hamburger patties, out in the sun. She'd turn them over. When they was dried out, she'd put them in a big gunny sack, and put them away.

Right after the second frost, we picked buffalo berries. I helped my grandmother go out and pick the berries. We'd dry these berries and put them away. Everything was raised out here. That's the way they lived.

Despite the hard work, it seems his grandparents rarely reflected discouragement or complained. Martin said:

I remember how my grandparents made their living out in the country and how they raised their own garden. They put in big gardens and they had a cellar. Back in them days, you didn't have to be rich to make a living. Grandmother Earth survived us. We put in all the potatoes, vegetables, corn, all these.

Go out here, my uncle used to have two horses, tied with reins around its neck, one plow with two handles on it. Day after day, he goes. Then he goes out with his jabber and plants corn, rows after rows of corn. We go out here and dig a hole and Gramma used to put in potatoes, rows of them. Watermelon, they raised them.

Comes in the fall, they have harvest of all their vegetables. The corn, Gramma used to half cook it and shell it from the cob, lay it in the sun to dry. When it was all dried out, we'd sack it up and store it away. *Waštúŋkala*, we call that.

In the fall, they'd all dig those potatoes. I used to help them dig potatoes out. We'd go with a plough, root them all up. What they want to keep for their winter feed, they put it in the cellar. My uncle lines it out with hay and they haul all their potatoes in there and cover it up with hay again. Then they close the cellar up.

And so, these are the ways that I was raised. I don't remember growing up that my grandfather or grandmother ever go to town every day and buy groceries. I remember my uncle saddling the horse up to go into town to buy flour. The only thing I remember them buying is a couple hundred-pound sacks of flour, baking powder – and they smoked ... about a sack of Bull Durham would last them pretty near two weeks because they wouldn't have more than one or two cigarettes a day. That's all they smoke. They might buy a little sugar sometime.

They wasn't coffee drinkers. Most of the time they drank their own peppermint tea. Gramma goes out and collects *čheyáka* (peppermint leaves) around the swamp area and she dries it and puts it in great big sacks. So there wasn't hardly anything they bought in them days.

There was nothing that they spent money on. Like today we have to get up in the morning, run to the store and buy eggs and bacon, bring back and cook it. Dinner time, run to the store and buy a few cans of groceries and come back and cook. That's an everyday deal. We have to run to the store every meal to get this chemical food. Now we're eating a lot of these foods that are already cooked and put in cans on the shelves of these stores. This is why I've always told people, don't lose your can opener. You lose that can opener, you gonna' all starve to death. That's the system. No wonder our lives are short today. We grow old before our time.

The Grandfathers told me to tell the people, "If you want to survive, let Mother Earth, our only Grandmother, Mother Earth, survive you. She is here waiting for many moons." And so, this is why I've always told people, "Don't wait 'til it gets to the shelves in the stores, because you may not get it." I told them to put in their gardens like the old people used to do. I know how it is. I was raised by grandparents. It's been so many years now that that has been happening. It can be done. It has been done. We can do it again.

MARTIN'S SISTER MELDA REMEMBERED

Martin's sister Melda, remembered life in their family during the 1930's and the role Martin played as the oldest grandson:

Martin, he is the oldest one in our family. He hardly stayed with us because he was at Grampa Sam and Gramma Rose's out at LaPlant, north 8 or 10 miles on a ranch. The two brothers, Joe and Martin, they were a big help with the cows and they rode horseback. Whenever they come home, they will go to work with my dad out of town to make a living.

LaPlant is where we lived too. Martin is always busy. Whenever there was work, he left home. He turned cowboy. He broke horses for saddle horses. Him and my brother Joe broke horses to work pulling a wagon. He is a good hunter with my brother Joe.

Martin loved to joke. He was always in a good mood, even when times were so bad. He also was very helpful to mom as we had to haul water, chop wood. We were always working. Whenever he was around it made work lighter for my dad and mom.

I never heard him get mad or swear so I grew up not using rough language because my brothers never used that kind of language. Our grandfather told us not to use God's name in vain, and also our mom told us that too. He is so kind to the elderly. He drives cars for them to the Cheyenne Agency to the Government office for business which is often.

Martin had quite a talent dancing all kinds of dances, but he was the best in Charleston. I never saw him, but mom told me. He really amused the guys at the pool hall in LaPlant. I liked to hear him whistle to tunes. Me and my friends enjoyed him whistling. Sounds like a bird to me.

DAY SCHOOL AT CHEYENNE RIVER

To Martin, real education was the daily exposure of life living with his grandparents and his experience in the world of nature out on the land. He loved listening to the stories of his grandparents and learning from their experiences.

He participated in their ceremonies and other cultural traditions. He observed their strong kinship relationships and the rich cultural values of sharing and giving, respect and kindness, optimism and humor interacting with one another. He studied the birds, animals and the medicinal plants on his grandparents' ranch. He loved traditional food, especially what he harvested with his grandmother. To him, this was the real education.

Martin spoke of his experience starting school at LaPlant Day School. He was nine years old before he was enrolled by his grandparents. Young Martin's experience at the day school was challenging but not as traumatizing as for other Indian students. He was not subjected to forcible removal from his home and family by authorities like so many other children. He went to day school so he continued to live at his grandparents' home.

At school, however, he was forced to learn a foreign language. He could only speak, read, and write English at school and since he had only spoken Lakȟóta at home, he was constantly punished by the teacher for speaking his language. He was made fun of and ridiculed by the other students for this.

He also lacked experience relating to and playing with other children. When the White children teased and bullied him, he would react by fighting with them. He was then punished for fighting. The teacher began to restrict him during recess. His uncle and the janitor had to escort him to and from school. He was not allowed to go outside to play during recess so he was forced to stay in the classroom while the children played outside. He shared memories of day school:

> I think I was nine or ten years old before I went to school. I was out in the country raised all alone. That time that I went to school, I started learning how to speak English. I never learned how to speak it before because my grandparents never spoke English. They spoke Indian all the time. When my parents came out to visit me on the weekends, they all spoke Indian to me, so there was no word of English that anybody ever used, and this is how I grew up.
>
> So when I didn't speak very good English, they teased me. Then I start fighting White kids. On the way to school, there's an Indian janitor at the school. He meets me. He escorts me right up into the classroom. So during the school year, I always stayed fifteen minutes after school was out for the day after all kids left the campus. Then the teacher turned me loose. So until I went away to boarding school, I never had recess.[52.]
>
> My father lived right behind the big schoolhouse. I always remember when I'd go to the little store after groceries, all the little kids would be playing outside having a lot of fun. And when they would see me coming down the road towards the store down town, all the kids would hide from me until I got away from the store and back home. Then they would all come out. I got along with their parents, but the kids, I guess I never could get along with them. I also got along good with the Indian boys. I played with them after school.

Going to Boarding School

Martin thought that his grandfather had him attend boarding school partially because of the conflicts with White students at LaPlant Day School:

---

52   There was one exception to Martin being restricted from recess. One of Martin's teachers liked to work with him during his recess time. He told how she taught him how to tap dance during recess. Then, in the early 1930's, when Lawrence Welk and his band came to LaPlant, Martin showed off his tap dancing skills to the crowd that had gathered, dancing to the music of Lawrence Welk.

In them days, you have to live so far from a public school before they can send you to a boarding school, so for two years I went to day school where Indian kids and White kids mixed. The third year they sent me to boarding school. My grandfather was the one who said to do it this way. The school superintendent, my grandfather and my dad agreed that I had a hard time with White kids. Maybe, they thought, it would be better to send me to a boarding school where I'd be among the Indian kids.

I didn't get very much schooling there. When I went away to boarding school, my last year of school, I ran away. The whole school was quarantined and I didn't want to be among that bunch so I ran away from school. They never came after me.

My grandfather, when he went to school, only went up to the third grade. That's all the school they ever had, so I always think when you get to the third grade, it's just like you're graduating from school. So that's the only education I ever had in my lifetime. But my granddad had a bunch of books. He was always reading books. I'd ask gramma. I said, 'What's grampa's reading them books for, them big ones?' And she always tells me, 'Them are the ones that the judge reads. *Wóophe*, the law.' That's what he studies, and that's how he taught himself back home, and so he was an educated man, but he had a lot of respect for everybody.

This is the way I grew up when I was a little fellow. I was raised by my grandparents this way up 'til I was old enough to work. But still, I always remember what my grandmother and my grandfather taught me. I grew up in that manner until my dad got sick and I went into town to help my dad.

STRENGTHENING SPIRITUALITY DURING SEVERE WEATHER

What wasn't killed off during the intensely hot summer weather of 1929, the winter blizzards in 1929 did. It killed the cattle and other livestock, finishing off many Indian ranchers, along with many non-Indians as well.[53]

Martin spoke of that winter:

They called it the Winter of the Late Snows. He said they thought it was never going to snow and that they would be suffering from drought that next year, but when the snows

---

53   US Senate hearing #12336, National Archives, 1929

came, they came hard, deep and heavy. Martin remembered how he helped his uncle dig out of their cabin to feed and water the cattle and do other chores. They couldn't travel to the reservoir to get their water, so they melted the snow for drinking water until late in the spring.

My grandparents survived with that, all winter long. Snow can get ten-foot-deep outside and blow for days. Blizzard! After a snowstorm, my uncle used to saddle up and I'd always stand at the window and watch my uncle. Sometimes snow would be so deep he wouldn't ride his horse. He'd get off, leave his horse and stay up on high ground.

Back in them days, in the winter, they tightened up more on the fur – deer hide or buffalo. They didn't have clothes as we do. They had fur blankets ... fur hides tied around them, just a breechcloth on them. The menfolk on horseback going out and looking for food, they used to carry two or three pairs of moccasins with them. If their feet started getting cold walking through the snow, if their moccasins are wet, they'd take them off, wrap them up, then put on a dry pair of moccasins. When they'd get where they could build a fire they would dry out their moccasins and go on again.

During the hard winter, there used to be maybe one or two boys who were orphans and had no place to stay, so they came out and chopped wood, hauled water and fed what little livestock my grandfather had. My grandmother used to open the trunk up and get this food out. That food is always on the stove. We didn't know anything about breakfast, dinner, and supper. Whoever's hungry can walk up and get a plate and help himself.

Martin remembered how some didn't always appreciate all of their relatives, but when someone got sick or needed food or shelter or other kinds of assistance, they always reached out to help each other regardless of their feelings, especially the families with children.

Some of those younger generations wouldn't prepare for the winter and would cause themselves much suffering because the 1920's and 30's were not a time of plenty. The elders knew the importance of preparing for the winter so they would over-prepare knowing they would be needed to provide help for the younger ones.

Martin's grandmother would say that it always seemed in the winter time that the younger ones would show up cold and hungry; they seemed to forget when the sun came out and the snows melted. "They were off and running again as if life didn't matter. They forgot that they needed to prepare."

Gramma Rose and other grandmothers were always concerned for their grandchildren. Because of the hard winters, the influence of alcohol and other hardships, those children were not always raised by the ones who bore them. Some grandchildren were not always getting enough nourishment or warmth, but they were family so grandmothers never turned them away.

Gramma Rose made sure that Martin knew that she didn't approve of the behavior of some of the younger members of the family and she let him know that she expected he would never become one of them.

Gramma Rosa's Resilience

Gramma Rosa's and Grampa Samuel's resilience carried their family through the economic downturns of the 1920s. They agreed to the Honor Farmer Project in 1930 and dedicated themselves to strengthening agriculture despite hot summer winds, drought, severe dust storms and insect damage along with thunderstorms and hailstorms that frequently destroyed crops.

However, it troubled Martin to see the suffering of Native farmers and ranchers as they lost their cattle to the government and their land to White ranchers.

The severe dust storms of the 1930s were well-known in the southern plains, but they also damaged the ecology and agriculture of the Northern Plains and far beyond.[54] Drought dried the tilled soil. High winds picked up the topsoil and created massive clouds of airborne dirt[55] that traveled as dust clouds as far east as the Atlantic Ocean.

---

54   Northern Rockies and Plains Precipitation, 1895–2013. National Climatic Data Center.
55   The Dust Bowl was caused by the failure to apply dryland farming methods and replacement of native buffalo grasses plus drought which dried the topsoil into powder. The high winds picked up the topsoil and created massive blasts of wind and dirt. Murphy, Philip G. (July 15, 1935). "The Drought of 1934" (PDF). A Report of The Federal Government's Assistance to Agriculture. U.S. Drought Coordinating Committee / Federal Reserve Archival System for Economic Research.

The winter of 1934-5, the red topsoil blew east as far as Chicago and beyond to New York City and Washington DC. Red snow fell in New England states when the red dust mixed with the snow.[56]

By 1933, dust storms, called "Black Blizzards," raged with now-legendary intensity in the Dakotas along the northern edge of the Dust Bowl.[57] Drought and grasshopper plagues in 1934, 1935 and 1936, plus 1939-1940, continued to cause Indian farmers' crops to wither and die.[58]

Throughout those years, Samuel was still operating his ranch with six horses and 22 head of cattle. He was able to pay the bills and provide for his family, and he continued to support his community by donating meat to celebrations and relatives for memorial ceremonies.

The Charger family was not alone among the families at Cheyenne Agency who endured the times of hardship. Other elders reflected the same cultural strengths.

FLORENCE ARPAN SHARED STORIES OF THE 1930's

Elder Florence Arpan, an *Itázipčho* (Sans Arc, or "the Keeper of the Pipe Band" of Lakȟóta) lived a few miles west of LaPlant in Green Grass. Like Rosa Charger, she described how their spiritual beliefs carried the family through two decades of economic downturns and severe weather:

> ...the whole reservation went under a drought and people had to sell their horses, sell their cattle. That was one year we never raised a garden. No rain. There was nothing but grasshoppers. The wind would blow them around like dry tree leaves. They would rustle in the wind. We had chickens, but the chickens refused to eat the grasshoppers. And we didn't want to eat the chickens if they ate the grasshoppers, because it added a funny flavor to the chickens. So we didn't kill the chickens, as hungry as we would get sometimes.

---

56   Cronin, Francis D; Beers, Howard W (January 1937). Areas of Intense Drought Distress, 1930–1936 (PDF). Research Bulletin. Research Bulletin (United States. Works Progress Administration. Division of Social Research). U.S. Works Progress Administration / Federal Reserve Archival System for Economic Research.
57   *The History of Agriculture in South Dakota: A Historic Context*, SWCA Environmental Consultants, Jul 2013, 21-22
58   "Northern Rockies and Plains Precipitation, 1895–2013." National Climatic Data Center.

We lived in a place where grass still grew but the government gave the orders to kill all the cows and horses. Some people managed to keep some of their horses alive, because that was what we used to haul wood and water. It was our only transportation. We didn't have to sell our cows because of the natural springs where we lived. There was hay up there, so our cows were in good shape when the government came and drove our cattle off. They didn't take all our horses. We had only four head of cows so they left a few head of cows.

It was the milk cow that kept us going. Our milk cow never went dry during that time, because there is a great Power that kept that cow going until it was over. We milked her. We had plenty of biscuits and milk gravy. That cow was a good cow.

How they ever survived, I don't know, but they lived. They finally gave us enough to buy us a little feed for our horses and cow. There was just enough feed for what little [livestock] we had left. My mother prayed one day and she said, 'I'm going to dig in the river bottom for water.' So we went along with her. And she had a shovel. So she said 'This is where I'm going to dig.'

And it seemed like she was guided by a divine Power of some kind, because she hit a water line. And we dug and dug, and that water was coming in so fast and it was good tasting water. And so my father managed to make a good curbing for the well as she dug it, and we were able to get our drinking water. It would fill up and we would fill our barrels.

And later my father went to town and bought a water pump and he bought a trough and he brought it back. So we put the trough down and we'd stand down there and take turns and we'd pump water for the few horses we had left. We have to pump water with the hand pump, you know. We'd pump for the horses. They'd come to water. They smelt the water so they come and they'll drink water.

I remember. It seemed like there were some times in those days, we didn't have enough food for three times a day, but we never got hungry. We never got hungry. We prayed a lot and it seemed like with what little food we got to eat, we would be full. I ate a lot of baked potatoes, a lot of biscuits and milk gravy. We lived on grass. We used to have cellars full of potatoes. There was no water, you know, so sometimes the potatoes didn't grow.

Finally, the government, in the wintertime, they brought frozen mutton from Montana and they passed that out. So we learned how to can mutton and we made meat gravy out of mutton. We learned how to eat it.

Some of them dried it, but we never tried that. We always canned ours in jars. We used to do our canning in the oven. Did you ever hear of that? How you can in the oven? A water bath. Yeah, we had water in the pan and we start timing our canned stuff as it began to bubble. We learned that from our German Russian neighbors. And we learned how to can and we canned a lot of mutton. It was good. We made gravy. We made hash out of it.

I learned a lot of things from my German Russian neighbors. They were used to hard times and they learned how to eat Ground Squirrel, what we call pispíza. They call them Prairie Dogs. We ate them. My mother tried a lot of different things and we were able to live on that.

We didn't have coffee. So we'd scrape elm trees and boil the bark and we'd have red tea. You take the outer bark off and you take the inner side and boil it and we'd have red tea. We learned to use things like that. I know some people really suffered, but it was the good Lord that kept us going. Nobody starved to death.[59]

MEMORIES FROM AUNT ELLEN IN THE WOODS

Elder, Aunt Ellen In the Woods, shared memories as a little girl traveling to visit families in LaPlant during the 1930's from their home in Dupris, on Cheyenne River Reservation:

> During the month of August, my dad used to take a lumber wagon with food, cows, horses and they used to go to LaPlant and Cheyenne Agency. And my mom was related to Julia and Louise Grey Bear. They went by Grey Bear. It seemed like everybody was a relative then. And we were kind of slow with everything. We visited each other and took time visiting. And when we make that trip to the old agency, on the way we stopped to see the Silver Stops family ... Joe Crow Feathers family. We'd meet the Pretty Weasels...
>
> But we had quite a few stops in LaPlant and then we'd go on to the old agency. And ole' Grampa Grey Bear was still alive. We used to go there. And we used to see Louise [Martin's mother] or Julie there. When we go there, they came

---

59   Oral history recording of Florence Arpan by Rose High Bear, June 2000.

72

to visit. And we knew old Gramma White Eyes. We had an aunt there. They call her Little Mollie, LaBeau's mother.

We met her and we met different ones like the Woods and Traversie's mother, Vivian ... Jennie Log and we met old man Log and his family. We had a lot of people to visit. At the same time, my dad was issuing out horses and cows to them.

And when we come back, we have a wagon load because they give things to my mother too. That's how they used to help each other and wherever they see her, they come right up to her and greet her. So that's how I knew them.

They all go down to the river. There's willows down there. They go down there and they make Sweat Lodge down there and they Sweat down and come back up.

And when they come back up, they have kind of a ceremony like in the tent. Then they'd open the tent door and I'd always be sitting in the corner listening to them talk.

They're all dead now. They were elderlies then. Mom had a lot of respect for them. She always had meat and stuff ready for them to eat when they got through.[60]

Martin witnessed deprivation of neighbors from economic downturns, epidemics, drought and the dust bowl. He was also aware of generations of traumatic events. What he didn't personally witness, elders shared details of massacres, U.S. Army control over the reservation, forced removal from homelands, forced separation of children from parents, coercion to sign treaties, forced leasing of their land against their will, and treaty violations.

However, throughout his oral narratives and personal reminiscences, we rarely hear him mention terms such as 'colonialism' or 'forced assimilation' so frequently expressed by others.

He and other Cheyenne River leaders were loyal to their cultural values and rich traditions of kindness and respect. They expressed their experiences in positive terms.

Possessing resilience, they sought solace from both the Great Spirit and Christianity. Their qualities of identity and strength, combined with spiritual traditions that survived underground for generations, continued to help them overcome and heal from collective trauma that had been inherited from previous generations.

---

60 Oral history recording of Ellen In the Woods, June 1999.

Martin speaking at Field Museum, Chicago, IL.

CHAPTER 4

MARTIN'S SECOND SPIRITUAL WORLD

Young Martin's Second Spiritual World began when he moved onto his own settlement in 1937. This extended into the 1960s. The time of his birth had coincided with the Agricultural Depression of 1919. The Great Depression that followed extended through much of the 1930's.

The Chargers and their neighbors had witnessed economic losses during those two decades. In response, they had strengthened their resilience. Their dry land farms and ranches were further exacerbated by drought and temperature extremes. The *"average moisture in Ziebach County was under fourteen inches a year and a temperature range of about one hundred fifty degrees."* [61]

The Cheyenne River Sioux Tribe managed a subsidy program during the Great Depression to purchase cattle and horses from the US Government and re-issue them to tribal members so they could develop and maintain cattle operations. Milk cows and sheep meat were also distributed to reduce food shortages among families, but many times starvation was so prevalent that some were forced to butcher and dry their beef in order to feed their families.

In September 1936, Martin's grandfather, Sam Charger, was hired as a Line Rider (or Boss Farmer) for the Extension Service to work in the neighboring White Horse District. He helped families care for their cattle businesses. Charger helped Native farmers with their leases, distribution of rations, documented farmers' complaints and assisted them in tribal court. This included helping to protect Indian farmers by keeping settlers off of tribal land and away from their cattle. Boss Farmers used their role to provide encouragement to strengthen tribal members' cultural survival as well as their farms, ranches, homes and gardens. The work required long hours, with him frequently leaving home before dawn and not returning until after dark.

---

61   South Dakota Ziebach County History of the Prairie, Ziebach County Historical Society, Dupree, SD, 1982.

It is not surprising that at the time of his eighteenth birthday, Martin chose to move and become independent on his own allotment. The tribe offered him a parcel of land, cattle and money as part of his Sioux benefits so he could start his own cattle operation. He also worked as a ranch hand where he could tame horses for a neighboring rancher and he also purchased a team of horses.

His sister Melda remembered that the rest of the family frequently used the horses for transportation. "Brownie and Blackie was Martin's team" she said. "Those two horses were so gentle that the kids could play underneath their belly. Mom and Dad used to fix them up and go to town to buy groceries. Mom and I also used them to cut hay."

Getting Married in The Old Way

Responsibility was not new to Martin. He was 8 years old when he began to help his father, who had a contract unloading coal from railroad cars onto the coal delivery truck for delivery to schools on Cheyenne River and Standing Rock Reservations.

Then, at age 12, when his father became ill, he stepped up temporarily to take over his dad's work responsibilities.

Martin's strong work ethic did not go unnoticed by the family of Elvina Little Eagle. Traditional marriages were still being practiced by some families, including Elvina's mother, Lulu Two Arrows and her father Edward M. Little Eagle who lived at the neighboring Crow Creek Indian Reservation. They approached Martin's grandparents and all agreed to arrange the marriage of Martin to their daughter.[62]

Meeting his Wife

Martin told the story of first meeting his wife, Elvina Little Eagle:

> And so I had a home. I had my own home. Not that I was going to get married, but I wanted to have a home of my own. I never went out and dated the one that I wanted to marry.
>
> I didn't expect to get married, but I got married in the old way. This family come to my folks and wanted to give their

---

62   Elvina Little Eagle was born 2/23/22 – died 10/20/83 U – 306, Prob. TC-411R-82). Elvina's father was Edward M. Little Eagle born 1869 – died 1943 (CC 404, Pro # 6549-45) whose father, Wilgus, was half French. Edward's mother was Red Bird Woman (CC-383 Prob #110488-15). Elvina's mother was Lulu Two Arrows born 1880 – died 01/19/1958 (CC-579 Pro #14234-58), Long Feather (CC-459) Fort Totten Sioux; Running Bird (RS-2169); Lulu Two Arrow's Father was Walks After Him and her mother was Her Blanket died 04/27/1923 (CC-576; pro #38897-24).(CC – U519, CC –

daughter to me to be my wife. They wanted me to be their son-in-law because I was a hard-working man. My parents and this girl's parents, they talked.

I didn't court this lady when I married to her. The folks talked about it. Time came, they brought her over. When I first looked at her I said, 'Is she going to be my wife?' I didn't even know who she was. She was from another reservation. And so I married a woman that I never knew before.

When I got married, we had a feast and giveaway and I went back to work. I left the same night after the feast. I had enough food for her to eat, but I didn't see my wife for three weeks, but I told my dad and mom to take care of her and make sure she had enough water.

When he began to start his own family, Martin followed the advice of his grandfather Sam Charger who had taught him that if he was going to have a family, he needed to support them and not rely upon others to provide for them.

One of the things my grandfather told me is very true and honest ... he said "Grandson, when you think about getting married, think about it. See that you can afford to support a wife. And remember, grandson, when you grow up, before you get married, first thing you want to have before you get married, have a home. But also, if you can provide and feed another person besides yourself, if you think you can afford to have a wife, if you can survive for her, feed her, then you can get married. And when you're married, you have to take care of her. Don't let no one else, your parents, their parents, take care of your wife. Work and provide for her. You wanted her so take care of her."

I always remembered all that so I went according to my grandfather and my grandmother, my grandfather especially. He taught me how to make a living. And I followed his instructions about my living conditions.

Another thing my grandad said was: "Whatever you do, tȟakóža – grandson, when you get married, think about it. Then wonder if you're going to have kids and if you can afford to support them. Make sure that you can survive and feed your kids. If you can provide and raise that kid and dress 'em and feed 'em, then you can go ahead and have kids. But if you can't, don't have kids. You're going to starve them somewhere. Then you'd be the talk among the people. That's a shame." he said.

The older generation, each one of the family had only one or two kids. That's all they have. I only had one Uncle. He used to take care of me. So this is the way my Grandfather told me a lot of things. Them are the strict orders my grandparents gave. This was the way I was taught.

I worked hard, made a living for my four boys and a girl. I had to feed them, dress them, make sure that everything went good for them. I taught them how to do things until they were all old enough to go off on their own. Even after that, when I see them, I give them a few dollars. That's to show I have respect for them.

The advice from Martin's grandfather meant that his work as a Medicine Man would have to wait. He had a family to raise first. He felt happy that he was able to do the work. It was a lot of hard work. It was not always easy, but it was what he had to do and he felt good at the end of the day.

At first, the young family made their home out in the country on Highway 63 near a junction between Eagle Butte and Pierre. A small rustic corral constructed of small trees and branches where they broke horses and practiced for Indian rodeos still stands near their homestead.

With some of his jobs, Martin was able to go home each day after work, but sometimes he could only go home on the weekends. Ranchers provided a bunkhouse where the ranch hands stayed during the week. These places never were very comfortable. Sometimes they had to bunch up hay to sleep on.

Martin Was a Horse Whisperer

Martin was happiest when he was taming wild horses. It gave him a sense of freedom when he was working *"by the seat of his pants"* with horses. It required a lot of hard work and patience but he seemed to have a gift of working with them.

He would first become friends with the horse, letting it know that it didn't have to fight him; that the two of them could work together. He would first get the horse to eat out of his hand and then he would get the rope over the neck. He would grab their mane very gently, pulling them one way and another. The horses knew what he was trying to accomplish, and he was successful because he was patient, gentle and calm with them.

He would try to break the horses without a saddle because he knew that was how his people used to ride them. The horses would be angry and try to get control, yet Martin would be gentle and reassure them, telling them that it was okay.

He remembered when he was young, he would swing his hat in his hand as if he was riding in a rodeo. It gave him an overwhelming feeling as if he owned and controlled everything. It made him feel as if he was master of the horse and master of the universe. He loved the feeling when the horses would buck high in the air on their hind legs and try to throw him.

He said sometimes the horse would actually buck hard enough to get him off his back. And then it would whinny. It seemed the horse was laughing at him, saying "Naa naa naa naa, I got you!" Martin would say in response, "Only this time!" Then he wouldn't leave the corral until he got back on the horse, even if that meant waiting a while for the right opportunity.

He loved the feeling when the horse finally broke. It was as though it would say, "Okay, you can have your way. I will work with you."

The horses always knew they would get oats to eat —the kind that had molasses and honey on them. They seemed to look forward to those things. However, if they had been bad that day, they wouldn't get any. They could smell it when the other horses would get it and they would not, so they began to realize their own stubbornness wasn't worth it.

Sometimes it took longer for some horses who were hard headed, but those were Martin's favorite horses. They wanted to run free and roam; their spirits didn't want to give up. But in time they would give up their dreams and feelings of running free. They would discover that they could run free when they rode out of the corral with Martin (even though they now had something on their back that felt a little uncomfortable).

He would walk softly and gently around the horses and make sure there was no fear around them. He would talk to the spirit of the horse through its mind and let it know it was safe and that everything would be okay. Some horses were wounded from being beaten by others who didn't know how to (or have the gift for) breaking them. These were the hard ones because they were very mistrustful.

Martin learned how to break horses without breaking their spirits. He would help them understand they could be one with the man and still have their spirit.

He once said, "If you break their spirit by hitting them with sticks and anger, and bring fear into them, you will never be able to trust them. If you break them with gentleness, kindness and love, they can become your best friend. You can talk to them and know they understood."

Sometimes Martin found himself talking to them because he felt they listened better than people. They would cock their head one way or the other, so he knew they were listening. His patience and gift of communicating with horses grew – which would serve him again when he began to work with stubborn and wounded Native people later in life.

HEAVY EQUIPMENT OPERATOR

Martin was hired as a Civilian Conservation Corps (CCC) worker under the program developed by President Roosevelt who authorized the government to expand the program onto Indian reservations, including South Dakota. Workers received $30.00 a month. The workers kept $5.00 of that and sent $25.00 home.[63]

Martin moved his family into the CCC camps where his skills as a heavy equipment operator continued to strengthen. The government had him first working with crude horse-drawn scrapers and later transitioned to heavy equipment to construct irrigation dams to support cattle and farming operations on the reservation. He soon became well-known for his ability to build small reservoirs. Martin's cousin Harry Charger and others later spoke of Martin being well known as one of the best heavy equipment operators in the country. The CCC program continued until the beginning of WWII in 1942.

Martin preferred riding horses over operating construction equipment, and he thought about the animals many times while he was working. He was also able to apply what he had learned

---

63   The Sioux and the Indian CCC, Bromert, Roger, South Dakota Historical Society, Vol 8, Fall 1978, p. 340.

with animals and horses to the heavy equipment operator work. He used his connection with the Spirit World to avoid accidents while operating heavy equipment. Many times when he was on the machine constructing a reservoir or a new road, he pretended that he was breaking in a new horse. He would pay attention to what the spirit of the birds or the spirit of the animals around him told him.

It always seemed whenever he began working in a soft spot that might cause them trouble, animals would show him where to be careful. Birds would dive bomb him when conditions became dangerous. He began to watch them as he worked so he could safely move earth around while constructing the earthen dams.

One time he was working toward an area where the ground was unstable. A bird started squawking and dive bombing him, letting him know something was wrong. He crawled down from his equipment and checked the ground. He could see that there was too much moisture from an underground spring to safely work and that the area was getting ready to slide.

He came back and told his supervisor why they shouldn't go according to plans. His supervisor had learned to respect Martin's judgment from similar experiences and realized they would need to go the other way, so he authorized Martin to change plans.

Martin also watched for animal tracks – prints from deer and antelope hooves; sometimes cat paws – to determine how stable the land was. He could see how deep their tracks were and this would tell him how soft the ground was and the best way for the crew to go. This kept him and his machine out of danger.

WORLD WAR II SERVICE IN THE US NAVY

After the Indian CCC camps closed, Martin joined the military. He served in the U.S. Navy from 1944 until World War II ended late in 1945. He served on the war front in the South Pacific assigned to the Seabees. They stationed him in Guam because of the skills he had developed operating heavy equipment in the CCC. He continued building his skills moving dirt, this time building air strips for the planes to land.

Martin's sister Melda and brother-in-law, Melvin Garreau, remembered:

The worst time for our parents and us kids was when he went to war, especially when he was in the front where the fighting was. He served as a Seabee in the South Pacific building roads so the army can keep pushing to the enemy. He also helped to bury the dead after battles.

My mom cried. We went to church every Sunday praying for him and the rest of the boys in our community. I'll always shudder to think if we had lost him, but he came home.

RETURNING HOME WITH POST TRAUMATIC STRESS DISORDER

Martin returned home from the war knowing it was time for him to help his people, but he didn't know how to make it happen. He had expected military service to change him into a warrior but his war experience had troubled and wounded him.

Instead of finding transformation and rebirth upon his return, Martin felt unsettled. Although he did not see direct combat in the South Pacific, the spirits of the Japanese that he helped to bury following the battles in 1944 and 1945 haunted him after he returned home. The traditional healing ceremonies once conducted for warriors returning from battle were being practiced less often in tribal communities since the government had made ceremony illegal, so his problem went untreated.

The disorder would not be discovered or named for decades, but he suffered post-traumatic stress disorder (PTSD), a common occurrence for Native American veterans returning home from war. Martin began a life-long habit of smoking cigarettes during his service, and also began using alcohol during the war, which he continued to do upon his return to the reservation.

Melda remembered his return:

> We celebrated his return, but he was very troubled over that war. He never saw direct battle, but he would go in after they had the battles in the islands. He had to help bury those guys in a mass grave. There were *wanáǧi* (spirits) of the Japanese who had died during the battles in the South Pacific that came home with him.
>
> He was quite a heavy drinker right after he got back from WWII. The spirits of those guys he had to help bury bothered him so badly that it gave him terrible PTSD. I don't

know how he ever got rid of the spirits of those guys. He will not talk about it. He only said, "Just think, I pushed a lot of Japanese into the trench holes. They were someone's babies. Their mothers worried about them and here I am..."

Martin's youngest son Leonard also shared memories of his father's experiences after returning home:

Dad never saw direct battle, but he really had a reaction to what happened in the war. He'd have something going on, like an 'experience' where he'd be dashing and hiding out in the yard and his sister would have to go and tackle him.

It's never easy to come home, but mom had another baby while he was gone, somebody else's. He was gone more than a year and here she had a newborn when he came home. That was Eddie, but Eddie got to be his closest son after Ronnie died.

Martin had a lot of memories upon his return. He thought about the years he had spent as a young boy with his grandparents. He remembered stories of his childhood when the elders told him that he was going to save the people someday. He reflected on them, hoping he could make more sense of it all.

As a young boy, he had visualized himself riding up on a horse and saving his people like he had seen John Wayne do in the movies. Now, he began to understand that he was not being guided to fight, or conquer the enemy, or become ruler of the nation as he originally imagined. He wasn't being asked to fight or do battle or be something he was not.

Martin mostly related to elders' stories about the Sun Dance ceremonies. He had been to a few Sun Dances that were held in secluded parts of the reservation. The elders had also spoke of the old Ghost Dance and its revival into the new Ghost Dance.

As he reflected on what that ceremony would do, he felt himself getting in touch with the spirits of his ancestors. Visions came to him by the spirits that were *wakȟáŋ* (holy). He felt he could see through the eyes of his ancestors and feel their emotions. Sometimes they seemed to go into (and through) his body and mind like lightning.

He started having dreams and visions. At night (after work) he spent hours talking and listening to the Spirit World. This went on for several weeks. He felt the kind of intensity that you get when you are in a *Haŋbléčheya*; when the spirits give you your vision. He felt these sacred experiences were the same as what his ancestors had experienced. He realized he was being guided to fulfill his dreams and the prophecy of his grandparents, and that they were helping him understand what he needed to do and what not to do.

When they came to Martin, the spirits told him they needed him to help bring the Sun Dance and other ceremonies back to the people. They reminded him why the Sun Dance is so sacred and that dancing with the spirits would bring healing and restore hope in the people. He was aware of the prophecy foretelling that ceremonies would endure and be passed onto future generations for the spiritual and cultural survival of his people.

In the back of his mind he knew he would someday be helping his people but he didn't see how he could help until after his children were raised. He also knew that if he were going to do his part to help the people unite, he would need to stop drinking. (His addictions to cigarettes and alcohol that he had picked up during the war lingered and he would continue for a few decades to struggle to overcome them.)

WORKING TO RAISE HIS FAMILY

The tribe gave cattle and horses to Martin and the other veterans after they returned in 1945. He kept his herd of horses out on his land and worked with them when he wasn't working for other ranchers. Although relatives helped take care of them when he was away, they eventually disappeared since rustling of livestock was still prevalent throughout the 1940s.

He was committed to supporting his wife and growing family. All of the babies were born in the hospital, except Ronnie, who was born at home with Gramma Lulu.

Following the guidance of his grandfather, he dedicated himself to providing for his boys and his daughter. Clifford was the oldest. Irene was second to the oldest. Another child was born who had died of pneumonia (his name was Eddie). Then Eddie was born followed by Ronnie. Their youngest son Leonard was born in 1949.[64]

---

64   Leonard was born in Pierre, SD on September 18, 1949. He traced his lineage on both sides of the family and thus earned the title of family historian. He and his older brothers, Clifford and Eddie, also relayed memories of the family for their father's biography.

According to Leonard: "All of us kids were born in the hospital, except Ronnie who was born at home with gramma Lulu. The family said that Dad was awarded horses and cattle after the war, but Dad wasn't home to watch them because he worked all the time. He would do anything or whatever was needed to support the family, so when he was gone working, and without fences and vigilance, horse thieves that still roamed the reservation in those days stole our herd."

MEMORIES FROM MARTIN'S SON EDDIE

Martin's son Eddie remembered the 1950s before he started school. There were times their family moved to follow Martin when he found new work to support the family:

> We lived at LaPlante before I started school. Back in the days when the railroad went right through LaPlante it was a booming town. We also lived in Phillip. I don't know what kind of work Dad was doing. Then we lived at Rapid at the Indian Camp along the creek in the 1950s. And then at Box Elder.
>
> Dad worked on farms and ranches and I worked with Dad too until age 16. He was a heavy equipment operator (scraper) for years. They have a bucket on a caterpillar with 2 tracks on it. He had to know how to remove the earth between the stakes and to move only within those stakes. You have to know how much dirt to remove and fill in.
>
> He moved dirt, built roads, dams, reservoirs on ranches, and he worked at Ellsworth Air Force military base in Rapid City. Then he was truck driving as a long-haul trucker for Old Home Bread and Blue Line trucking company.
>
> We lived at Hayes when the dam was built. My dad was doing ranch work around Hayes and he would come back about once a month. He built stock dams on ranches around the reservation so the ranchers could water their cattle.
>
> Dad was one of the best heavy equipment operators around and a smart man. He would survey the area himself and then build a dam for the cattle. He used to talk about his work making roads and irrigation reservoirs. The equipment was loud and he tried to stick cotton in his ears, but then he couldn't hear his boss's instructions.
>
> Then we left home to go to Cheyenne River Boarding School, coming home only at Christmas and for the sum-

mers. I remember in 1959 and 1960, in the evenings, we would go back home riding the school bus from the old agency to Eagle Butte. I remember driving by the old agency until it flooded.

When Clifford and Irene got older, they still stayed with Mom, LaVina and Gramma Lulu on mom's side down at Fort Thompson. When Leonard was still young, he stayed home with mom and sometimes at Gramma Lulu's ranch. When he was 14, he moved into the dorm at the boarding school in Eagle Butte and started high school. Ronnie and Leonard went back to the school dorms at Eagle Butte in 1962.

There was some of her land left on top, but mom originally had quite a bit of land at Big Bend[65] until most of it went under water. The Army Corps of Engineers were supposed to reimburse them or give them land in exchange, but they paid us little or nothing. 'You have to take what they give you,' mom had said. I should have been there to help, but I left to work with Dad.

LEONARD REMINISCED

Leonard sometimes served as oral historian of the family. He liked to share his memories of his younger years and their life with their dad and his varied ranch work:

I attended my first three years of school at Cheyenne River Agency at the boarding school down by the river. It was pretty down there with trees all over. Cotton tails jumping in front of you. Deer and cattle were sheltered from the winter down there.

In the winter time, he couldn't work because of the weather so we lived along the Cheyenne River and took care of cattle along the river down by the Cheyenne River 20 miles from Eagle Butte. They provided us with a cabin at an Army camp.

Dad sometimes worked with his Indian friend, Bullitt Peerman. Back in those days, they didn't always have equipment to bale hay so they used to go down there in the winter in a tractor and pitch loose hay on the back of the wagon by hand to feed the cattle.

---

65   Big Bend Dam is a major embankment rolled-earth dam on the Missouri River in Central South Dakota, creating Lake Sharpe. Built 1959-1963, it was constructed by the U.S. Army Corps of Engineers as part of the Pick-Sloan Plan for Missouri watershed development, authorized by the U.S. Government's Flood Control Act of 1944.

We lived like gypsies. Dad had a trailer house that they moved with and lived in while he was building dams. Dad took a lot of pictures of the family, and Mom had two big trunks with photos in them, but I don't know what happened to them.

Then when the dam was built, they moved us to the school at Eagle Butte. I remember Dad had jobs as a ranch hand for the local ranchers. He broke, trained and rode horses for everyday work. He fixed fences and put up hay. He also rounded up cattle on horseback and worked with bulls to prepare them for rodeo or auction.

EDDIE SOMETIMES WORKED WITH HIS DAD

Martin's son Eddie shared his memories of living at boarding school and also with the family along the Cheyenne River near Cherry Creek. The boys didn't have to work when they were small, but as he grew older, Eddie began to work with his dad:

When they flooded the old agency out, they checked us out of the dorms and we went home and they put us in public school in Pierre. We lived in Pierre all through the 1960s and I went to public school. We used to fight the White kids every day. They didn't like Indians.

Then Dad said to me, "You are getting old enough to work now." Dad ranched and fixed fence for neighboring ranchers on Cheyenne River, so I went to work with him doing farm work at a cow camp, ranching and working cattle until I was 19. I helped Dad repair fences. I drove the farm truck and operated the tractor. Grandmother Louise used to drive tractor and do farming too. The whole family would be out in the field.

In the spring, we plowed the fields and got the ground ready for planting. We put up hay through June and July. Sometimes, we mowed and baled hay. Sometimes there was no tractor, so we would cut, buck and stack the hay. In the fall, we disked the soil.

In the fall of the year, we used to have a big celebration, and a rodeo and fair. They had horse races, and bring in calves and bulls and heifers and they would have a rodeo. There was a lot of things going on then.

Back in those days, everyone had gardens. People would bring their crops in and they would be judged. They would bring corn, melon, cantaloupe, and they would get ribbons for their awards. Cucumbers, squash, tomatoes. They give prizes for the biggest crops.

Then in the winter months, we fed the cattle for the ranchers down there. The snow was deep at times and sometimes during the blizzards, we had to use a team of horses to feed them. There were a lot of trees and wildlife before the dams flooded the area.

We had one tame saddle horse. At night, we put it and the other horses in the corral and every morning the gate would be open. We would find the wire unraveled. I was never afraid of the spirits in those days, but they were around.

Those things Dad said ... sometimes we didn't know what he was talking about. He would say. "The old is coming back." and "You don't see that these days, but what is old is new." He knew things that were going to happen. "All these changes, like earthquakes, natural disasters and man-made things will combine to do a lot of damage." Once he said, "In the future, there will be a man 40 years who will look like an old man 80 or 90 years old." Now some of those things he talked about are happening today.

THE BIRTH OF ACTIVISM DURING MARTIN'S RODEO YEARS

Martin liked to compete in Indian rodeos as a Saddle Bronc rider. Sometimes when his sons, Clifford, Eddie, Ronnie and Leonard, were young and in their teenage years, they traveled together to rodeos in the Dakotas.

Martin's youngest son, Leonard, also loved the horses. He seemed so fragile that Martin was afraid for him to ride. He was afraid they would buck him off and break him. Leonard would plead and beg his dad to let him ride. Martin repeatedly told him not to, but when he turned his back, there he'd go.

Leonard admitted that he loved the feeling of running with the horses as fast and hard as he could. He said, "I taught myself to ride bareback. Dad didn't want me to ride. I did get broken up. I'm still broken up."

The horses seemed to like it too. Running that fast seemed to empower them. Martin could see the glow of joy and happiness on his son's face. It was so beautiful, as if the spirit had come down and touched him, so Martin began to realize he could no longer tell him to stop.

Martin's friendships with other Native cowboys grew into a strong allegiance at the Indian rodeos. In addition to camaraderie and laughter, they shared stories of trauma with one another. They lamented the century of abuses their grandparents endured since the nineteenth century, as the surge of missionaries and school teachers, nuns and priests, Indian agents and White ranchers moved into Indian communities and imposed boarding schools, churches, grazing leases, farming practices and starvation, all designed to assimilate and control the Lakȟóta.

Martin understood the anger of his friends on the rodeo circuit. They spoke of how America portrayed itself to the world as a refuge from religious persecution while government and church leaders declared centuries-old Lakȟóta beliefs and spiritual traditions illegal. "...And then they tell us we still can't practice our ways of the Sun Dance, that we can't practice our ways of the water ceremonies, sweating and healing, our ways of medicine and herbs. Those are what Creator had given us! How could they take away what didn't belong to them? Even this land didn't belong to them. How could they keep taking more and more away?"

Martin didn't need to be a scholar of United States history or European theology to understand how deeply this had affected his people. He knew the frustration of the men as they spoke of multiple injustices deliberately perpetrated without their consent. He felt their weariness from being birthed and living daily in deep poverty, racism and internalized shame. He listened to stories of Indian boarding school abuses and how parents and grandparents had been forced to convert to Christianity. They spoke of the unprotected young children who were subjected to sexual abuse by school priests, nuns and other religious leaders, introducing cycles of sexual abuse and historical trauma into decades of Indian families.

He painfully remembered the rampant fraud that robbed their grandparents at Cheyenne River and Standing Rock of rich grazing land just a decade or two before he was born. Many desired to operate their own cattle businesses where they could raise beef to provide them with a livelihood and at the same time, help families ward off starvation. Instead, despite strong objections and impassioned appeals of tribal leaders and Indian ranchers, large cattle companies worked with the Department of the Interior to impose grazing leases upon Indian ranchers and moved them off of their land.[66]

THE OAHE DAM

Martin also witnessed Eminent Domain imposed upon the reservation with the Oahe Dam construction, creating destruction by flooding of the tribe's prime Missouri River bottomlands. After the dam was constructed, the people were removed from along the riverbanks of the Missouri. Tribal members related the spiritual, emotional and material blows parents and grandparents suffered as they lost their homes and access to the river. Many felt there was nothing they could do about it.

Martin's son Leonard was only ten years old, but he also remembered: "1958 was when they flooded our best homeland. We had lived there in the winters when Dad and my brothers took care of the cattle. Then the Army Corps of Engineers moved the old agency up to Eagle Butte. It destroyed old Cheyenne Agency and where great-great Grandfather Chief Martin Charger had settled Charger's Camp in 1870."[67]

The timbered areas were the shelter and feeding ground for wildlife that provided food for families. "*More than 400 deer, several hundred beavers, and thousands of rabbits and raccoons lived year-round in these woodlands while thousands of pheasants and other game birds wintered there each year.*"[68]

Wild fruits and berries that had provided essential nourishment and enjoyment to Indian families were destroyed by the flooding of the bottomlands, including chokecherries which they mixed with dried buffalo meat to make pemmican. The full moon in August was named after it, "the Moon when the Chokecherries

---

66   Letter from Harold C. Frazier, Tribal Council Chairman, CRST, to the US Department of the Interior telling that in 1889 (the time of South Dakota statehood), the US Government divided the Great Sioux Reservation and took 11 million acres of land transferring it to the railroads, cattle barons, settlers and state governments. Between 1889 and 1934, tribes lost an additional 6 million acres under the Allotment Policy, July 2 2018.

67   Authorized by the Federal Flood Control Act of 1944, thousands of acres of prime river bottom were condemned by Army Corps of Engineers and taken by eminent domain for construction of the Oahe Dam. One of the largest artificial reservoirs in the nation. The dam covers 150,000 acres and provides electricity and irrigation to a large section of the north central United States. When the valley flooded in 1958 15,000 acres of woodland was taken, including 90 percent of the reservation's timber. It had been the only source of fuel for at least one-fourth of the tribe and a source of free lumber.

68   "Reservoir and Reservation: The Oahe Dam and the Cheyenne River Sioux," Lawson, Michael L., Univ. of Nebraska, Omaha, NE, 1973.

Turn Black," signaling the time to hold the Sun Dance. This plant and its medicinal juice were essential to the Sun Dance ceremony.

Families had also harvested black currants, wild plums and serviceberries there as well as the buffalo berries that were used during young women's coming of age ceremonies. Sprouts from wild plum trees were gathered for use in healing ceremonies.[69]

Families also mourned the loss of mouse beans. Grandmas would travel down to the river bottom with their canes and bags of dried corn. They searched under the trees for wild peas that the field mice had stored in piles under the leaves. They always honored the mice with prayer and replaced what they harvested with dried corn.[70]

At least eight Indian cemeteries with over a thousand grave sites had to be relocated, along with some private Indian burials, a monument to Indian war veterans. The Medicine Rock monument also had to be relocated.[71]

As families packed up and relocated to new settlements, they sometimes found only austere prairie with no access to water, timber or traditional foods they had cherished for generations. They especially grieved separation from neighbors they and their families had grown up with.

Then the US Forest Service started to require that the people pay to set up their tipis at the river. Access to the river was important for conducting water ceremonies (although it was still forbidden to hold ceremonies by the water, or pray and fast, or conduct other traditions critical to their spiritual health). It was almost a century before Native people would legally be able to openly hold Sweat Lodge and healing ceremonies.

MEMORY FROM ELLEN CONDON-IN THE WOODS

The late Lakȟóta Elder Ellen Condon-In the Woods remembered the elders going down to the river for ceremony even when it was illegal:

69   *Uses of Plants by the Indians of the Missouri River Region*, Gilmore, 1977
70   Wisdom oral history, 1999, plus U.S., Smithsonian Institution, Bureau of American Ethnology, "Uses of Plants by the Indians of the Missouri River Region," by Melvin Randolph Gilmore, Thirty-Third Annual Report of the American Bureau of Ethnology (Washington: Government Printing Office, 1919), pp. 43-154.
71   S. Rep. No. 1737, Ibid.; MRBI Rep. No. 29, Ibid., pp. 16-18.; U.S., Department of Interior, Bureau of Indian Affairs, Location and Census of Indian Cemeteries, Cheyenne River Indian Reservation, South Dakota, MRBI Rep. No. 120, Billings: Missouri River Basin Investigations Project, 1951, pp. 1-3.

We stayed by our family. We had time to play. We had time to work. We did all that. We never lay around or sit around. The only time we sit around is in the evenings after supper when we sit around and sing and do things.

And then there were some older people that come visit us and they had their Pipes with them and my mother would say, "Well, my cousin is here and they will have a ceremony, but don't you tell anybody. If you tell, you'll put them all in jail."

They all go down to the river, there's willows down there. They go down there and they make Sweat Lodge down there and they sweat down and come back up and when they come back up, they have kind of a ceremony like in the tent. Then they'd open the tent door and I'd always be sitting in the corner listening to them talk.

They used to have a big tent around our place that they would pack and come and fix up their tents and they'd camp around there. At that time the government didn't allow the Indians to have Sweats, but they had one made towards Cheyenne River in thick willow trees and they had a Sweat Lodge made down there. So they'll all come in like Blue Hair and Black Bear and Joseph Eagle Chasing.

So they all come in and they all talk and go down to sweat and they have a meeting after the Sweat. And they used to smoke their Pipe. They each had their Pipe. Some of them were Medicine Men. They were my mom's relatives. They're all dead now. They were elderlies then.

Mom had a lot of respect for them. She always had meat and stuff ready for them to eat when they got through. At a certain time they all come in from Red Scaffold, Bridger, Cherry Creek, even from Thunder Butte and Iron Lightning. They all go down there and spend a couple of days down there and then come back up again. So the police would come and want to know where the men folks are at and we just don't know where they're at.

MARTIN SHARED ELDERS' MEMORIES

The people had always gone freely to the water, got their fish and did whatever they had to do to survive. These were the sacred places they went to do ceremony, get deer and elk and all the kinds of foods and medicines they had hunted and gathered for hundreds of years. They felt they should have the right to continue to do this.

After that, if the people left the reservation to go hunting or fishing or for any other reason, the government would try to have them arrested for leaving the reservation. This angered the people, because they needed to hunt to survive. The government didn't provide enough food for families to survive, so for many generations they had to become sneaky for their family's survival. It was bad enough that the people had to be put on reservations. It angered them even more that they couldn't hunt to feed their people.

When the hunters followed the deer or whatever animal and it happened to go across the boundary line, they were thinking about their family going hungry.

The elders would say, "The White Man doesn't own the animals. The sacred animals gifted themselves to the people and people don't have a spiritual right to say you can go or you can't go. The boundary lines were not made by *Thuŋkášila*. They were not spiritual boundary lines."

The loss of their fuel and wood supplies was economically devastating. They were forced to find new ways to heat their homes. They also lost the wood supplies for buildings and fencing they had always harvested from the bottomland without cost.

Timber theft along the Missouri River by steamboat operators had been common since the days of Martin's great-grandfather (Martin Charger) having battled the government over the same issue. His letters in 1883 to the Indian agent and the US Government described how islands and bottomland on their reservation were being clear cut to provide wood to fuel steamboats and other vessels increasingly traveling the river. No documentation was found confirming that Chief Charger was paid for the timber after he requested reimbursement for his losses.

He wrote: *"Do the White have a right to cut down our green wood, when the agent will not let us cut it down for our own benefit? They are cutting near my place on Bullberry Island, which I know and I have ordered them off. But they will not move. Can I make them pay for it? I have spoken to the agent about it and he says he is not able to help me. I think the wood is ours and we want to cut it ourselves. If it is to be cut, we want the money ... for us."* [72]

---

72   Letter from Martin Charger to Mr. C. H. Howard, Eng.,21 August 1883, Nation-

GROWTH OF ACTIVISM

More than a century of government actions continued unfolding during Martin's second spiritual life. In 1956, on the heels of the Termination Act, the Hoover and Eisenhower administrations signed the Indian Relocation Act into law. Also called the "Adult Vocational Training Program" it was designed to decrease subsidies to reservation Indians.

Congress appropriated $3.5 million a year authorizing the Bureau of Indian Affairs to transport adult Indians for vocational training to urban centers hundreds of miles from home. Families were encouraged to accept a one-way bus ticket and settle into urban areas for job training.[73]

Martin observed his people relocating to urban areas and doing their best to adjust to city life. They wanted to find work so they could support their families, provide a better education for their children and reconstruct a foundation for their grandchildren. A February 1960 report from the Bureau of Indian Affairs reported that the US Government had successfully moved more than 31,000 Indian people to cities and that 70 per cent were now self-supporting.[74]

It didn't feel like success to Martin. He listened to the stories of some who had relocated to urban communities during the government's Relocation Era. He saw that some had successfully enrolled in school, learned new technology and found work, but the move to distant relocation cities caused some to become more disillusioned and impoverished than before relocation. Although many did find temporary work, some were soon unemployed and became homeless in the cities' ghettos, languishing in a state of alcoholism and despair far from the support of their families and the reservation community back home.

Martin observed that his people, as they settled in their new communities, were continuing to be put down as a nation. Wherever they turned they saw the fresh face of racism and rejection.

---

alArchives, Washington DC

73   An estimated 200,000-300,000 Indians received assistance to travel to eight cities designated as Relocation Centers during the 1960s. There had not been such mass removal of Native Americans since the Trail of Tears in 1838 when Cherokees were forcibly moved to Oklahoma Territory.

74   Walls, Melissa L.; Whitbeck, Les B. (June 14, 2012). "The Intergenerational Effects of Relocation Policies on Indigenous Families." *Journal of Family Issues*. 33 (9): 1272–1293.

They felt ashamed of their skin color and for the way they looked and dressed. They became frustrated; their anger heated up as their cries of protest expressed the mistreatment of family members and neighbors.

He realized some of his people had left the reservation because poverty was severe and unemployment was high. Education and health care were inadequate. Many were bitter over alleged inexperience and corruption in tribal government. Some were also ashamed of some relatives whose lives had become side-railed by alcoholism and abuse. They felt ashamed that their cultural heritage had eroded. They felt let down by the elders who had grown silent.

Martin predicted there would be devastating long-term effects of families leaving Cheyenne River during Relocation. He could see that their lifestyle in their new homeland was interfering with their spirituality. Some of those who obtained work found that living with jobs and technology interfered with the cultural values that had kept their families united together through decades of hardships. There was a threat that by moving off of the reservation his people would become disconnected from their spiritual connection. As they began to lose touch with their own history and culture, their memories also began to fade.

THE ADVENT OF INFORMED CONSENT

For decades, the voice of Native people had been ignored. Lakȟóta were excluded from critical decision making regarding their own lives, their families and communities. Congress, Department of the Interior, Bureau of Indian Affairs, the State of South Dakota, the cattle industry and even state institutions of higher education had successfully used the erroneous concept of 'race-based demonization' to exclude them by erasing the concept of tribal sovereignty originally expressed in the treaties.[75]

In 1953, the State of South Dakota introduced Public Law 280, in which State and Federal government leaders banded together to transfer authority for tribal affairs from federal to state government.[76] Officials publicly exposed their open contempt and disre-

75   Ibid. Walls, Melissa L.; Whitbeck, Les B. (June 14, 2012). "The Intergenerational Effects of Relocation Policies on Indigenous Families." Journal of Family Issues
76   The state asked to be subsidized by the federal government for the financial burden of assuming authority over tribes.

gard for Lakȟóta people, making it clear that no one was willing to acknowledge the sovereignty of South Dakota's tribal governments. At the same time, policies remained in effect that White people would not be prosecuted for confiscating Indian land and cattle, killing Indians, or committing other violations against tribal members on reservation land. Their racial stereotypes publicly characterized the Lakȟóta as inherently lawless savages who imposed a social and economic burden on South Dakota. This plan was supported by the South Dakota Bar Association, and even faculty at the University of South Dakota's Institute of Indian Studies.[77]

The South Dakota legislature stated in the jurisdiction bill that control of tribal members be gained *"through forced consent,"* inferring that the reservation-based court system and law enforcement was incompetent. The traditional tribal justice system was widely regarded as more humane and rehabilitative compared to the more punitive state and federal courts. It demonstrated more concern for fairness. However, government officials were unable to recognize that tribal justice relies upon close tribal kinship relationships within families to remediate wrongs.

In February 1959, the House Subcommittee on Indian Affairs scheduled a routine congressional hearing on H.R. 3737.[78] Robert Burnette, President of Rosebud Sioux Tribe, unexpectedly appeared and delivered testimony before the subcommittee:

> I knew if this amendment became law, all Indians on reservations would be at the complete mercy of state authorities, whose primary aim would be to divest the Indian of his land and to destroy the tribal system. I imagined Indians in state courts, facing a jury of Whites; Indian children taken from their parents and placed in foster homes; Indian children in schools dedicated to the eradication of their heritage; wholesale discrimination against Indians and the Indian way of life.
>
> I decided to make my testimony a report of the injustices that had occurred since Public Law 280 had been enacted... it would be not only cowardly but unwise to shrink at this time from a direct assault on a legal weapon that Whites had

---

77   *Not Without Our Consent: Lakota Resistance to Termination 1950-1959*, Edward Charles Valandra, University ofIllinois Press, 2006, p.219
78   Ibid, pp. 245-6, *Not Without Our Consent: Lakota Resistance to Termination 1950-1959*, Edward Charles Valandra, University of Illinois Press, 2006

fashioned to harass, subjugate, and ultimately devastate the reservation Indian.[79]

His testimony erupted into a scandal. It was a scathing indictment of South Dakota's racist history, policies and institutions. Lakȟóta tribal leaders launched legal action through a referendum along with a massive public relations campaign that exposed a century of discriminatory treatment they had received from South Dakota's White community which had excluded Native voices from the decision-making process.

Because of the emerging political influence of Indians, their protest effectively exploded through the media nationwide. Using South Dakota's political tradition of the referendum process and a statewide vote, the Eighth Circuit Court of Appeals instead affirmed Lakȟóta sovereignty.[80] This became a historic turning point for the Lakȟóta. From that time on, the voice and consent of the Lakȟóta in government decisions became a permanent prerequisite and "an expected norm."

As Lakȟóta tribes gained support to preserve tribal sovereignty and self-governance, the defeat of House Bill 791 was regarded as "the single most stunning political upset in U.S.-Native relations in the twentieth century, meriting far more print than this discussion allows."[81]

THE DIVORCE

As Martin approached his third spiritual life, he continued to see greater public awareness emerging of injustices his people faced at home on the reservation and in urban communities.

A century of misguided federal Indian policy had created conflicts inside Lakȟóta communities. The people continued to take sides whether they were Christian Indians or Traditional Indians; Reservation Indians or Urban Indians; Full Blooded Indians or "Breeds" who had intermarried into other nations or colors; Invisible Indians – reluctant to teach their ways to their descendants; focal Native activists – proudly declaring their ancestry to their children, grandchildren and the world; Indians fluent in their tribal language or those who only spoke the English language; Indians

---

79   Ibid, pp 245-6.
80   Ibid, pp. 165-6
81   Ibid, pp. 252-3

addicted to alcohol and drugs versus those who had remained or became clean and sober.

He knew that it wasn't just relocation that was disorienting them. Martin felt strongly that it was important for Native people to leave the cities and come back home where they could recover their spiritual connection. Their ancestors had suffered so their descendants could regain the rights to their land and could participate in their traditional ways again.

At the same time, as his boys and daughter, Irene grew older, Martin and his wife continued drifting apart. Martin's grandfather had told him it was his job, the man's place to provide for the family, so he honored his grandfather's advice and continued to do his best at whatever he did. He sometimes expressed that he felt he was like everybody else, trying to be strong and doing whatever was needed to provide for his family. He would say, "That's what a man did. A man is supposed to be strong."

Their youngest son, Leonard, observed his parents' quietness. Throughout his growing up years, the family sometimes separated due to Martin's work, but sometimes they were able to travel together to his various work sites. "We moved quite a bit, and hardly ever lived on the reservation. It was always a hard time. Mom was a quiet woman and dad was too. They never argued. It didn't seem like they had enough time together so they grew apart."

Newly divorced, Martin continued to live near the reservation, working irrigation construction jobs and then he took a job as a truck driver.

EDDIE EXPRESSED HIS FEELINGS

Remembering the time in 1965 when their family split up, Eddie shared his sadness over their divorce:

> By then, we were all grown up and mom and dad divorced. I left around 1965 or 1966 and went to California. I went into construction and then mechanics. Ronnie was with me on the West Coast about a year until he left and joined the army at Fort Ord. Then I moved to Colorado and worked construction.
>
> Ghetto (Leonard) went to Faith. He worked there and at Cheyenne Agency all his life, and at Pierre. Clifford became a policeman and he worked in Eagle Butte for 16 years. Later on, when Dad became an Old Home bread truck driver, Clif-

Martin with his sons, Clifford and Eddie High Bear, 1993.

ford rode with him on his routes. Irene left too. Some people from Cheyenne River lived near Chicago, so Irene sold her allotment and moved to Chicago.

Martin's second spiritual world accelerated through the 1960's. He was still reliant upon alcohol, but that didn't numb him from showing kindness and compassion to others who were suffering. He continued to gather with friends from his reservation and neighboring tribes on the reservation, rodeo grounds, the streets, in meeting halls and bars. Some had lost perspective, becoming more disconnected from what was real, making them more vulnerable to loss, incarceration and even death.

Martin fully realized his people needed to reconnect themselves with what was real. They needed to relearn their old teachings and life ways so they could participate in ceremonies. He knew it was time for him to do his part to help the people restore their cultural and spiritual traditions. He spoke up and shared his perspective of peaceful activism with others.

He acknowledged how the century of repression and losses was causing too many to grow angrier and more vocal. He expressed that when he was younger, he too had vocalized the need for the people to restore their rights. He too was doing ceremony when it was illegal. He was also fighting for the rights for them to go hunting so they could conduct their manhood ceremony and prove themselves as men. He expressed his feelings:

> These ceremonies were created by Great Spirit to make the people healthy and strong. I saw so much destruction that I could no longer sit back and say it was right. I'd heard all my life of the wrong being done to the people, not just to the Sioux but to all Native people all over ... I believed in fighting for the rights of the Sun Dance and other ceremonies by doing them, whether it was legal or not. My understanding of the importance of the elders and their stories deepened.
>
> I knew it was essential for us to heal. We needed the spirit to come back so we could understand the freedom the ancestors had lived with on the land before the Europeans came. They called it stolen lands.
>
> I could also see that some of my people were not ready to listen. I continued to use alcohol, but I tried to teach that alcohol use during ceremony was death to the people. I had fought that myself since my military days. The time was coming for me to quit.
>
> It was this kind of prayer that would stir up the ancestors in the Spirit World and stir up the people down here. That prayer would bring the ceremonies back. It would help to restore self-respect. It would bring warriors back to the right state of mind and bring the women back to their spiritual role. It was time for all Native people to stand up and find the balance between their spiritual worlds.

ALCATRAZ

Martin supported the Native networks that were emerging during the 1960s. They were reawakening hope among his people. There was enormous unrest from social protests of the 1960s with the civil rights movement, the war on poverty, and anti-Vietnam War protests raging through America. The enactment of the Voting Right Acts of 1965, although designed to provide protection and assistance to Native people by prohibiting discrimination on the basis of race; provided minimal relief when the South Dakota state government responded by imposing multiple barriers to block federal legislation.

Native activists needed their voice and their rights to be restored. They felt by walking together, they could provide strength in numbers and accomplish great things for future generations. They condemned multiple abuses and pledged to support Native American self-determination, civil rights and sovereignty.

Their primary focus settled upon the protection of their legal rights, especially spiritual traditions which had been illegal for nearly a century. They wanted sacred sites to be returned to them, including the Black Hills and Bear Butte, so they could resume ceremonies that had been practiced there. They also wanted better economic conditions and education support for Indian people living in city ghettos and on the reservations.

Much like the desire for Black Power among African Americans, intertribal organizations such as the Red Power Movement and the American Indian Movement began to support one another to restore their rights. Red Power became the chant of Native men and women who had relocated to Oakland, California.

In Oakland, Indian groups began to gather at the Intertribal Friendship House to discuss conditions in an effort to fulfill the needs of tribal people who had migrated into the area from all parts of the country. They grouped up in several dozen political and social groups and began to protest Indian treaty and civil rights abuses.

One of the most famous demonstrations was the 1968 takeover of Alcatraz Island in San Francisco Bay. Calling themselves "Indians of All Tribes," they launched the Red Power Movement-Alcatraz and claimed the island by "Right of Discovery."[82]

Five years earlier, in March 1964, a group of five Dakhóta Sioux, with an attorney from the American Indian Council had traveled to Alcatraz Island and briefly claimed the facility. They were unsuccessful in securing their claim to the island citing their right to surplus government property.

Their tactics were different from that of African Americans and Hispanic Americans as they began seizing control of government property as a result of the legal backing of a Sioux Treaty claim stating that they could obtain surplus federal property under terms of Article Six in the 1868 Black Hills Treaty. The US federal government had closed the Alcatraz federal prison as of 1962.[83]

82   American Indian Activism: Alcatraz to the Longest Walk, Troy R. Johnson, Joane Nagel, Duane Champagne 1997, p. 2.
83   Like a Hurricane: The Native American Movement from Alcatraz to Wounded Knee. Allen, Warrior, Robert, New Press, 1996.

As national media began to follow their activities, it raised the awareness of the public to American Indian injustices and helped increase national and international publicity. Sympathy and support from the public grew.

On the West Coast, a group of Indian Native activists from Little Rez, San Francisco's Native community known as the United Indian Bay Area Council plus students from San Francisco State University and UCLA.

MEMORY FROM MICHAEL TWO FEATHERS

One of Martin's Sun Dance helpers, Michael Two Feathers, who is now an *Itȟáŋčhaŋ* (Sun Dance Chief) and also carries a Medicine Bundle, told of being drawn to Fisherman's Wharf one day in the fall of 1969:

> I was traveling, hitchhiking, trying to find myself. A Choctaw friend, Joey and I ended up in San Francisco. We had hitchhiked and ended up at Fisherman's Wharf. We saw this big crowd of people looking over the edge.
>
> We thought, "Wow. They must have caught a big ol' fish. Let's go and look."
>
> We looked over the edge and saw a few Indians loading boxes onto a boat. All along the railing people were watching these Indians. I wondered what it was all about so we walked down.
>
> I asked the elder Indian there, "What's going on?"
>
> He replied: "We took over Alcatraz and this is donated food and water that we're taking over there to support the occupation."
>
> "Do you need any help?" I asked.
>
> He said, "Are you Indians?"
>
> "Yeah!" we said.
>
> He said, "Yes, grab some of those boxes and help us get them on the boat."
>
> So we started helping. It was a pretty good pile that we loaded onto this 40-foot boat. I only had a backpack and my friend the same, because we were just traveling on our thumbs and going from meal to meal. They fired up the boat and we left.
>
> When we ended up out there, I became part of the crew that worked with the boat and I also did different things here and there.

When we got there, I asked the elder from the boat, "Where can we camp?"

He said, "Anywhere you want."

So we were looking around. All the regular living quarters, like the guard houses, were already taken. So Joey and I walked up into the prison. We were looking all around, kind of adventuring around, and we found this one area where no one was. It was a cell block on the second floor. 'Gee, we can have a whole cell here to ourselves with beds' I said. So we threw our stuff in there.

And then I got this feeling that someone was watching me. You know how the hair on the back of your neck stands up? I had this funny feeling but I kind of put it aside. When my friend and I walked down the hallway and opened this big door, it turned out to be the gas chamber where they strapped the people down. Where we had put our camping stuff was death row! They had killed a lot of people there and I thought about it later. That is why I had this feeling that I was being watched. The spirits of the people that they killed were still there.

I remembered when I was 8 years old, my dad took us, me and my sisters, to a powwow. He bumped me on the shoulder while we were standing there watching, and he said 'You are Indian.' That is all he said to me about it. That made me feel "different." I was a different color than most but I didn't know much about my culture.

When I got to Alcatraz, I spent some time sitting with the elders. This one old man was my first contact with the Lakȟóta. We would sit around the fire at night and this elder fellow, I don't even remember his name, he would tell stories.

He said, "Our cycle of life is like a circle and it has four quarters. To us Lakȟóta, it is represented by the four legs of the buffalo. Each leg is a quarter and each hair is a year." And he said "That buffalo is standing on one leg with not much hair left, so there is a change coming. We are getting to the point where a new cycle is going to start."

That went pretty deep for me. I was 22 years old and didn't know much about ceremony yet or any of that. We stayed there for a while, but we were starving. Donations were nice but they weren't enough. Some others showed up but weren't there for the original reason – to turn the island into a cultural and educational center so that people could learn that all Indian people are not stupid and lazy. It seemed like some came there to party. My friend had to leave and I had to take care of other things in my life, so we both left.

DEAN BARLESE SHARES HIS THOUGHTS

Martin's lead Sun Dance singer, Dean Barlese, also spoke of the Paiute elders who visited Alcatraz and came away with renewed pride. The takeover of Alcatraz Island strengthened their pride of their Native heritage. Indians were not ashamed to be Indian anymore:

> I had a gramma, Minnie Thompson (Minnie Brown) and her sister, Rose Williams. She was born in 1900 and in her 60's, going on 70 already in the late 60's, early 70's, when they started traveling. They went to Henrietta, Oklahoma to a big gathering there. I think it was a national AIM convention.
>
> When they started traveling back this way, Richard Oakes[84] was in the hospital in Oakland. So they traveled from Oklahoma into New Mexico and Arizona and came up through Southern California and into Oakland. They talked about how Richard Oakes wound up in the hospital, that they went in to pray with him, and how later he died.
>
> She always tells us about that. The Alcatraz occupation was going on, and here my grandmother Minnie was out there. She was ready to turn 70 and she turned militant. Then she started telling us 'You should be proud of who you are'. 'You guys should do this' and 'You should do that,' her and her sister Rose would tell us. And they traveled up to Washington during the salmon fishing protest on the Nisqually River. These old grammas, 69 and 70 years old, and they were out there in the world being all militant. [Chuckles]
>
> If you really think about it, at Alcatraz and the protests that happened in the late 60's, it brought a lot of pride back. A lot of our people at Pyramid Lake, once people started standing up and protesting, when they started standing up to the government, they started feeling pride again.
>
> The school administration, like the county school district, they didn't like that because we started wanting to grow

---

84   Richard Oakes (1976-1972) was a spokesperson for the Red Power Movement during the Alcatraz Island takeover. His 12 year old daughter Yvonne fell during the occupation and was taken to the hospital. She died there on Jan 8, 1970 as a result of her injuries. https://diva.sfsu.edu/collections/sfbatv/bundles/238413

our hair again. It started to touch our collars again and that was a big *"no-no"* to them. They thought we were trying to be hippies. We didn't feel so oppressed and depressed about who we were. We started feeling proud again.

The Alcatraz Island occupation lasted 19 months until it ended in June 1971. Despite dissension within the ranks and their failure to achieve certain demands from the government, the event became a major turning point in the history of American Indian activism. The takeover demonstrated that activism could bring broad public exposure to critical issues and provide stronger support for Indian rights. The occupation became a symbol of unity for Indians, not just in the San Francisco Bay area, but throughout the country.

Tribal leaders gained national and international media attention from the Alcatraz occupation. It helped raise the public's awareness of the wide range of issues and grievances that had existed under the radar for more than a century on reservations. Indian governments and activists began to demand that the government address the cultural repression of more than a century and other injustices.

Martin High Bear traditional dancing at powwow in Coos Bay, Oregon.

CHAPTER 5

MARTIN'S TRANSITION INTO HIS THIRD SPIRITUAL WORLD

By 1970, Martin began to work on giving up alcohol. He knew it was his destiny to help his people with the brown skin turn away from the "poison-water" so they could relearn their spiritual ways and restore their traditional beliefs.

He felt ashamed of some of his family members who drank and partied, but he especially felt ashamed of himself. He spoke frequently of going out to find what he was supposed to do to help his people. Then he would get sidetracked.

His life was intensifying, showing it was time to learn the ceremonies, go on Vision Quest and strengthen his connection with the Spirit World. He spoke of this transition:

> Then I had all these dreams and visions, but I was busy working. Then when the boys and my daughter grew up, I finally went back and met up with this old Medicine Man. I told him about my dreams and what was happening to me. So I was in my late age when I went up on the hill and fulfilled what I was to do. It was maybe twenty years before I done that. I always had the vision to do it, but I say I was too busy. I had to grow some kids.

Martin continued to have dreams and visions and to feel that special connection. His body, mind and spirit began to heal. That understanding grew as he spent weeks in connection with the Spirit World and attended ceremonies. He felt he could see through their eyes the old sacred ways of his ancestors when they were first having their visions. He could feel their feelings. They taught him about the old Sun Dances and why their revival would restore hope to his people.

He began to understand more clearly what his grandparents and other elders had meant when they told him as a young boy that he would help to save his people. The ancestors were not instructing Martin to guide the people to fight and conquer to regain their rights as Indian people in the traditions of the Europeans. Instead, they were guiding him to help the people regenerate and restore their spirits so they could restore their spiritual greatness. They needed to relearn and internalize the ancient values of respect and honor so they could follow the ancestors' teachings of unity and harmony. They no longer had to be something they were not.

Because of the early years Martin spent with his elders and the teachings they had shared, especially about the suffering his people had endured, he realized he had no choice. He knew the Spirit needed to be given back to the people and it was important that he do his part to help. He realized his people needed to recover their spiritual connection so they could once again have hope and healing. They needed to stand up and reconnect themselves with what was real so they could recognize their own destinies with respect and honor.

JERRY FLUTE'S RELATIONSHIP WITH GRAMPA FOOLS CROW

Jerry Flute, the late Tribal Chairman of the Sisseton-Wahpeton Oyáte, tells the story of how he met Martin and Medicine Man Felix Green,[85] from Rosebud Indian Reservation, through Grampa Frank Fools Crow:

> I first met Felix through Frank Fools Crow. To us, as Sioux people, Fools Crow was like the pope. He was the highest spiritual leader that we have in this century and the most powerful and highly respected person. I met Fools Crow the first time at a Pipe ceremony at Green Grass at Stanley Looking Horse's house, and that's also where I met Felix. I got to know Fools Crow to where I went to his house in Pine Ridge several times.
>
> Fools Crow was the one to encourage me to go on the mountain for a fast, and he sponsored me the first time I went on a fast. The second year I was going to go for a prayer

---

85   Document: Brotherhood of the Native American Peacepipe dated April 6, 1974 stating: "The Board of Directors recognizes Felix Green as a Medicine Man, and authorizes him to give medicine and conduct spiritual ceremonies with the Sacred Peacepipe." Signed by "President Arvol Looking Horse, Vice President Stanely R. Looking Horse, Secretary Arlee F. High Elk."

fast, he called me up and he said, "My wife is in the hospital." He never called me himself. There was a guy, his name was Matthew King – Noble Red Man. Yeah, he was like the secretary, Fools Crow's interpreter and secretary.

Matthew called me up and he said, "The old man wants you to know that his wife is in the hospital and he can't come when you go for your fast, so he wants you to call Felix Green." He said "You go to his house in Cherry Creek. He'll be waiting for you."

I didn't know Felix at that time. I didn't have a clue who he was, but I figured as long as Fools Crow said, "He'll be there and he'll sponsor you, and he'll put you on the mountain," I said, "Well then, I'll go there."

So when we were ready to go fast, we went to Cheyenne River. I'd never been to Cherry Creek before. I found my directions and I got to Cherry Creek and asked where Felix Green lived, and of course everybody knew him because he's also a highly regarded Medicine Man. So they directed me to his house and we pulled in his driveway, and here's this old man. He's sitting outside in the shade. I introduced myself and he said, "I've been waiting for you. The Sweat Lodge is ready and we'd better get in there right now." So five minutes later we're sitting in the Sweat.

He said, "The Sweat Lodge at Bear Butte is no longer usable so you can't Sweat over there. So we'll Sweat here and get all your stuff ready here, and then I'll take you right there to Bear Butte and put you on the mountain. When you're done with your fast we'll come back here to have a Sweat. Okay?"

So that's how I first met him. And then I got acquainted with him and he was a lot different than Fools Crow. Fools Crow had a lot of humor. He found levity in a lot of things. He was humorous, but Felix Green was a comic. He found humor in everything. He was really a comic. He'd make you laugh all the time.

I went to Bear Butte almost ten years in a row. I would call Fools Crow and if he was available he would put me up. If he wasn't available I'd ask Felix, Felix would put me up. I think I had Martin put me up after he was given an altar. Martin put me up once or twice at Bear Butte. But I got to know Felix pretty well to where he would come here, spend a week, two weeks. Probably the longest he stayed, maybe a month he stayed here with us. And he was teaching me all the time. Fools Crow was no different, you know, he was always teaching.

When I first went to Bear Butte, Fools Crow actually recommended that I not go to the summit. He said that Bear Butte was a dangerous place to fast, and that too many people had been killed by lightning up there. And he said the last two men that were killed by lightning were Cheyenne. They wanted to fast at the top, and lightning hit them. He said now the Cheyennes go to the top to leave offerings, but they never fast up there at the top. And he said, "I don't even fast at the top. I fast at Chimney Rock," about half to three-fourths of the way up.

He said, "I don't know why you want to go to the top."

So I just told him, I said, "You know, my ancestors have fasted there for centuries and if lightning hits me, it hits me, but that's where I want to go. I want to go to the top."

He said, "All right."

I mean we debated a little bit, but he respected my desire to fast at the top, so that's where I went. I fasted at the very summit, and never had the lightning hit anyplace close to me so I was okay, I guess. A lot of bad rainstorms and a lot of lightning and hail, but nothing that ever affected me.

It might have been during that Wounded Knee takeover or right after when Matt King called me up. He always referred to Fools Crow as "the old man." He said, "The old man wants you down here at 10:00 o'clock on May 8th," or whatever day it was. He said, "He wants you to come over here."

I said, "Well, do you know what he wants me over there for?"

He said, "No, he just told me to call you and he wants you to be there. He wants you at the Kyle Community Center." So I told my wife, "Well, if he wants us to come over there we must be of some importance so maybe we should go over there."

So we went to Kyle and got to this community center and there's a lot of people in there, maybe seventy-five or a hundred elders, most of them elders. So when I got into the building people told him that I was there, so he motioned me. He was sitting at the front of the room with his wife.

He motioned me and he kind of introduced me as I was like his nephew from here, and that he wanted me down there to do him a favor. And right where him and his wife were sitting they had a great big portrait that was covered up with a star quilt. And he took that star quilt off and it was a portrait of him and his wife when they were first married.

He had a buckskin outfit on with his war bonnet. She had buckskins on, and I think they'd been married for sixty-some years and somebody had done an oil painting of them. And what he wanted me to do was he wanted me to carry that painting around to show everybody that was in there.

So I carried that painting around. I let everybody look at it, all the way around like that. Brought it back and after that was done, that's the first I knew that that was his wedding anniversary. So they did a blessing on the food and they ate, and when the meal was over with, they had a giveaway. And that star quilt they had covering that painting, he called me up there and he give me that star quilt for taking that picture around for him. There were a lot of other things they gave us too. So we had kind of a relationship there, the old man and I, and his wife.

We have a medicine here – they call it bitterroot – but our language it's *šiŋkpáŋka phá*. He liked that but it was hard to get over there. So my aunt and I used to harvest that in the fall, and I'd get a big bundle of it, dry it, and I'd give that to him. And he really liked that. He used that for himself, and when he was doctoring people he used that medicine. And he wanted me to bring him a root one time that was not dry. Behind his house he had a little creek there and he was going to plant it, see if it would grow there. So I took him several roots and they wouldn't grow there. He was very disappointed. The soil was different, I think.

He and I had like a grandson and grandfather relationship, and I think one of the other reasons why we hit it off so well was that I'm fluent in Dakota. His preferred language was Lakȟóta, and he could speak English but his preference was Lakȟóta. So we could converse in our languages. He liked that, because at that time there weren't a lot of twenty-five, twenty-six-year-old men speaking their language. They were all speaking English at that time.

They were going to do a Sun Dance at Green Grass and he invited me to come out there. So I packed up my family and the day he wanted us to be there, we got there that day. But the Sun Dance arbor hadn't been built yet. There was some logs out there but there was nobody working and instead there was a powwow arbor.

I don't know if you've ever been to Green Grass. They've still got that pow wow arbor. You go past the church and then you get to Looking Horse's place. So we camped there at the powwow arbor and late that afternoon Fools Crow came in. And before he got there Pete Catches pulled in, so he was camped right next to us, and then Fools Crow camped next to Pete Catches.

I had a pipe bag that actually came from a BIA museum. I don't remember how it came to me, but I had this very old, old pipe bag. And Fools Crow wanted this bag. I mean, he kept hinting that he wanted this. And early the next morning my wife got all excited and she said, 'Look what's hanging outside.' So I come out of the tent and here's a great big eagle feather bustle hanging there.

So later on that day we were sitting over there at Fools Crow's, and he asked me, "What do you think of that bustle?" I said, "It's a good one." He said, "You know, the very first World Champion Dance Contest, someplace in Denver or something, I won that. I'm the first World Champion Indian Dancer."

And then he was telling me, "You know, when Fools Crow makes a bustle, like that one, I get a thousand dollars for that." And he said, "You think about it." He wanted to trade that bustle for the pipe bag. I said, "Yeah, I'll think about it."

That night they had a powwow. They still hadn't started work on the Sun Dance. I had my outfit with me so we danced that night. He and his wife were sitting there, and whenever I danced by them, he'd point to that pipe bag because I was carrying it. So that evening after the powwow was over we were sitting over at his tipi and he was telling us about how he had these three rocks.

Fools Crow said, "I call them Íŋyaŋ škaŋškáŋ. They're tiny, about the size of a buckshot. These are triplets, brothers. I use these in my doctoring ceremony. One time some guys came from California. They come to my house for a Sweat Lodge. I used those inside the Sweat Lodge. When we came out I put them on the buffalo skull, put all three of them there. We went to the house and I forgot about them. So the next morning I went out and one was gone. Looked all over for it and couldn't find it. So I took those two and I put them back in the bag, and they were crying. They were crying for their brother. They were restless all the time. I kept looking for it. I thought one fell off on the ground. I couldn't find it."

A couple days later one of these *Íŋyaŋ škaŋškáŋ* told him, "You better do a ceremony and bring him back because he's very unhappy where he is." So he did a prayer ceremony and he wanted that third one to come home. He said, "Wherever you are, come home." He said that next day he was back. That third one come back.

My wife was sitting there listening to him. And when that third one come back he said, "Where did you go?" He said, "One of them guys from California took me and put me in his pocket, took me back to California.' And he said, 'I couldn't get away until you sent those spirits to come after me. Then I came home." And he was happy. He said, "I'm happy to be back with my brothers because this is where I belong." So my wife was listening to him.

So we went to bed. The next morning she's shaking me, she says, "Look what's out there now! Here that big bustle was still hanging there. Great big porcupine roach was hanging with it. Boy, one of the most beautiful roaches, a great big long one like that, hanging there. You know, you better let him have that pipe bag. If he can bring a rock back from California, he's going to take that pipe bag away from you. He's going to take it away from you anyway, so you'd better get something for it."

So that afternoon, they still didn't start working on that Sun Dance ground, you know, and I told them, I said, "We got to go home." So he was asking me, he said, "What do you think about that pipe bag?" I said, "Yeah. I'll trade it. I'll give it you." So I gave him that pipe bag and he gave me that bustle and porcupine roach.

JERRY FLUTE'S FRIENDSHIP WITH FELIX GREEN

Felix Green was from Rosebud Indian Reservation, but he would travel just a horse ride away to the Cheyenne River Sioux Tribe where he lived sometimes. Jerry Flute shared his experience meeting Felix:

So I found my teachers in Fools Crow and I really liked him, and he honored me. It was through Fools Crow that I became acquainted with Felix, and then through Felix I got to know Martin. I think the older guys kind of took me under their wing because I was probably in my twenties then, and I wanted to learn. I was looking for my own religious survival. I was searching for that, and here, at that time, everybody was a Christian. There was no traditional people here in that time. They were all Christians, and I wasn't satisfied with that.

Felix told me about Martin. He said that Martin had been drinking quite a bit down in Rapid City and he got into a car wreck. He had a hole in the side of his jaw from that car wreck. They couldn't heal it.

Martin's mother was living with Felix at the time and she asked Felix to doctor Martin to heal his jaw. And Felix told Martin's mother, 'I can't doctor him unless he quits drinking.' He said, 'If he quits drinking then his medicine will work on him.' So his mother went down there to Rapid City and she brought him back. She brought Martin back to Cherry Creek, and after a couple weeks when he got sober, Felix started taking him in the Sweat. And same time he was giving him medicine because that hole went all the way through his cheek and inside his mouth, and it wouldn't heal.

So after a period of time, Felix continued to doctor him and that hole healed up, and when Martin was sober, Felix wanted him to learn these ceremonial songs so he could help him when he does doctoring. So Felix started to teach him the different songs that go with whatever kind of ceremony, doctoring ceremony.

He's one of those guys that probably knows a thousand songs, and he was one of the people who was teaching Martin songs. And of course Felix taught him the primary songs that you sing when you're setting up an altar and when the Pipe gets loaded. You know, in the ceremony there's a protocol of songs that have to be sung in a certain order, and those songs, Felix taught those to Martin. And then there's other songs when you're in the Sweat Lodge. There's a series of songs that are sung in a particular order. And if you're doing a Sweat Lodge the old way, there's no such thing as four doors to a Sweat Lodge. I mean, you go in and you come out, that's it. You know, if you're in there an hour, two hours, you don't open the door for anything. And in the old way there's a succession of songs that are sung, and Martin learned those too from Verdell and probably some others over there.

I didn't know him when he was drinking. I don't know how long he had been sober, but Felix was doctoring him when I first met him. And he still had a patch on that jaw because it wasn't quite healed when I met him. So I didn't know him during his drinking days. I met him just as he was kind of weaning himself off booze, and he was being treated by traditional medicine. But I knew from listening to him, his alcohol stories. I mean we all have stories we can talk about while we were drunk. You know, we're all the same way, so I heard a lot of his stories—where he hung out and places he got thrown out of, and how many times he was in jail. I heard all of that, yeah. But I didn't really know him while he was a practicing alcoholic. I knew him when he was getting doctored and knew him as he was getting further into spirituality, to the point where he was given an altar to help people.

Martin was around at Wounded Knee time but I never went down there when that was going on. I mean, I went there but I wasn't at Wounded Knee. I was over in Kyle and Pine Ridge. But yeah, I'm sure he was there. Fools Crow was there. I don't know of Felix ever going there, but I think Martin might have been there.

I knew Martin's mom, and they had a pretty good relationship from what I could see. I don't think I ever spent a lot of time visiting with her. I would hear her if there was a conversation between she and Felix and Martin, and her son-in-law was Melvin Garreau, the chairman at Cheyenne River at one time. She was a traditional woman and I think she was a very kind and gentle woman. She wasn't very tall, and she wore the long dresses and cotton stockings, and always wore a kerchief or scarf over her head. She never went bare headed. And even though she could speak English, her preference was to speak Lakhóta.

She had a lot of concern for Martin and that's the reason that she kept after Felix to doctor him, because Felix wouldn't do it for a long time. And he said, 'He has to quit drinking. This medicine won't work if you're drinking. It just won't work. He's got to quit drinking first.' I think she convinced Martin that he had to quit drinking for Felix to work on him because he finally came home and Felix healed him.

Martin's relationship with Felix – they were very close. Martin had been going to the VA hospital after he got in that car wreck in Rapid City. And I think he was very surprised that Felix healed him with Indian medicine where western medicine couldn't stop that infection. It couldn't heal. You know, when he got in that car wreck, and whatever happened he had that hole in his jaw and they couldn't heal that. But Felix did, and I think Martin was forever indebted to Felix for doing what he did to heal him. Not only to heal him in that fashion physically, but he healed him spiritually. So they had a very good, very close relationship.

Felix got him pretty involved with ceremonies and teaching him how to sing, and he became a helper for Felix. After four or five months, if Felix was going to do a doctoring ceremony for somebody, Martin would set up the altar for him. Then when the ceremony started then Martin would sing for him. He did that for a couple years anyway, maybe longer.

Then I don't remember what year it was, I suppose it was 1973 or 1974, there was a ceremony at Stanley Looking Horse's house at Green Grass. Felix called me up and he wanted me to come out there. I had been to several Pipe ceremonies there, and at that time there was only a few people who would come. The first Pipe ceremony I went, there must have been in 1970 and there was maybe seven or eight people came. And then the following year there might have been twenty people.

But when Felix invited me out there, it wasn't for a Pipe ceremony. He said there was going to be a number of Medicine Men going to be there. He asked me if I wanted to come out there and just kind of Sweat with them and see what was going on, because Felix was kind of my mentor. He was teaching me about the Pipe, the ceremonies.

And so I went out there for that meeting. Some Medicine Men came up from Montana. Pete Catches was there, Fools Crow. I can't remember all of them, but there was probably six or seven Medicine Men that were there. And they did a ceremony by themselves about midnight, one o'clock in the morning. The rest of us were all sitting outside. We had a fire going, had soup and coffee outside.

Then when they finished their ceremony, Stanley Looking Horse came out and said, "Martin, they want to talk to you." So Martin went in. He went inside the house and they were in there for quite a while.

It must have been about three or four o'clock in the morning when Felix came out to where we were sitting out there and he said, 'These old guys have given Martin an altar.' And apparently what they did was they kind of tested him. He had maybe two or three years of experience with Felix by then learning all these songs. So when they asked him to come in there and set up an altar and to do a ceremony for these older men, he apparently did so well that they thought that he could have an altar of his own.

That night they gave him an altar. They said, 'You have the right to conduct ceremonies and doctoring and whatever.' So at sunrise they had another prayer ceremony and Fools Crow came out and recognized Martin to where he's able to do ceremonies. They recognized him in front of the people that were there and I was there when that happened.

Stanley Looking Horse told me years after that ceremony when these old guys tested Martin that it was Felix's insistence that they test him. I'm not aware of any person since that was given that kind of a test to see if they knew everything involved in having an altar, setting it up, the prayers, the protocol. I'm not aware of anybody ever being subjected to that since. I mean, maybe they did that for everybody before, but I wasn't privy to that, but I was privy to the fact that they did, in fact, test Martin, and in their view, he passed so they gave him an altar. Stanley said that Felix is the one that wanted them to try him out and he passed. So they bestowed an altar on him. And they said he's entitled to have this altar and all the prayers and respect that go with it.

So yeah, they had a very close relationship. There was a lot of respect between the two of them. There might have been some other guys over at Cheyenne River that had some role in Martin's evolution from being a skid row drunk to a highly respected spiritual leader. I know that Verdell Blue Arm was very instrumental. He taught Martin a lot of ceremonial songs. We have Seven Rites to the Pipe, and each one of these Seven Rites, it has its own protocol. Each one has their own distinctive songs that you must sing when you're doing these ceremonies.

For a while, Martin continued to help Felix, and then Martin started going on his own. He used to come here. Felix used to come here too and spend maybe a month with us, and then he'd come with Martin and you know, we'd have ceremonies here. We'd have Sweat Lodge and a lot of people would come here for doctoring. And then periodically Martin would come by himself and we continued to do the same thing. We'd have Sweats and ceremonies here, and more and more people got to know Martin from here.

And all this was going on at a time when we, a small group of us here, we're trying to revive the Dakhóta religion. Before I went on my fast down to Bear Butte there was no Sweat Lodges. There was no Sweat Lodges. There was no ceremonies. Nobody had Pipes. Nobody was praying with a Pipe. We're still trying to bring all that back.

More people were getting acquainted with Felix. They were inviting him into their own places for ceremonies, and then Martin started to come. More people, including the Thompsons and Ed Red Owl, were getting acquainted with him. Ed Red Owl is a friend of mine. We were on this quest together to revive this Indian tradition here. Ed became good friends with Martin, and Ed introduced Martin to his family. Jake Thompson is Ed's half-brother, so they would invite him and he would stay over there with them for maybe a week or two weeks and then he come over here and then he'd go back to Cheyenne River.

I guess it'd be true to say that I knew him before he was given that direction to carry a ceremony on his own. I knew him before that, when he was a drunk down in Rapid City. And then I saw him develop where he quit the drinking. I saw the kind of doctoring that Felix Green did for him. I watched him learn songs and ceremonies, because that's what I was doing myself. My intention was never to have an altar, but to know about these things. But I saw Martin go beyond that. He learned well and he was able to heal people. So that's how I knew him.

BUILDING THE FIRST PRISON SWEAT LODGE

Jerry Flute shared how he continued to work together with Martin, including in 1975 or 1976 when they helped the Indian inmates in the penitentiary in Sioux Falls:

The Indians had a lawsuit against the State of South Dakota because they wanted to put a Sweat Lodge in there. And the State said, "No, they couldn't have a Sweat Lodge."ß

I became acquainted with the warden. We both kind of had a little confidence in each other, so I set up a meeting with the warden, myself and Martin. Martin and I went over there to Sioux Falls. We sat there with the warden and two or three of his deputies and we talked about the Sweat Lodge, the importance of it, and how it's a healing for our people. We convinced the warden that they should have a Sweat Lodge there. So Martin and I built the first Sweat Lodge ever in the state of South Dakota in the penitentiary. They still have a Sweat Lodge in there.

They tell you that when you carry this Pipe, you can never predict where that Pipe is going to take you. You never know where it's going to take you if you're practicing with it. If you put it away and you're not practicing with it, well, it's not going to take you anyplace. But if you're practicing with it and you're praying and you're running ceremonies and trying to help people that Pipe will take you.

Whether Martin was ready to go beyond that or not, he wasn't able to control his destiny there because the elders – very influential Medicine People, including Fools Crow – controlled his destiny that night. They put him on the road and said, 'Go!' He had no choice, so that's where he went.

I wasn't prepared to live that way. I wasn't prepared to live out of a satchel and sleep in the back of my truck. I had no desire to do that. You know, when you go places for doctoring they don't give you money. Sometimes they give you money. Maybe they give you a tank of gas. They might give you a tire or give you a blanket or something.

That was one of Melvin's complaints to Martin was that, Melvin's two-car garage was getting full of Martin's stuff. It was getting full of Pendletons and buffalo robes and tipis, and tires, and televisions. You know, he'd go someplace and he'd be up in Canada for a month or whatever. He'd come back with a whole bunch of stuff. He'd unload it in Melvin's garage.

I was over there with Felix one time. We went to see Melvin. We went to the garage and we looked in there and I was surprised. It was like going in Walmart. He had a lot of stuff in there – tires and televisions, and you name it, that people gave him.

MARTIN BEGAN RUNNING SUN DANCES

Jerry continued:

The first Sun Dances at Green Grass, Grampa Fools Crow ran it in 1978, and he couldn't come in 1979, so he asked Martin to run it. Martin had received a vision and he went to

Grampa Fools Crow down there to Pine Ridge and he told those elders what his whole vision was. He had the vision of all those dance movements and the altar. He got it all in a vision. And they said yes, they'd seen those dance movements, so it was clear to them that he was to do it.

I'm not sure who all was there. It would have been Matthew King and some others. In fact, Matthew King came out to the Sun Dance at Mt. Hood and so did somebody else. Other Medicine Men who came out to Mt. Hood and they would give speeches to people and teach them and all this.

One Sun Dance was the Looking Horse International Sun Dance. The first year at Mt. Hood Sun Dance was 1979. They were trying to help the urban Indians out there. People came from Canada, Washington, Montana, California, Oregon. A big group from Nevada was Paiutes, and so they started having a Sun Dance at Mt. Hood and he ran that until around 1992. Vernal Cross came out and took it away from him because there was an attitude that they didn't want non-natives to be there. Vernal was willing to go along with that and Martin couldn't, because by that time Martin had this vision that all the races needed to get along.

Then Martin started running Sun Dance down in southern Oregon at Four Nations Sun Dance Camp. He ran the dance up at Secwepemc (Shuswap) country at Alkali Lake, Chase, B.C. He ran a Sun Dance at Crow Agency, Montana, because those Crow Medicine Men came and told him 'Well, we've got a Shoshone Sun Dance but we don't have a piercing dance here and would you be willing to come and do a Lakȟóta Dance for us Crow boys? It would be a reconciliation between the Crow and the Lakȟóta,' they said. So he came and did that dance.

And then he took over a dance that Wallace Black Elk had stepped away from down in Ashland, Oregon. Wallace stepped back because somebody wrote that Wallace Black Elk book. The author of that never gave Wallace any royalties and that author was down there in that Ashland area. So Wallace refused to come back to do that dance. Martin had to take it over part of the time. It also was run by the Chips people. So that was five dances he would do in a summer sometimes.

So I guess the spirits said it was okay for him to do, but it wasn't an easy life for him. He really had a hard life. You know, poverty, and people would always say terrible things about him. He sometimes picked the wrong friends and his friends were kind of, what do you call it? Not the most ethical people in the world, and he would be implicated by his friends' behavior.

We spent a lot of time together, and I suppose to a certain extent we were learning at about the same time. We would talk about what we saw in ceremonies, the spiritual things going on, and it was always good.

MARTIN WAS NOT IMMUNE TO TRAGEDIES.

Despite all of his spiritual training as he became a Medicine Man, Martin continued to suffer deep personal loss. Karen Timentwa shared her memory of Martin from the 1970's after his son Ronny's death from suicide:

I was living in Ashland when Martin called me one night.

He said, 'What are you doing?'

I said, "I'm not doing anything. What the heck are you doing?"

He said 'I'm getting ready to get on the road.'

"Where are you?"

'I'm in South Dakota. I'm heading your direction.'

"When do you think you will get here?"

'I have to take my time.'

"I'll make sure there's some food. Bring whoever you want."

A couple of days later, he called me in the evening and said, 'I'm about six hours out.'

I stayed up and got some food going, bread and everything. He and his son, Eddie came in around two o' clock in the morning. I did not know why he had to take so much time. I figured he was stopping and doing ceremony.

I told his son where he could stay so he went to bed, and Martin stayed up.

He said, 'My boy died. That's why I had to take my time.'

The first day after the burial, he could only go ten miles. Then he had to stop for the day. Then the next day he could go so many miles. For those first four days he was only allowed a certain amount of travel. Then after that fourth day he could complete his travel.

He said, 'Of all people, I should know.'

He said that his boy had taken out an insurance policy. 'He was telling me different things. There were signs,' he said.

121

He was feeling really bad about burying his son. We stayed up all night long that night, and talked all night long until the sun came up. He said whatever he needed to say to get it out. That was pretty hard.

He told me, 'Don't tell anybody I'm out there. Give me a week.'

There were just five of us living here. I said, "When you are ready, just tell me and I'll let people know you are here. Otherwise, I won't say anything."

Eddie and Martin stayed here resting for about a week.

Then one day he said, 'Okay. It's alright.'

I let people know. He ended up doing ceremony. People came over. He stayed there with us for two or two and a half weeks that time. You have to do that to take the pressure off.

That was the first time I got to know Martin in a whole different way. He was like one of my family, my Uncle. He was somebody that you really respect and get advice from, someone that you trust. It was really hard to see him so hurt. He really had a hard time. That was his most traditional son, Ron was.

Martin said, 'He would be downtown in Eagle Butte and he'd see an older couple trying to get across the street, and he'd park his car and walk them across the street. He came back from Vietnam...'

It's a hard life to be a medicine man. I had told a friend of mine at one point, it's hard to be who he is.

I know. I grew up around elders. My grandmother was an Indian doctor. It was no big deal. One thing about that happened with Martin and I, and I'm sure it happens with a lot of medicine people out here, people just swoon at you. They forget that you're also human.

All they want to do is ask all these questions about spiritual this and spiritual that, and they forget that (medicine people) have a sense of humor, they get aches and pains, they get irritated, they have a favorite thing they like to go and do.

Sometimes they just want to just be part of the family, part of the little group of people, and not feel like they are on the spot all the time, turned on.

So I saw my friend suffer through that loss. It's not an easy thing. I don't know if I would wish that on anybody. It can be really isolating in a lot of ways.

Ed Red Owl Narrative

In an oral narrative from Martin's adopted brother, Sisseton-Wahpeton Oyáte Leader Ed Red Owl, he eloquently expressed his appreciation for Martin. Ed had attended seminary and was studying to become a Catholic priest. When he was reintroduced to his ancestral spiritual traditions through Felix Green, Martin and others, he stepped away from the priesthood and became a tribal leader for his reservation:

> My name is Ed Red Owl. My Dakhóta name is the same: Red Owl (*Hiŋháŋ Dúta*), and Martin High Bear is my adopted brother. Martin, I first met him in the early 1970's. He came here with his stepfather Felix Green, and we attended our first Dowáŋpi ceremony as we understand it today. And from there we were taken to Bear Butte and made our Vision Quest for four years in a row.
>
> We, (the Sisseton-Wahpeton Oyáte), have had an agent here since 1867. We know this person as the superintendent. The early superintendents here, up until approximately 1918 into the 1920s, were all missionaries appointed by the government. One of the first missionaries, a man by the name of Moses Adams, he would call the Traditional Treaty Council in and tell them, "I don't have any documents to rule or to govern you. And the reason for it is because I only have and will only use one set of rules to govern you, and that set of rules is the Ten Commandments. That is the only rule I need."
>
> And based on that then, in 1867, there began what we now call the Era of Oppression. All the traditional rites and ceremonies, customs and cultural ways of our Sisseton and Wahpeton from 1867 until 1980, when the American Indian Religious Freedom Act was passed, were outlawed and oppressed.
>
> Couples could not live in camp or village as they had known for centuries and centuries. They were provided a house, a barn, livestock. They were provided farm implements and expected to till the earth and live as farmers. Some of them began that process, but it is very difficult. The period of time in the late 1860s through the 1970s and particularly in the 1890s were ones of drought.
>
> The Sisseton-Wahpeton were different in the sense that although they had annuities, monthly allocations of food,

123

they were predominantly Presbyterians or Congregational. They believed that evidence of one's salvation and the after-life could be determined to the extent that one was self-sufficient as a farmer and had wealth through earned labor as a farmer, and therefore the families were split up in that fashion on the allotments, and the entire personality of the individual was subjected to forced change.

In approximately 1892 in the same period that the allotment act was occurring, the agent implemented the second instrument of forced assimilation and acculturation. That was to send the children from the age of five until the age of eighteen to the boarding schools. For that entire generation commencing in 1892, and continuing until the 1960's, children were all required to attend either the federal or the church boarding schools. Children, over a period of more than a hundred years, were coerced to attend boarding schools.

And at the boarding schools, the Dakota language, you could not speak it. It was forbidden. All of the customs were forbidden. They were outlawed. One had to be either a Presbyterian or Episcopalian or a Catholic. Those were the three main line religious denominations at Sisseton-Wahpeton that one had to belong to.

So what would happen from the time of the allotment in the 1890s and continuing until World War II, the agent and the Indian clergy would assure that every family would attend church on each and every Sunday. If one did not attend church faithfully every Sunday, there would be sanctions and punishment. If you were entitled to any goods, monies or funds owing from treaty obligations, you were put on hold. You could not access that. There were certain benefits that you were denied during this period of time.

There was a tremendous movement here wherein the traditional ceremonies of the Sisseton-Wahpeton People went underground. There is much apparent activity where people did practice the ceremonies. However, they had to do so underground. It would have to be secret.

The Sun Dance was outlawed. The Sweat Lodge was outlawed. The entire corpus of traditions utilizing the sacred Pipe was outlawed from 1892 until 1980.

And at the time of death, family members who had known to have attended Sun Dance or erected a Sweat Lodge or gone on Vision Quest, their remains would not be taken into the church. They could not be buried in the cemeteries their grandfathers and grandmothers and grandparents had been buried in.

It is ironic today because those churches still exist today, and very much a dominant force, and to such an extent that these churches are called Indian churches. They are not integrated with non-Indians. They have had from the 1860's and '70's Indian clergy, members of the congregation of those families who have contributed, members of their families who have served either as lay ministers or as ordained ministers or priests. And that particular tradition has continued and was sanctioned by the government.

The second issue is that we were all coping with issues of alcohol abuse, issues of domestic violence, and issues of physical and emotional damage that comes from those types of abuse. In the process, we wondered, well perhaps it is because we ourselves are evil people. We must be evil. We don't know how to do anything other than those things.

MARTIN AND THE SISSETON-WAHPETON OYÁTE

Ed Red Owl continued to share the history of his relationship with Martin:

In the 1950's, the destitute unemployment here was 92 to 96 per cent. The Bureau of Indian Affairs implemented the Relocation Program and people were transferred to Minneapolis, Cleveland, some to New York City, some to San Francisco. The idea was that once they left their allotments, their land could be sold and the settler descendants then could acquire that land for little or nothing.

That is the climate in which Martin High Bear came here to Sisseton-Wahpeton. There were others who came, other spiritual leaders from Standing Rock, Rosebud and Pine Ridge. However, the reception towards them was severe, very very severe. Those families that had invited the spiritual leaders from the other reservations were severely criticized.

Many of those families were excommunicated from the Christian churches. And at the time of death, those family members who had known to have attended Sun Dance or erected a Sweat Lodge or gone on Vision Quest, their remains would not be taken into the church. They could not be buried in the cemeteries that their grandfathers and grandmothers and grandparents had been buried in. We approached that knowing we had all been subjected to Sunday ... after "Sunday of sermons" from preachers and the clergy.

The majority of the families that would greet Martin would focus on the spiritual needs that we each had. When Martin came, we did not want to subject him to that. Even with the declaration of the Freedom of Religion Act in 1980, we continued to keep him underground. The number of families he networked and served were kept out of public view. And the reason for it is that many of us felt it was very important to protect each other from the process of being ostracized or being excommunicated, although in fact many of us did become excommunicated.

I think the work of Martin High Bear was to demonstrate the power of the traditional ways as demonstrated in the Sweat Lodge and Vision Quest and in the healing ceremonies here at Sisseton-Wahpeton. That process began in earnest in the 1970's, fully before the Religious Freedom Act.

We knew that we were existentialists, or more specific, we felt that we were without any salvation. And yet we felt that we could not acculturate. We could not become non-Indian because in our community, from time of inception to the present time, the non-Indian immigrant and their descendants do not accept Indians, and not only socially or economically, but also religiously. We felt we were not going anywhere.

So with Martin that was the first lesson. We had, I recall, one of the very first ceremonies at the home of Jerry Flute. Martin was there with his stepfather Felix Green. And Martin had a ceremony and the purpose of the ceremony was "We were looking for a ceremony" that would put some personal meaning in our life.

What happened at that ceremony that Felix and Martin conducted – we call it today a *Dowáŋpi* ceremony – is that for the first time we experienced the spirits who came into that room and talked to us. We could hear them and understand what they said and we learned more than we had heard throughout our lifetime in our churches. In fact God and his powers had spoken to us. That was the first time we had that experience.

And through the Sweat Lodge, we attained a condition of what we call *wowakȟáŋ*, purity. You can go into that Sweat Lodge and become reborn, recreated in a sense. Inside the Sweat Lodge, we learned that God did not make garbage, that we are created in God's image and making and likeness. And we learned that from Martin that we can do that again.

We have a long ways to go, but those teachings persist. The way it was done here was addressing specific issues that the families had. Working with Martin, whether it was health, psychological or physical, it was approached in the context of ceremony, in the context of outcome.

And so the spirituality has translated into everyday living. It isn't something that is cerebral and without substance that we can't talk about. In fact, it does have real substance. We have become who we once were when we were self-sufficient.

Apparition of the Buffalo Calf Maiden, by Frithjof Schuon

CHAPTER 6

THE LEGEND OF THE SACRED BUFFALO CALF MAIDEN

Shortly after he became a Medicine Man, Martin went up on the hill on *Haŋblécheya* Vision Quest ceremony. While he was fasting, and praying inside of his altar, the Grandfathers came to him and recited seven teachings, revealing that these were ancient cultural values from the Sacred Buffalo Calf Maiden who had gifted the sacred *Čhaŋnúŋpa* (sacred Pipe) to the ancestors.

The Grandfathers then instructed Martin to live his life following these ancient teachings and to share them with the people of Turtle Island. If he could help in that way, today's Indian people could begin to regenerate the respect and honor that once prevailed among the Red Man and help to restore their spiritual way of life.

The Grandfathers also revealed that this set of indigenous cultural values was to be shared with people of all colors, that if all peoples could develop greater awareness and understanding of Indian culture, they would learn to appreciate this wisdom and knowledge. In this way, all colors of people could live with respect and in harmony with Indian nations.

Martin made a commitment to share the teachings of the Sacred Buffalo Calf Maiden. It became part of his life's work. He called his vision "The Seven Commandments of the Sacred Buffalo Calf Maiden." He sometimes referred to it as the Seven Laws of God or the Seven Directions of God's Laws.

For more than two decades, wherever he traveled, he shared this vision. Along with his doctoring work, he honored his commitment and followed his instructions. He taught his own people, and he shared with people of all colors, reciting it countless times in living rooms, lecture halls, Sweat Lodges and spiritual camps all over Turtle Island.

Gradually, he became adjusted to the hardships of road travel and frequent criticism, even blackballing, by groups among his own people who accused him of leaving his reservation to profit from his heritage.

The narrative is in Martin's own words and comes from recordings made during the last decade or more of his life. Because he had limited schooling, his English translation sometimes lacked proper grammar. It also lacks the richness and depth he could have provided in the Lakȟóta language.

Martin also shared his version of the Coming of the Sacred Buffalo Calf Maiden as recorded by Gordon Bird with Featherstone Productions in the 1970's. Gordon gave permission for the transcript of Martin's recording to be included in this biography.

THE STORY IS TOLD IN MANY WAYS

Martin said on many occasions, "We are going to talk a little about the arrival of the White Buffalo Calf Pipe." Then he would tell the version of the story that he was taught:

Years ago, when the Calf Pipe was given to the Indian people of the Teton Sioux tribe, the nation, at a certain time of the year, they all meet. And the old saying was, "It was the time when the chokecherries, the fruit, turned ripe."

Each band consists of around two or three thousand people. And the chiefs were all talking about how they're going to survive through the winter months.

The Sansarc was one of the Seven Bands of the Teton Sioux Nation. We call it the Seven Tipis, the Seven Campfires. And after they had this meeting, the Sansarc band was on the move, headed west, suffering and hungry. And so they camped and the chief sent scouts out to look for something to eat. They wanted to see if they can get a herd of buffalo, and also at the same time they want to find a good spot to camp for the winter.

And so when these two scouts left, they talked about going in different directions, but they agreed to meet in a certain spot up on a hill. So they made their circle and met up on the top of the hill.

They were talking there when they seen what looked like a buffalo coming up on them. So they were watching it and it changed. Looked like a woman coming. And so they watched it until it come close enough. Here was a Woman in a buckskin dress. She was carrying a fan and fanning herself. And when She come up close to them, they noticed that that fan was sage, made like a fan.

One of the scouts wanted to attack the Indian Maiden.

He said, "Let's attack Her."

But the other scout backed away and said, "No." He knew She was no human.

A cloud of smoke come up – a big fog between Her and the scout. As this one scout stood looking at the cloud, it cleared away. The Indian Maiden was standing where the cloud cleared away, and there lay the bones of the scout that had bad ideas. The bones had snakes and insects crawling out.

That was the day when it was shown – the good and the bad. I was told when She met these two scouts, it was shown – the power. Before that, everything was good in what they lived with. They didn't know what bad was until the White Buffalo Calf Pipe Woman came and one of these scouts tried to attack her.

This other scout looked down at his friend's bones and looked back up at Her.

So the Indian Maiden said, "You have a very good mind in you. You go back and tell your chief and your people that I have come from the Buffalo Clan. Tell them to make one big tipi for his people all set up inside thick with sage. I have come here to bring you people something. I shall bring a message from God and a gift that they told Me to bring."

He was ready to leave. She told him not to look back, but to take back the message. And so he turned around and went back like She said.

"Don't look back." So he didn't. All the way through, he knew that this Woman he was talking to was a spirit.

And so when he come close to the camp, people noticed this scout come running back to the encampment all by himself. He was running on a zigzag trail. That's the old ancestors' way, the way the old people used to do, telling there was trouble. Back in the old days, when anything happened, when the warriors or scouts got within sight of the encampment, they were running a zigzag course. That is the way they knew it is important.

He came back with the message and went right to where the chief was. And he told the chief he met a Lady in buckskin. She had a fan that was made out of sage. She had leggings and moccasins. She had braids – a beautiful Maiden. And he told them what She said.

"She told you to make a big thípi and line it out with sage and tomorrow She'd be here to bring what She has brought for us here."

He told of the tragedy of his friend and buddy, lying up there in bones. So right away the word went out.

And so the next morning, they built a big tipi. The women folks took some tipis down and sewed them together and put one big tipi up. And they had a buffalo skull there and they had an altar kind of set up. And they lined it out with sage. And so you see, this sage is one of the most important medicines.

So when everybody was ready, they saw this Indian Maiden. As she was coming, the scout that came back with this message went out and escorted the Indian Maiden into the encampment and to the tipi they built. The scout asked Her into the tipi where the chief was. And so She went in with him.

She was dressed the same, the buckskin dress, the leggings, the moccasins. Only She had painted Her face red, with vertical stripes and Her hair was braided on one side. The other side wasn't. Her hair was loose. Where She had braided, She had buffalo hair tied as a hair tie.

When She went inside the thípi, She turned to the left at the door and went clockwise all the way around, back to the door of the tipi. Then She went to the center where the chief was sitting.

When She went in, they noticed that She had this Pipe. She told the chief and the people that She had a message and a gift from God.

She said, "This is what We have brought. These are some of the messages that are with it. You people are starving, and so this Pipe was for Me to bring over here from Wakȟáŋ Taŋka, from the Buffalo Clan."

She came over and presented the White Buffalo Calf Pipe. There are eagle feathers on there. And She had this braid of sage, sweet grass, buffalo chips.

So when the Maiden brought the White Buffalo Calf Pipe, She didn't give much orders to the Lakota people about it, but She gave instructions of how to use the Pipe. She told them about the Pipe and showed them how to fill it, how to handle it to use in the Four Directions.

So She told them to fill this Pipe up and "Pray to God, Wakȟáŋ Taŋka, with it in the Four Directions, Up and Down, and you shall get help. There's two eagle feathers on the bowl of this Pipe. One represents 'Whenever you people are in disaster, smoke this Pipe. Great Spirit will help you.' And the other eagle feather represents 'If your people are starving, smoke the Pipe and pray to God and you shall get food.'"

And so She showed him how to smoke this Pipe. She prayed with the chief. She filled the Pipe up, smudged it with the sweet grass. And She sat down and smoked this Pipe with the chief. When they had water to drink, she took the sweetgrass and dipped it in it. That was the way she drank water.

And after they got through smoking the Pipe, the White Buffalo Calf Pipe, She stood up and she said "Now, my journey is over."

Before She left, She talked to the menfolks and told them how they should provide and take care of their families, what they were supposed to do. She gave them instructions.

She turned to the women folks and She spoke to them. She gave the womenfolk instructions and She told them how to provide for the family and the children. Then She turned to the little people, the children, and told them what they are supposed to do, how to learn and understand, respect and help.

When She was here among the Lakota people, She looked at all the women folk. The only thing She said that very clearly identified Herself was, "All of you women folk - you are all My sisters."

She looked at the men folk and said, "You are all My brothers."

And "This is all My brothers and sisters." She meant the little children.

She looked down at the chief that was sitting there, chief of the band. She looked at him and told him, "You are My oldest brother. Now I have fulfilled what they told me to do. So I must go."

So when she was ready to leave, the scout was going to escort Her back out. She said, "No," that She didn't need no escort, that She'd walk out of the camp by Herself. And so when She left, they all came out and watched Her when She went away from the encampment.

So when the Indian Maid left the encampment, She turned, smiled, and waved at the people. She rolled over and when She got up, She turned herself into a buffalo. That was when the buffalo grasses were tall. She went down and each time She went out of sight into the buffalo grass, She turned a different color. The last time She got up, She turned herself into a White Buffalo and loped away from the encampment. And that was the last time they saw Her. He told of the tragedy of his friend and buddy, lying up there in bones. So right away the word went out.

All that time, She was a Spirit. And so you see, these are the ways that God has given us the Red Man's religion. So that is the *legend of the White Buffalo Calf Maiden. The legend was told in different ways in many different stories, but it all means the same.*

HOW OUR INDIAN RELIGION WAS PUT TOGETHER

Martin continued to tell the story following the coming of the Sacred Buffalo Calf Woman:

And so, God gave us the White Buffalo Calf Pipe and this is how our religion came to us. And so it had to take our ancestors quite a few years after that – 40, 50, 60, 70 years – to dream, have visions and to put this religious structure together.

Today the White Buffalo Calf Pipe is still with us. It is still back home where I come from. It has been here many moons now, handed down from generation to generation. Today, this Pipe is nineteen, twenty generations old. Underneath it all is lined out with sage, one of the first medicines.

This is why, when She came, She told us "Line that *thípi* out with sage and I shall come and bring what God has told me to bring."

Now, today it's here and it has reached out to the Four Directions of this island. That's the way the Calf Pipe is. It has even reached out farther. And so this is why I'm very happy to tell you how we got the Pipe.

And this is why in my prayers that were taught to me from the Grandfathers, I say, "*Uŋčí*, who has walked above the Earth who turned Herself into different colors of buffalo." That was the Grandmother and that's the White Buffalo Calf Pipe Woman. This was given to me in my prayers, in visions when I was up on the hill. And so I use that today to honor and respect the Pipe.

So this is why, to this day, the Christian people say: "When the end of the world comes, Christ will return." The way the Christian religion was created, Christ will be back then.

And to us, we say: "When the time comes, the White Buffalo Calf Pipe Woman will come back." And so these are the things.

RETURN OF THE WHITE BUFFALO CALF MAIDEN

So the Indian people living on this spiritual island have what has been handed to us many moons ago – the sacred White Buffalo Calf Pipe. This Calf Pipe was brought to the people, to the Lakhóta, handed down on Mother Earth from the Buffalo Nation. There were millions at that time, and that's where the Calf Pipe came from – the Buffalo Clan.

There's stories behind that about the buffalo and how we pray so the buffalo would give its life up to the people so the people could eat the meat, use the bones for utensils and the hide to make tipis and bedding.

It was the Moon When the Chokecherries Turn Black when the White Buffalo Calf Pipe was handed down to the Indian people. So then all things started falling into place. So that's why they honor August as a spiritual month and they are still performing some of the biggest Sun Dances in August.

So the Sioux nation takes care of the Pipe for the people right in the center of this spiritual island, within the Four Corners of the Four Winds. We still have it here. So today when they see a White Buffalo, people always think that is Her that came back again. So the White Buffalo is pretty well honored, because they think it's the One that brought the Pipe to the people.

You know, here a while back, here this past August [1994], there was another little white buffalo came. And I know some stories about that little calf that came. A female. The other was a male. Now this is the female. The first one was born in 1933 and died in 1959.

When She came, it was the time when the chokecherries were turning black, when She brought the Pipe over. So today, we call it the month of August, the Moon the Chokecherries Turn Black.

And pretty close to 200 years later, the White Calf came, a female. She, too, came in the month of August. So after 200 years, that's how far apart that these calves are. So it's important for people to honor and respect the White Buffalo. It's a rare color.

Already I know stories behind that, why that calf came. And I have stories that represent towards the Indian people, what should be done, what's going on. So this White Buffalo meant a lot to the people. This calf that came has put a lot of things in the people's minds.

It's like Arvol Looking Horse said, "People from all over the world flew over just to look at the calf."

The calf came to the people to awaken the people. Whoever named that little calf Miracle had a good idea. So she's called Miracle; which it is, a miracle. The message this little white calf has brought is not just for the Indian people but for the four colors.

Also that little calf came here so the people can live in peace. And a lot of these wars are going to be over with. It will help make people realize why they're fighting.

I presume God is pretty sorry about the people today. He wants everybody to live a happy life. He wants everybody to do what is right, like walking that Red Road.

So these are the things that we often have to talk about. Like they always say, *"Peace on earth. Good will to men."* That's been lost.

It was here on this Island. Now you'll have to look for it. So find it. Memorize it. Pick it up and use that word, "Peace on earth. Good will to men."

MARTIN'S VISION OF THE SEVEN COMMANDMENTS

The narrative of Martin's vision is in his own words from recordings made during the last decades of his life:

And it was when our ancestors got this Pipe that there came the Seven Laws of God. The Seven Commandments was told to them by visions. So the Indian people were created under the Seven Commandments and this was the way it was handed down from generation to generation among the Red Man.

So these Seven Commandments was handed down to me when I was up on the hill; four days and four nights. And this is why different people wanted to tape me. So they taped the Seven Directions of God's Laws. Some people called it the Seven Commandments. These are laws from God, the Creator. We call *"Him"* the *Great* Spirit. And I explained what that means beside Christianity's Ten Commandments. We teach these to people. And so we are so much closer to God because we have our culture strong.

So I shall recite them as the Buffalo Maid that brought the sacred Calf Pipe from the Great Spirit. I'll try to explain a little about what these seven really mean and see if you people can understand and study it. They might be talking about you people. And so that was the way it was told and this is how the religion has been put together by dreams. And our ancestors followed up on these dreams and went into the Sweat Lodge, and up on the hill to Vision Quest. And they had Sun Dances. They suffered themselves for four days, four nights – no water, nothing to eat. They talked with the spirits about what this means and they brought the answers back, the messages.

And so each man has a certain animal they respect a lot in their visions, their dreams. Any old people, our ancestors, Indians, really respect these animals, and the birds because this is where they have their visions. And I've noticed that they study these animals, their ways, their movements, their innocent ways. And also with birds. If they do these, they can come up with a lot of things that help.

So this is the way they put this religion together. And so the Indian religion was set up by dreams and visions by our elderlies. And we have to obey and listen to them. And now they have gone back to the Land of the Fathers, gone back to the Spirit World. And this is why I say, now the religion is together. They worked hard for it. And so this is why I've always told people it took a long time to have this religion put together, and so I always tell them, let's not lose it. It's for us to work hard for it and take care of it so the little people and the unborn can take it from here.

And so this is why, today, we still have Medicine People. We still have people back home that can work and use these supernatural powers. And so this is why today Medicine Men have visions. If they come up from a line of Medicine People, handed down from blood relations, generation after generation, this is why they are Medicine Men today. And they know who their ancestors were, their grandparents.

They have to go up on the mountain and vision quest, four days, four nights, and find out, kind of iron out what their dreams were, their visions were. And so you see, it's a great deed and it's a great gift to be given a nice beautiful religion. We communicate so close with the Great Spirit today that everything we say and do, it never fails for us, 'cause I guess God communicates with us, not with His words but with the power.

You put these spirit powers all together with one mind, it's pretty powerful. This is why I'm talking about this supernatural power. This is why God gave us this power. We can make things happen. We tell the spirits, "Do this, do that." And they go out and do it. The miracle, the mystery that has no beginning, has no end.

Martin at Sun Dance sitting in front of tipi.

CHAPTER 7

THE FIRST COMMANDMENT:

WIČHÓZANI

THE PEOPLE SHALL LIVE WITH HEALTH

THEY PASSED THE WORD ON ABOUT THE HEALTH OF THE PEOPLE
His voice, with its compassionate, patient tone, resonates through the hush of the classroom. The room is packed with students, some circling the back corners and standing along the walls, straining their ears to hear his words. Sunshine streaks through the flowering trees on this warm May afternoon, but today no one stares out the windows. All eyes are on Martin High Bear.

He takes off his cowboy hat and drops it down on the chair next to him. Caught in the moment and his spiritual presence, it is easy for students to ignore the portable oxygen tank in the back of his electric cart and the plastic tubing winding its way to his nostrils. They hardly notice the little lapel microphone clipped on the collar of his striped cowboy shirt or the video camera in the middle of the room.

The class is a first-year course in Naturopathic Medical Philosophy at Portland's National College of Naturopathic Medicine. It is 1994 and Dr. Jared Zeff has invited Martin to speak about the spiritual perspective on healing. Martin looks fragile and no longer gets around without a lot of assistance. However, the power of his message and a twinkle in his eye reveal a lively spirit. Fully immersed in the moment and enjoying the attention of his students, he flashes a warm smile their way.

As always, he begins with a prayer in his Lakȟóta language, thanking Great Spirit for a good day and asking for blessings and guidance for this group of students who are on a special path of healing. Then he leans forward, resting his elbows on the steering column of his electric cart and begins to confide in the students:

The first teaching is: "The people shall live with health." The Seven Commandments always started from health. People back years ago, many moons ago, used to live with health. That was the old way back in the old days.

People were healthy. They ate fresh off of Mother Earth. They ate from the buffalo where the meat was fresh. They drink the holy water from this spiritual island with health, breathing nice clear air. Nothing was there that they had to look for because God created everything for them to live with. That's the way our people lived two, three, four, five thousand years ago. They lived under God's instructions. They prayed 365 days out of a year.

And a lot of us, when we get up, we still pray to God. Thank him for yesterday. Thank him for last night, 'I had a nice rest. Grandfather. Thank you, a lot.' And this is the way, I guess, He knew who out of a family would live this life and would be strong enough to take it.

And this is where they started with the visions and dreams that had come to these holy people, the Medicine People. They studied those dreams and visions. It was explained to them and so they passed the word on to one another about the health of the people. They were pretty healthy. No disease. If there was any, there was Medicine People and medicine in these herbs to heal each other.

COLLECT AND STUDY HERBS

When I first became a Medicine Man, the Grandfathers told me to go start collecting plants and medicines, and so I did. So I have learned different plants. We call them plants, but they are herbs. They grow all over out here. These are the things we have to study, just like students in school, only I have to study through nature. No books. No pencils. No paper.

Today we work with herbs. Plants, flowers, you call them. Out among these trees out here, the foothills, maybe up on the mountain, up on the trees, there's plants up there. You have to study them. Each plant represents something. Each plant can heal a different illness or disease, so we have to study the plants and what kind of flower they have. Even the trees help. They can heal people, the root of the tree.

I have to concentrate and ask the Grandfather Spirits, "What is that? It caught my eye, Grandfathers. You caught my eye and I know it means a lot, this beautiful plant with flowers on it." And so the Grandfathers recite it to me.

If the Grandfathers call for a certain medicine, you have to study it. This is the way we have to work with medicine. The spirits tell me what kind of herb to use, but I have to know the herb. It's in my Medicine Bundle.

When I listen to people telling the spirits where the illness is, what they think it is, I know what herb they need. I have had ceremony for the same kind of illness so many times that I know what kind of herbs to use and how to use it for different parts of the body.

Sometimes, with this ceremony, they call for that medicine. The same kind of illnesses over here that you're going to heal, they call for this other medicine, so we have to study it. Why do they call for different medicines when it's for the same illness? This is why you study it out and find that these plants are related. This plant here is a cousin to that plant only this one heals that person. And this other one heals another person.

Some plants resemble one another. Each one has a healing power that can heal a certain illness. One will have a different color of flower than the other one, but the leaves will be the same. Maybe another two plants look alike with the same kind of colored flower on it. Only one has smaller leaves on it. The other has bigger leaves. But they can still cure the same illness. They're related. They're cousins.

So I found out a lot about different herbs and medicines. They're all related, just like the spirits say everybody is related. Everybody is a sister or a brother to all nations of the four colors in the world so this is why the plants are related.

THERE ARE FOUR KINDS OF HERBS

One of the things you may understand and think about: When God created all these medicines, he knew the kinds of illness, certain types of disease, that was going to be happening in the world. For instance, let's take diabetics, blood medicine, heart medicine, bone, all these. You name them all. There's a plant out there for that, but you have to study it.

This is why I have always told people, "When God created these plants, 600 or 400, the tobacco ties – represent 400 to 600 different types of herbs that grow all over the world." Like we say, we have many. In ceremony, when we use 405 tobacco ties, they represent over 405 plants that are in the medicine we use.

This is why I say, when God created all these plants, He knew what the illnesses were going to be. People don't know. They go up here and chop them down and say they're weeds. Take an Indian, he'll find that plant and dig it, then put it away. The spirits tell me this is the way we are supposed to do.

There's four different types of healing medicines that I have learned. There's the Great Plains medicine. I have some of that with me. Back home in South Dakota we have these plants growing among the grass, even along the creeks, with different colors of flowers on them. They are growing in the pastures, in the draws, among the grass. Different colors come out in the spring. Some of those plants have flowers that stay out all summer long, then shrivel up in the fall. Some grow close together, about that tall. Some have white flowers, some are yellow, some have purple flowers. Each one is for a different illness.

Then we have the foothills medicine at the foot of these mountains. Then we have medicine clear at the top of the mountain. Up on top of the mountains, it's mostly trees and tree bark, plus there's plants up there. You have to climb that mountain to get this medicine. Some of them we have to dig. We have to dig until we catch the root. You don't cut the root out. You get yourself a good sharp knife. You cut into that. You get part of the bark and part of the tree root, and then cover it back up again. Use that as another type of medicine. Then it grows on trees, like the moss on the trees.

Then we have swamp medicine. I have plants from up in the swamp area. We have to put on hip boots, kind of wade through the water into these higher places that are soggy and muddy. There's plants out there we have to dig out. I carry some of that with me in my Medicine Bundle. So this is why for some of the herbs that I have collected, I go down there to the other side of Detroit, Michigan and I get some of this swamp medicine. It's a blood medicine. And there are some that are kidney medicine, but you have to wear hip boots to go inside the swamps, up on the little ledges where this medicine is. Plants grow right in the water and come up. You have to dig right in there and get the roots out, dry them out to use them.

I used to go up in the swamp area up there in Ontario, Canada. I'd get some of that swamp medicine and give that medicine back home to people in this area. Back home in the Great Plains, this medicine would work real strong to them people. Then I'd take this Great Plains medicine and take it to Ontario and make them medicine or give it to them and it was real strong over there. It seems like the swamp medicine works better over here and the Great Plains medicine works better over there. I found that out a lot.

I don't know the herbs by English names. I know some of those herbs have names that long, but I don't even know how to pronounce them. Tongue twisters, but I know the Indian words in my native tongue. I know what the plants mean and what they're good for.

I presume a lot of people all over the world at one time knew their areas. There's medicine you can get out there in Arizona in the sand area. There's medicine here that grows in the sand. They use it over there. That's their medicine, the Hopis and the other people there.

Here on the coast, they have the fish. Plants that grow under the water, they have a lot of that plant medicine in their fish. There's some parts of the fish you can get, just like we have the beaver. As far as using the animals, we have medicine that we can take out of different animals like the lady that was healed with a beaver, part of the beaver. This eye medicine that made that woman see came off of the beaver. You can use a part of that and put it in a jar. That's good for anybody who's got glaucoma. You can put it on and cure yourself.

I put a part off the beaver in a glass and diluted it with water. I always try it on myself to see that it doesn't burn me. If it burns, I put a little more water in to a certain point and squirt it in the person's eye. I healed a lady that was blind for twelve years. We had a ceremony and the spirits told me to use that medicine from the beaver. After five days, she could see. She was surprised after twelve years of darkness, the cars, the television and all that. She had to study the past twelve years again. And so there's medicine coming out of plants and also the four-leggeds.

Today, the White Man's got Murine. In the old days, did you ever see an old Indian wear glasses? They doctored their own eyes. There was no such thing as glasses in them days.

They can see like the eagle. That's as far as you can see. If anybody's over there, we can see them. Today we have to have binoculars to see these things. So you can study that out in the old Indian way.

Today there's a lot of different medicines that are starting to come into this country. I know some of the people that handle these herbs from other countries like China and Japan. There's a lot of herbs that are coming in here and they started learning ways, like your acupuncturist. To us, we don't do that, but still we honor it because it does the kind of work that we do to heal bodies, to build spirits up, to build this body up the way it's supposed to be.

WE PRAY WHEN WE GATHER HERBS

When we take anything, we pray. We leave tobacco. We take just what we can use because we can always go back and get a little bit more. This is the way we were taught. We wasn't greedy for it, because we always know this was the way we were taught and this was the way God created things to be.

So after you pick what you want, wash it off good. Some of them you have to use the root, and then comes the stem that can heal another illness. Wash that out good and dry it out. Wrap it up and put it away. Sometimes you have to have a good shovel with you. You dig the foot of this tree and catch a root, then carefully cut some of the root of that tree out. You take what you need, then put tobacco on there and cover it back up. Put Mother Earth back. Don't leave a hole there. Honor Mother Earth. She's our survivor.

These days, they're meeting all over the world to talk about the planet, Mother Earth, how She is going to survive, and how you can help Her survive from all the wounds they put on Her. But the most important thing is when you go digging these herbs, you have to pray. Give tobacco and tell the herbs what you want to use it for, to heal people, so people shall live with health.

And so this is something I have always wondered about. How can they cure cancer? Now we got into AIDS. Some of these illnesses we have no cure for, and there's some more illnesses and disease that coming up that they've got no cure for. One of the things that I'd like to say....There are plants out here to heal that illness. God created these medicines to be out here. All you have to do is look for it. They're out here because God knows different illnesses will be coming in. And there's some more that you can't cure that's coming. We may not see it, but this next generation will run into it.

You can go see your doctor and tell him this Medicine Man says there's a cure out here for cancer. You can look for it. There's no chemicals in it. It's right out here. You just dig it up, wash it off, cut whatever you want. Boil it. Drink it. Cure yourself. So these are some of the things I'd like to share with you people here. You pass it on.

There are several months when these herbs have to be picked. Then maybe next month, you have to pick these other herbs up. You want to get plenty of them, so you can have them during the winter months. You might run out in the spring, but as soon as spring comes, then the herbs and plants start growing up and flowering out and you can tell when they're ready to be picked. There's a lot of medicines between May and August.

Back home, we used to have a saying, 'After the choke-cherries are dried out, it's about that time when Mother Nature shows her best colors'. That was the time. You know, back in them days, they had no calendar, but each month had a saying. So they say, 'When the trees start changing colors and Grandmother Nature starts showing her beautiful colors,' that was the time people talked about. The leaves all start changing beautiful colors, so them days they go by that time. That's the end of the herb picking because they're drying out. That's when Mother Nature, Mother Earth, starts going into hibernation.

KEEP THE PLANT'S SPIRIT ALIVE

It is very important to give tobacco when you dig your herbs up. You have to put tobacco out and pray with it and tell that plant 'I'm going to take you home with me, because there are some people that you have to heal.' When you take this plant home, you wash off the dirt. Leave it out to dry, save the stem, then wrap it up good and put it away.

Take what root you need and either grind it up and use it as a salve, or boil it and drink it. If you want to make tea out of it, pray with it. If you have to grind it up, grind it up, but keep the stem whole. You keep the spirit of the plant because the spirit of that plant is going to go inside that person. Your body and spirit will work with the spirit of the plant. So that is one of the most important things.

God created everything, and everything God created has a spirit. Those are some of the things we have to study so we can work with those spirits. So when you gather an herb, you are gathering the spirit of that herb. When the spirit of that plant contacts your own spirit, that's where the healing is. The herb makes contact with your spirit and heals you. When you contact your spirit with this plant's spirit, you can have a healing. It sounds unbelievable, but if you study it, you will recognize it because there's something great in there. It's a miracle. Like we say, 'A miracle that has no beginning and has no end.'

So this is why these plants are very important. God created them for the elderlies back in the old days. Everybody used to carry these plants and heal one another.

You've got to keep that plant's spirit alive. That's why we always say, when you dig into it, you have to pray and give tobacco. God has created these medicines so the people can use them. This was before the hospitals or the doctors or the pharmaceuticals. So we always tell them, if you want to use this plant, use it right.

So they go in there and take the disease out without even opening your body. They don't believe in this knife that cuts your skin open. That knife is used for some other purpose, not to butcher the human body. There's a lot of infection in the hospitals. When you open the body up and let the air in there, it causes another disease.

That's what they told me. I know they're holy. There's nothing holier than them spirits on this earth, because they were sent down here by Grandfather, Great Spirit, to watch these Four Directions like it was their own, and so to this day, the way God created everything. He put these spirits to watch these four corners and they're still watching this to this day, and so that's who we work with.

Response from The Students

The knowledge Martin shared with the naturopathic college students was new to them. Professor Zeff shared later:

What I saw on most of the students' faces was awe, thought-fulness, a great deal of respect, and really a sense of wonder to hear this man talk about plants as living beings, with spir-its that want to work with us, and that would bring healing. The students wanted an understanding of how the spiritual aspect of the person, how the spirit of the person relates to why people are ill and ultimately why people are healthy and happy. And Martin talked about some of that.

Martin was gifted with the ability to communicate with the Grandfathers. He would call them *Tȟuŋkášila*, or Grandfather, or "my little Grandfathers." Whenever he used herbs to heal in cer-emony, after someone had prayed for healing from a certain dis-order, the spirits would tell him what was going on. Sometimes they would advise him to use a certain medicine from his bundle. After the ceremony, he would have the medicine made up, usually a quart or half gallon of tea to be drunk. He would advise the indi-vidual to drink a small cup first thing in the morning and then at bedtime for four days, or until the tea was gone. The spirit of that herb would make contact with the spirit of the individual and help to heal them.

WE PRAY TO THE GRANDPARENT PLANTS

After a short break, Martin continued speaking to the students about the communication between the spirit of the plant and the spirit of the person:

> In order to gather herbs, we have to pray. God created all these medicines, and these plants are just like humans. You have relatives. These plants have relatives, so wherever you find this plant, you look around because there's a grandfa-ther plant in this bunch. When there's a plant you want to pick, you have to look for the Grandfather or Grandmother plant. There might be a lot of it that's growing out there. We look through that to find the Grandfather of all the plants. The Grandfather plant is most generally the tallest one where they grow, maybe two or three inches or maybe taller than the other plants.
>
> You have to ask to take some of his grandchildren to heal people. You go up to it with your tobacco and you pray. You tell them you want to take some of their grandchildren home

because they're going to heal somebody. "Grandfather, I'm going to have to take some of your grandchildren because people are ill and need your help. I'm going to need some of your children, so here is tobacco.'

Then you give out tobacco and start on the outside edge. Start digging and get the root and the stem all together. I always say keep the root and stem together. That way, you keep the spirit of that plant. Then just take what you need. Wash it, dry it out and wrap it up. And then put it away.

Respect the herbs. When you respect them, you can carry the spirit of this herb. Whatever God created has spirits. And so this is why the spirit contacts the human spirit and makes people well. That's in our prayers.

We like to say "Grandmother." We always pray to *Uŋči*, our Grandmother. You know, when the Pipe was handed down to us, this Indian Maid brought the Pipe, so some of us Medicine Men that know this, in our prayers that was given to us, we pray to this Indian Maiden. We call her "Grandmother:" - *Uŋči*, who brought this religion down to us. She's our Grandmother.

The old ancestors say when the time comes, Gramma will come back again to visit us. It's the same message as the one that says when the time comes, Jesus will come and visit the people again. He may not come on this island, but He'll come back to where He was born, where He was crucified. But here, our Grandmother, the Indian Maiden, will come back, the Sacred Buffalo Calf Pipe Woman, She'll come back.

One of the most important things we use back home is sage. When She came, She uses sage. Sage is one of the spiritual medicines to be used in many different ways. It's a good remedy. It's good for anything. When we make a prescription of herbs to make medicine for a disease, a lot of times we add a couple or three leaves of sage to boil in it. You can take a sage leaf, clean it up good and put it in your mouth. You can have that to cure your sore throat and headaches.

The sweetgrass is another. You can boil it and drink it. When She came to visit, when they gave Her this water, She took the sweet grass and dipped it in water and sucked on it. That was purifying. Today, we use that to smudge, to call the spirits. Sometimes we have to use a little of it to boil and drink, so these are the two most important herbs that was shown to us, sage and sweetgrass.

When you have difficulties in your stomach, use cedar. Take a little cedar, not much. Boil it and strain it and drink that. It'll cure any kind of stomach disorder.

They use a lot of bitterroot. The bitterroot can be used in a lot of different medicines. It is one of the main medicines, chopped up and used for a sore throat, to heal babies if they have pneumonia. You can use that for skin, like a kind of lotion. There are different things, but that's one of the important ones.

You'd be surprised how beautiful some of these different herbs smell. Some of these herbs, you take the root. Some smell like some of these medicine that we use. Some got kind of the same smell, but it is for a different illness. Some of them smell like licorice, you know that licorice candy?

And so this is why today we can talk about the herbs and which herb can be used to cure. God knew what was going to happen, what illness and disease was going to fall upon the people, so He put plants out there for us to use to heal each other. For the past 100 years, or 200 years from now, there might be some more illnesses that can be cured. So we can say that there are plants out there that can heal anything. Knowledge can be passed on generation after generation that there are flowers or herbs out there to heal it, any kind of disease. They're working on it, so maybe they'll come up with some of these plants, trees, whatever, to help people get cured. They might if they run into the right medicines.

WE HAVE CURED CANCER, HEART DISEASE AND DIABETES

Just like the news reporter asked me, "What's the most important disease?"

"Well," I told him, "There's three of them that are killing people right and left. That's heart disease, and cancer, and a lot of them have gone from diabetes."

The most important disease that's killing people today is cancer. There's different types of cancer. There's a plant out there, maybe three, four plants out there, prescriptions together, that can heal cancer. But you have to go out there and find out about them, which plants these are. And so you see, it means a great deal to the people. The people are still trying to figure out how they are going to heal cancer. We have cured cancer.

And this heart problem is mostly handed down from generation to generation. I know among the Indian people, diabetes is one of the strongest diseases, that when once they have it, it is hard on Indian people. Every time I go somewhere and my Grandfathers are going to have to doctor people, it's either one of these three diseases. But we have herbs that when the Grandfathers ask, we give these herbs in tea. So we have cures for all these. Today these herbs are coming back strong. We can heal any kind of illnesses.

How they can heal these poor kids, mentally ill? We have medicine to cure that. One time, I was going to work with a doctor who was going to put up a big hospital. He was going to group up and work with kids where they are neglected in these mental hospitals. So I told him that I would be willing to help.

So in the meantime, in a ceremony, I asked the Grandfathers to show me some herbs that would heal these poor kids and they showed me an herb. And this herb is in the state of Montana. Maybe one of these days, if I can get the time, I can get the right person to help me go up there. He knows what this plant looks like. And I would sure be glad to get some of that. I've seen so many (disabled) kids. It makes me feel sad when the Great Spirit says that He created people to live with health, and this all has taken place.

I know some lady that had a broken back from a car accident and she was going to have a child. And the doctor told this lady that she's not going to have a normal child because he had to use radiation on her back to heal her back. So this child she was going to have will not be a normal child. She come up to me and told me about it. And so I had a ceremony and I got a medicine from China, mind you, way over there in China, that can cure this radiation poison in the human body. And so I give the lady a few teaspoons of that in water. I boiled it and she drank it. To this day, she has a normal baby. Before it was too late, they took out all this radiation poison that they put in her back to cure her.

Plants Can Cure Future Diseases

Now we come to the main other killer, AIDS. There's plants out there that can cure AIDS. They came pretty close to it, but not quite enough, when they started on trees. The trees are medicines, as much as the plants, the flowers.

As years come and go, maybe the next hundred years from now, there might be another disease that comes on earth here that can't be cured. There's a plant out there for it. God put these all out there and he knows what disease will need to be cured. So this is why I say, there's going to be a lot of different diseases that are coming out. The herbs are here. There's herbs to cure cancer and AIDS. There's herbs that are going to cure any kind of illness. We have to know about them and understand where the herbs come from. God knows there are incurable sicknesses, but there's plants for that.

THE SPIRIT OF THE TREE OR ROCK CAN HELP YOU

I've always said if you are having a hard time, go to one of these trees. If you need help and there's nobody around to help you, go up to a tree. Give it a little tobacco and talk to it. Tell it, 'I need your help.' Then the spirit of that tree will go and help you.

Hug that tree, even if you have to cry. Go ahead. Nobody can't stop you. Bring it all out. Don't carry it around with you. That tree spirit will help you. This is all here to help. So if you have the time, give a little tobacco to a tree and that tree will help you. And when you come back again, give that tree a little tobacco again. Back in the old days, it was called kinnikinnik. So pray with that tree. That's the way God gave us.

Or go out there and give tobacco to the water, any lake or anything. Give it tobacco. Pray to that water that you need its help. The spirit of that water will go wherever you want it to go.

Pray to that rock. This is one of the most important things. I always tell people to do that. Don't try to wait for a Medicine Man or something like that. You can do it yourself. You can pray. Pray to God and the spirit of that water or tree or rock.

If anything happens, help each other. That's the old Indian way. People help each other. If someone needs help, there's a lot of things you can do for each other. That's one of the commandments: "Help one another."

We have to pray to God who created all. Everything consists of the religion. The Great Spirit didn't grow these herbs out here for nothing. He grew them for you to pray with, or part of the tree, or part of the water, because our body consists of the water, all these. So we have to use them. We have to depend on them. If we don't, nothing will help us.

AFTER THE LECTURE

Dr. Zeff reminisced afterwards about Martin's impact on his students:

> It was a great experience as well as a great honor for me and my students to have Martin come and talk. What I was impressed by was the clarity and the order with which he spoke and of course what he had to say.
>
> The students talked about that for the rest of the year. They were, all of them, which is unusual, impressed. The general tone was one of deep appreciation. They wanted to know how to get to know the plant medicine from the kind of perspective that Martin presented, in which the plant is not just a bag of chemicals, but is a being that has a spirit and even a consciousness that participates in the healing that it's asked to participate in.
>
> How to approach plants. How to gather plants with respect and that sacredness. It was these kinds of things that Martin talked about. Nowhere else in their education, really, are these things discussed. That was the source of the awe.
>
> There is also a mystery. Martin opened the door for some of them to see or even know that it is there. There is a realm of life beyond that which we normally, in everyday walk, experience unless we are really in tune with that spiritual aspect. They saw in him someone who did that, someone who lived in communication with the spirit. That is the thing that they seek, but for which they have very few teachers or very few experiences to guide or direct them and this was one of them. Consequently, that small time they spent with Martin became a high point in the education of some of these people.

SHARING PROPHECIES

College classrooms and the open minds of students were not new to Martin. For more than two decades, he spoke at colleges and universities all around the country. In 1984, Martin spoke to students at Humboldt College in Northern California. This was the original homeland of the Yurok and Hoopa peoples, and a number of Native American students attended college there.

Martin frequently shared prophecies, not just about the health of the people, but also about the health of the planet. On his way to

Humboldt College, he drove through the coastal mountain range and ancient redwood forests bordering Oregon and California. His mind lingered on this endangered species which he called the Standing Nation, the Tree People. He sometimes prayed with and gave spiritual support to environmentalists who were working to save remaining old-growth redwood stands:

> Many years ago on this island, what they call North America, when the Red Man lived here, they had no interferences of any kind. They were healthy people. But back in the 1800's, they talked about this pollution of the water, the air, and what the people are going to make of themselves, and what they are going to do to destroy. All these have been talked about by my elderlies and been handed down to us.
>
> The Grandfathers told us to be aware of years of hardships. Our Grandfathers, the spirits, are our guidance. They tell the future for us. This is where we Medicine People use the supernatural power that's been handed down to us, the miracle, the mysteries.
>
> Our people back home on the reservations, we had a hard winter, disaster area. That's nothing new among the Plains people back there, so every time we had to pray and all this, Sweat Lodges, Vision Quest. This is the way the religion was set up. The Red Man lives in hardship every year. This is why a lot of the elderly say, 'It's hard to be Indian.'
>
> We lived on the land, the island that God created the Indians on, and we lived in harmony. We believed in it. We believe in God, the Creator. He's our Grandfather, Great Spirit. He has handed down a religion to us. Back in the old days, the people breathed fresh air. They drank healthy water, while today we're trying to survive. I have often told about this to people.
>
> But today, it's different. Today one of the biggest things happening, and this is one of the things that has been happening here, is efforts to save Mother Earth. Mother Earth has been waiting to give aid to any of her grandchildren to provide some of Her food, but nobody has even thought about Her. These are the things that are happening to Mother Earth.
>
> Our Mother Earth needs a lot of help from us. The ocean, the big bodies of water, need help. Bad things have been happening to them. They're cutting down all the old growth of

timber. That's taking a life from that tree. There's a reason why God grew them timber, the trees. Now they're cutting them down so they can make money off them. Polluting the water.

As I was coming over here, when I seen the redwood trees, I said to the people that drove me here, 'Oh, look at the great, great grandfathers. They have been for years, centuries. Now what is going to become of them?' They never did nothing to people. They never caused no people no disaster. In fact, they bring you refreshments. They're the shelter of the tree of life. It has lots to do with your circle of life from childhood back to childhood.

But we're glad that we have the trees here yet to purify a lot of things for us. They are here for a reason. The Great Spirit created it here on these sacred mountains for a reason. It's up to the people to sit down and study these, why they are here today. I supposed he's sometimes very unhappy because people don't mind. But what is going on today is one of the reasons, like I was saying. Time has come to pray and to use God as our guidance because they need all the prayers.

And this is why I've always said, 'The old is coming back.' Keep some of it. We need it. Study it. It means a lot. Some of the sicknesses that are hitting us today, we're praying to stop some of that. People's lives are going to be real short and so that's why today we call it a fast life and die young. We're in that stage now. Back in the old days, people used to live a long time, their circle of life. They ate a lot of herbs. They lived on herbs to keep themselves healthy.

At that time, the air wasn't polluted and the water wasn't polluted. There were no cars, no airplanes, nothing there to pollute. Today, it's different with polluted air and even the water's polluted. What we eat, our ways of living, chemicals, the things like that, we've lost a lot.

They didn't dig up Mother Earth. They lived off Mother Earth. They respected Her. They prayed to God every day. They lived a beautiful life. So I was told people used to live as high as eight or nine hundred years old. Mind you! That's how old they get, because there was nothing there to interfere with them. They didn't live this fast life, die young. They lived a beautiful life, nothing to worry about.

Let's go back maybe 20 centuries ago, or 20 generations ago. They used to live to be two or three hundred years old. And here, a while back, I was told, there was an old lady back up in the mountains. She just died here a couple or three weeks ago, one of our grandmothers. All they can remember back of her age, some of the boys were telling me, she's around 130 years old. And so you see, it sort of shows some of the elderly can easily live to 100 years old.

So the life of a person today is around 70. You're pretty old then. At the rate of how it is going, the life of a human is getting shorter and shorter. One of these days, you'll be 40 years old, and you'll be an old man. Since we got all these chemicals, drugs, alcohol, it shortens your life up. You live maybe up to 60 years old and you're pretty old today. You're humped up. You got a cane.

And so, by joking, I've always said, "Well, I've seen it. When I get that old, I'm going plum around it, so I don't get it." In a joking way, I've always said that. And so these are the things.

Martin was referring to himself in that joke. Years before he became confined to a wheelchair, he'd had a dream of himself. In the dream, he saw an old man who was being wheeled down the sidewalk in a wheelchair, with an oxygen tank strapped on behind. Martin was approaching from behind and as he began to walk past, he glanced back at the old man. He saw himself.

STUDY THE MEDICINES TO HELP THE PEOPLE

Martin was invited to Germany in 1992. A group of friends from West and East Germany, Italy and other countries gathered to see Martin and hear him speak of spiritual matters. A small child was sneezing and coughing. His nose was running and he was feeling miserable. Martin frequently carried a piece of root in his chest pocket. He would sometimes take it out and smell it or give it to someone to smell. This time, he took a piece of the root out of his pocket and placed it on top of the hot wood stove. Pretty soon, tiny wafts of smoke drifted through the room and the sweet odor began to fill the air. Within a few minutes, the child had stopped crying. His nose cleared up and he was happy again. The smoke from the root, combined with Martin's prayer for the child, rapidly healed him.

He would sometimes have a tea made for patients with colds or lung disorders, combining several herbs into a heavy cooking pot filled with water. He would instruct people how to prepare the medicine and take it off the stove after it had simmered for about twenty minutes. Some of the tea would be set aside to be drunk afterwards. Then they covered the sick person's head and the steaming pot with one or two thick towels while they sat in their own little steam bath, breathing the hot steam into their lungs as long as they could tolerate it. Then the patient drank a cup of the warm tea and laid down to "rest up" while the medicine worked on their lungs. We frequently made this same formula for Martin. He would take his steam bath and a cup of tea for four days and nights whenever he got a cold or lung infection.

PEOPLE WHO DREAM ABOUT THE BEAR

Martin frequently advised friends who had visions or repeated dreams about the bear to study herbs. The spirit of the bear works as a helper to the herbalist, so they could learn to heal with herbs. In 1992, during a trip overseas, we stayed with a family in the German countryside. Their spiritual community had been learning about and participating in Native American traditions, including the *Inípi* (Sweat Lodge ceremony) and the *Haŋbléčheya* (Vision Quest ceremony) Brave Buffalo, Martin and others had taught them since the early '80's.

This mother of two small children had rarely gone into the ceremonies. She had always preferred to stay in the background, prepare meals and watch over her children as well as friends' children at ceremony time. That year, following *Haŋbléčheya* camp (which was held on the hillside above their home), she became very emotional and was drawn to climb that hill to pray for a while.

During her walk, she had a vision. A very large bear came to her and told her he was going to help her. "He was two and a half times the size of an ordinary bear," she said precisely.

To honor the bear, she decided to prepare a feast for him. So the next day, she cooked for the bear. When she walked up the hill with the plate of food, she set it down on the ground where she had met the bear's spirit. The bear spoke to her, "Don't fix separate food for me. I want to eat the same foods that you eat."

So from then on, she knew to share a portion of her own meal (what we call a spirit plate) with her bear, to honor him who'd now become her spirit helper. Martin later advised her, as he had advised many others over the years, that having the bear for a spirit helper meant she was to learn the herbs.

He explained to her that this vision meant she would be an herbal healer:

> The bear is the only animal of the four leggeds that respects and honors herbs. He lives on herbs. This is why people say, back home, *'When anybody dreams about bears, he's dreaming about being an herbalist'*. You are going to have to use these herbs. So you are going to have to go out here and study about the medicine. Some of them get a lot of help from elderly people. There are a lot of herbalists.
>
> Back in the old days, there were no doctors, no hospitals, no electricity. But the plants out there, that's what they healed themselves with. People used to live and use these plants to heal each other. I know back home, the old people used to have their own Medicine Bundles. They'd go out and dig the herbs, wash them up, put them away. During the winter months, they'll have plants, herbs to heal people.
>
> Grandmas had their own little sacks of herbs. Some had little boxes made out of buffalo hide, dried out and they made a little box and made a little medicine bundle out of it and put medicine in there. And so they cured each other. If you catch a cold, fever, flu, pneumonia, there's medicine to cure it. That's the way our ancestors lived, because they didn't have no doctors. They were healthier people, so today we study it out.

ADVICE TO HERBALISTS

In 1992, when we hosted a gathering at our house, a group of Portland Baha'i friends came over. We had just rented a little duplex on Southeast Twenty First Avenue that would be our home for more than a year. They wanted to learn from Martin about healing with herbs. So as our friends crowded into our living room and kitchen space for a couple of evenings, Martin spoke about the traditions of an herbalist. He also encouraged them to learn from the books and from other elders from their tribes:

> I have a bundle, a Medicine Bundle. But one of the main important things is that, being a Medicine Man, I can't doctor myself. I've been ill but I have to go to a Medicine Man and

get doctored. I have to get another Medicine Man to doctor me. And so this is why I have to go back home sometimes and have a Medicine Man work with me.

The old Indian way is through a Medicine Man, through spirits that they work with. These spirits work with them and that's the way they do all their doctoring. So the bundles and herbs that we carry means a lot to people. I've always told people we are no different. Through these herbs, the medicine and the plants we call medicine, the human body, flesh and blood, is no different between us. That's why we have to use the herbs in order to put the good back in our bodies, and live with health.

Maybe you want to be an herbalist. Maybe you are looking for herbs. If you want to be an herbalist, fine. I wish there were a lot more like you. We always like to teach people about the herbs, because it means a lot for the people. A lot of this they picked up from the elderlies and they took pictures.

Before you start, you put out some prayers and tobacco ties. Sprinkle tobacco on Mother Earth. Then take your time and pick the herbs. When you get home, wash it out, dry it out, wrap it up good and put it away.

That's why he put all them plants out there, but people don't realize it. A little flower grows up in the yard, they'll chop it off. They chop it off and throw it in the weeds. That could cure, maybe take care of the whole family. They don't realize it because when they take sick, they run to the doctor and to the hospital, instead of learning about the herbs. They could save a little money on themselves by learning what that herb's good for.

If one grows up in your yard, right in your lawn, give it tobacco and dig it up. Plant it over in some corner where it won't be disturbed. Transplant it. Honor it. Maybe smell it. That is why I said, "You can help one another heal yourself. Give this medicine to each other. Keep it on hand." It will make you live healthier. It's a miracle.

One of the medicines called "Bear Medicine" has a beautiful odor. You carry some in your pocket. It smells like perfume. It really smells good on Mother Earth, but you don't know. We walk on it, that's all we know. But we don't know how beautiful the smell is, the bushes along the creeks, under Mother Earth. There are a lot of beautiful smells. You won't know it until you pick one of these plants.

They all got a different taste, the majority of the plants. Some you boil and drink and it's really bitter. It's hard to take, but if you want to heal yourself, you've got to toughen up and drink it. If you can drink whiskey and all that stuff, you can drink the bitter herb.

For heart disease there is heart medicine. For any kind of blood problems there are different kinds of blood medicine. Diabetes, bone medicine, you name them all. It's out there.

Headache medicine. A headache medicine used to grow on trees. It is kind of like a sap. It grows kind of like a wart on cedar or pine trees. Take that sap and have them smudge with that and it will cure any of these headaches. The headache will go away real fast. People have headaches and they say, 'I don't know what's the matter' and they take aspirin. If you smudge yourself a little with that tree medicine, you'll never have a headache again. It cures headaches.

There are different types of bone medicine. You take elk antler. Take a chunk of that and file that until it's real fine. Take that and pray with that. You put it on a broken leg and wrap it up. Leave it on there. It'll heal up. You go to an x-ray machine, you'll never see where that broken spot is. You'll never find it, because it's spiritual. That's the way the old people used to heal themselves, a broken arm or broken leg using these antlers, deer antlers, and different things. Use that to heal each other. There are herbs that you can take in liquid form by boiling it and make your mind stronger so you don't forget things.

There is a big soap weed bush. The root goes down about 15- 20 feet into the ground. You have to dig it out and it's so big around. People used to use that for soap for spiritual cleansing. Chop it up and stir it a while, and it soaps up. People used to wash themselves with it.

There's all different kinds of herbs out there. There's another thing they use, like a drumstick. You see it growing in swamp areas. They turn brown in the fall. About that long. They used to bust that open and take all that silk out. When they have a baby, they put that on. Today you have Pampers. We didn't have those Pampers, so there's a lot of different things that the old ancestors used to use.

Raspberry bush, chokecherries, plum, different kinds of wild fruit. Each one can heal a different illness. There are different types of medicines especially in these trees. Cottonwood buds, when they start budding out you can get up in that tree with a ladder or something and start picking the buds. You can use them as medicine. Red willow is medicine. You can heal each other with these.

One of the trees around here in Oregon means a lot. I heard they were picking on this one tree because they found a cure for cancer in the Pacific Yew. They were hauling it out by the truckloads. Somebody told them that you use this tree, the bark of this tree to heal different types of cancer. Now they're getting tons of it. They're going up in that old growth forest, getting that Pacific Yew bark.

There's different ways of healing with herbs. You have to use these herbs in a lot of different ways. You can put it in a form such as a tea and drink it to heal yourself. Some of them you have to smudge with. With a lot of medicine, the stem cures something and the root cures some other disease. And so these are the things with these herbs. Sometimes you have to use nothing but the leaves, or some of the buds, if you get it early.

We have to believe in the spirit of that plant. Always carry whatever you can of that plant, because then you're carrying the spirit of that plant with you. But one of the things we found out, when you have this plant, you have to keep the spirit of that plant protected. You can't grind it all up, or you could kill the spirit of that plant. Then it's no good, but you can grind it after you take a little chunk off to carry, maybe the stem or root. If you have to, you can then grind some of it to use as a salve. You still have the spirit of that plant through the juice or in the salve form.

These are the miracles of what can happen. This is what has been taught to us, so these are the things we have to tell others. Miracles can happen to you regarding what you study here. It's a mystery. The miracle that has no beginning and has no end is Mother Earth.

The herbs are one of the most important things back in the old peoples' lives, and we can make it that way today. This is why we always advise people to pick this herb. Dry it out. Write down what it's for. Write it on your package and make yourself a little Medicine Bundle and put it away. Maybe somebody wants to be doctored and wants this. You can get your Medicine Bundle.

Boil this medicine, maybe put it in a salve or something. Give it to them, and you can heal people. That's what that medicine's for. That's what God created it for, so that people could live with health. That means a lot to these people.

You can then teach others about it. What you learn, share it. Share these Medicine Bundles with other people. That is the way God has given for the people to heal each other and live with health. The Number One commandment is health ... health of the people. That's the way God gave us of our seven. And so I just want to pass the word on.

Martin High Bear in Green Grass, South Dakota 1992.

CHAPTER 8

THE SECOND COMMANDMENT:

WIČHÓUⓃČHAĞE

THERE SHALL BE GENERATION AFTER GENERATION OF THE PEOPLE

After a short break at the Naturopathic College, Martin continued to speak to the students, this time about the Second Commandment of his vision: "The people shall live from generation to generation." During this second lecture at the college, I watch the students' facial expressions as Martin naturally creates feelings of intimacy, filling their hearts with good feelings. Perhaps it stirred warm memories of the students' own grandparents.

Fascinated by his every move, they listened to him speak of the miracle of children, respect for elderlies, and how the essence of this Second Commandment has, since time immemorial, preserved ancient indigenous cultural values and traditions for today's and future generations.

Dr. Zeff shared with us later that the students wanted more understanding of who he was. "Some of them wanted to work with him," he said. "Some of them wanted to know how they could get training to become a Medicine Person. They didn't realize it is not the kind of thing you go to school for. It is handed down in one's bloodline from generation to generation."

TAKE CARE OF YOUR CHILDREN, THE GIFT THAT GOD HAS GIVEN YOU

Martin Continued:

They said there shall be generation after generation of the people. This is the second commandment. And so that is the way the Great Spirit has created the Indian people on this island. A lot of things have been handed down from generation to generation. And so things were here before, maybe ten thousand years ago. This is the way the people lived. This is the way the people were.

The miracle that has always happened to us families (and they respect it very much and are thankful to God that this miracle happened) is our children. The babies born from a woman, formed into a child and come on earth: That's the miracle. And so this is why this miracle works in different ways. And this spiritual power is still on earth in this way.

God never misses a thing. Everything He puts out to His children.... You are all his children and so He put them all out so you can use it, generation after generation. That is why, today, you are here. That comes under the second law of God.

This is why every time I come to speak to people at different places, there's so much to speak about, so much to tell about what our ancestors left us. And we need to figure out ourselves where we come from, who we are. These are the things that we have to understand.

We're all old enough. We are not little children anymore. And so today is the seventh generation. This is why I've always said, "Take care of your children, the miracle that God has given to you." And this is why we always talk about it, not for ourselves, but for the young people and into the "unborn" who aren't here yet. And so this is very important to us.

I hear young people say, "I wish I was born back in those days." Back in years, years ago, there was no such thing as alcohol. There was no such thing as child abuse, women abuse. And then today we see younger kids going around hell raising. And so these are the ones that we have to teach.

We need to teach the little people. We teach them not to do things. Everybody has their chance. Let the younger generation live their chance. They have to learn what they have been taught so they can pass it on, because we are not going to be here tomorrow to teach any more of that. That is why, today, I'm glad to be here to speak to you girls and boys. You know, that's what the spirits always say, to talk to the children. Even though you're one to one hundred years old, you're still a child. If you study it, that means a lot.

BUFFALO PEOPLE

The spirits told me that as long as the river flows there shall be populations of the Indian people on this spiritual island. So today, when they say there shall be generation after generation ... if they didn't say that, we probably wouldn't be here.

Back in the old days, in the 1830's, there used to be over forty million buffalo roaming this range – forty million buffalo and maybe more. When the White Man came, the hide and fur companies came in here and started buying hides. They started killing buffalo. They was only getting $3.50 a hide in them days. That's when they started slaughtering these buffalo, two, three, four hundred a day. And when they had overstocked the hide and fur companies, they started buying them for 60 cents a hide.

They leave the carcasses laying out there all bloated up, rotting, and they took the hides. So they kept it up and up. They didn't want to believe in what Great Spirit has created. But the feeling they had was, 'If we clean these buffaloes out, maybe we might starve the Indians all out of this.' And by around the 1880's, they wiped out all the buffalo.

But still today the Indians are living. Like the old saying, *"As long as this river flows, there shall be Indians."* And if the river ever slows up, I know the Great Spirit will turn it loose again, 'cause He created the Indians on this island – what they call North America.

Martin was referring to the Buffalo Disaster, when in a three-year period between 1881-1883, an estimated 320,000 hides were shipped out from buffalo country. The northern herd of buffalo was almost totally exterminated. Estimates of earlier nineteenth century buffalo had ranged between 30 to 200 million, with 60 million the most common estimate.

Between 1840-1860, they were divided into southern and northern herds by the migration of people west along the Platte River and by the building of the Union Pacific RR. An 1858 disease epidemic that destroyed the buffalo remaining in the Platte River valley, completed this division into two herds and brought about dramatic changes among Great Plains peoples.[86]

---

86   North Dakota History, Vol. 50, No. 1, Winter, 1983, p. 23-30.

The massive number of bones left all over the prairie were eventually rounded up and sold to the fertilizer industry in what became known as the Buffalo Bone Commerce, including the Devil's Lake buffalo bone trade.[87]

MEDICINE MEN COME FROM A LINE OF HEALERS

Martin explained:

Our Medicine Men come from generations after generations. You have to be from a Medicine People. And so it forms into a person automatically to all these. It is a God given gift. And so, my ancestors were Medicine People. I came from a line of Medicine People in my blood relations. I got this power through my great-great-grandparents on my father's side. So this is where I got this power to work with spirits to heal people and to give medicine – herbs. So this is why it is my turn in this generation to be a so-called healer, "Medicine Man."

My dad was to be a Medicine Man, but he didn't. So when I became a Medicine Man, I had to start from scratch. There was a generational gap from my great grandmothers and great grandfathers, but I took care of it and went up on the hill on Vision Quest. That is why I kept up the tradition as a healer, so this is why I was appointed to be what I am today.

If you are going to be a Medicine Person, it is in your blood relation and is passed on. Like now maybe one of my grandchildren may pick it up from me and carry it into the next generation, but he has to have these visions. If one of my grandchildren becomes a healer, the spirits will give him a vision. It is passed on like that. We either will have to train one.... Maybe he might not go for it, but this is why we are here today.

A vision is like a dream. When you study that dream, you don't forget it. If you think you're going to forget, write it down.

You may dream about it over and over. It might be some animal that you dream about a lot. You might dream about a sick man or a sick woman. Then pretty soon, in the next dream, they're up and spry, you can tell they got healed. That tells us that you were born from a line of Medicine People.

Things like this is working for the people, the ways the Great Spirit has created things, how to work with this in ceremony, all these. It's never forgotten and will always be here.

---

87   Ibid p. 23-42) (see photograph) https://www.history.nd.gov/publications/ndavailable.html

These are the things that I always talk about – spiritual – advising people."

Prophesy from Holy Men Guided the People

Back in the 1700's, 1600's, way back, the old holy men back there stated prophecies. The experiences they had in them days, they knew ahead of time, what was coming. Back in the old days, when prophecy was coming out, some of the old people talked about it and handed it down from generations to generations.

"And the air will be polluted; the trees will be dying; People will be dying; the animals will be dying; the birds-feather nation will be dying." That was a prophecy from way back. Today we're seeing it. At that time, they knew there would be something that "they" would be doing. Instead of respecting the living things on this earth.

In the old days, this was told way back among our ancestors and they talked about it. They talked about things so we would understand as generations come after generations.

It's not just talk from one human to another. There is something there that is deeper and more holy than we can ever think of. That's the way our ancestors lived. They knew whatever was going to come – the next twenty years from now. They knew that. The changes of things; the weather, the changes of Mother Earth, the trees, the water. They knew all these.

They could look up in the stars and look at certain stars and predict the weather. Them days, they'd look up at the spiritual stars up there. How they twinkle. The movement. How they beautify themselves. They make it work. They tell the weather report, sometimes maybe for a year.

So they get down and talk to each other so they can prepare for that kind of weather changes. Today, you have to watch television to tell what the weather is going to be tomorrow. But before the television and radio and everything came, they knew all that.

These Commandments Were Passed Down

The Seven Commandments that He has handed down, these commandments were here before, maybe ten thousand years ago. This is the way the people lived. This is the way the people were. I can say for one sure thing. When Indian people were given the Seven Commandments, God created the Indian people in these Seven Commandments. So obey them commands – how to live under the Holy Sun; how to walk on Mother Earth; on the Red Path that the Great Spirit has sent down to us; how to live happily with our spirit power.

We remember God, our Grandfather. We were taught to do that, and we honor Creation, what God created. It is all holy. We thank our Grandfather for everything. And that's the way it's been handed down from generation after generation after generation. So this is why tonight, I have left a few messages before I leave here.

I enjoy it sometimes when I get a chance to recite some of these things of the old way. These are the things that we talk about back home. Our elders know these ways, so they can live with it. And they know what is going on and how they can live with respect and honor. When my grandmother and mother were living, they would talk about that.

Now we're realizing where we are today. We're not supposed to forget about it, so we live with it and pass on some of this information that we are given. We're giving it back into this young generation that's working to bring it back strong.

So now, they're using this culture and religion today, and I think the Great Spirit has seen these Indian people, these children, using a religion and a culture that He has laid down to them on this spiritual island, so Great Spirit is happy. He would have said a lot of good things to these Indian people on this spiritual island.

I imagine if He was down among us, He would say, "My children, you have made Me happy. What I have taught, what I have brought to you, you mind; and you're doing what I wanted you to do."

GO TO THE ELDERLIES

A lot of things have been handed down from generation to generation. And the ones that can speak the truth are the ones that listened to their grandparents, listened to their parents. So that's why we never lost any of our culture. We still have our ways. The majority of the people still speak their language. We always say God gave us this language, this tongue, so let's not forget it.

I often tell the people, every place that I go, if you want to know about something, go up to the elderlies that are living yet. That are still of an age where they have a good strong mind. They remember things. Go to these elderlies. Call them grandfather or grandmother, every elderly.

That was the way I was taught. Every old couple that comes to the house, they are somebody's gramma or grampa. Their experiences were very different from ours today. You can learn what is going on and then you'll know how things are, why they are that way. If you don't, they are going to take it with them and you will never learn.

I've always said, give them a gift. Give them a blanket, or take some food and tell them, 'Grampa, I want to learn some of this.' Sit down with them and ask them for help. If you have a tape player, take it along and ask permission to tape what they have to say. They will tell you some of the old things, some of the old memories. Then remember them.

A POWERFUL EXAMPLE

Ed Red Owl, *Sisíthuŋwaŋ Waȟpéthuŋwaŋ* (Sisseton-Wahpeton) tribal leader and historian, shared his family and tribe's experience with Martin's teaching: *The people shall live from generation to generation.* For Ed, this involved participating with Martin and his stepfather, Felix Green, in the traditional ceremonies of their people to overcome historic oppression. It is also a journey that translates to this day and beyond into everyday living on the Red Road:

> Here at Sisseton-Wahpeton, we have what is called very rich agricultural land and good range land and good tilling soil. So therefore, every square inch of our reservation was surveyed – every inch. And what that meant- that our being scrutinized by the forces of acculturation was 24-7; 24 hours a day; 7 days a week, we were inspected, monitored and coerced to be programmed to be something that we were not historically in a cultural or religious perspective.
>
> In relationship to Martin's teachings, the issue that he undoubtedly encountered was that everybody here had been programmed. We were more Christian than the Christians. We were more committed to education than the non-Indians. We were more inclined to be middle class than the middle class. We were more committed to agriculture than were the farmers.

The problem is we didn't have our natural means to do it or social acceptance. And our entire religious view was that of the churches. And we only had faint memories. So therefore, as a spiritual leader, I would often think that it must have been very frustrating for Martin to deal with us because we had been programmed.

We were only allowed to do one type of cultural thing on an annual basis and that was our Fourth of July Powwow. That was it. And that started with the government scouts at Fort Sisseton, when the commander would allow the Sisseton-Wahpeton to bring out their drums and dance in observance of Fourth of July. That is all we were allowed. We couldn't do more than that. Everything else was done underground. So we had a pervasive attitude of negative self-perception. We did not think we were worth anything.

Martin and Felix would often challenge us with our basic Sisseton-Wahpeton identity. They would say to us, 'You have to make a decision.'

And we would say 'What type of a decision?'

They would say, 'The power is in your mind. It is in your entity. If you want to turn yourself into a buffalo, if you want to turn yourself into a bird, you can do that because that is the type of people that you once were. You are the Sisseton Wahpeton Bands. You are the mother. It was from here that the entire religious and cultural patrimony came, except on you came the worst oppression that could come to any bands of our *oyáte*, our nation. And so that is what your challenge is.

As an example, your people used to fashion small men, little tiny men, and your people knew how to turn wood into flesh. And that these *čhaŋóthila*, these little men carved out of wood, could speak and talk and act. That is part of your patrimony. But you cannot do that until you make a decision about everything that has happened to you.

With regard to the Second Commandment, "Living From One Generation to the Next," we knew that we were existentialists, if you will. Or more specific, we knew we were nihilists to the extent that we felt that we were without any salvation. And yet we felt that we could not acculturate. We could not become non-Indian because in our community, from time of inception to the present time, the non-Indian immigrant and their descendants do not accept Indians.

And not only socially or economically, but also religious-ly. There are two Presbyterian churches here, the Indian and White, and there are two Episcopal churches here, Indian and White. And yet we felt we were not going anywhere.

In the 1950's, when the Bureau of Indian Affairs had imple-mented the relocation program, and our people were trans-ferred to Minneapolis, Cleveland, some to New York City, some to San Francisco. And the idea being that once they left their allotments, their land could be sold and the settler de-scendants then could acquire that land for little or nothing.

And in the 1970's when Martin came here, many of those families began to return home, but it wasn't working. The destitute unemployment here was 92-96 per cent, and so we decided we would have to do something with that as a people.

And that was the challenge I think of Martin High Bear is that he had a knack of being an *ikčé wičháša* – common man. But yet we knew he was a healer and he had a healing altar. We didn't understand. Often it was difficult for us to have to give up, not give up, but become deprogrammed.

So with Martin, that is the first lesson. We had, I recall, one of the very first ceremonies and that was at the home of Jerry Flute. Martin was there with his stepfather Felix Green. Martin had a ceremony, and the ceremony was "look-ing for a ceremony" that would put some personal meaning in our life.

And what happened at that ceremony that Felix and Martin conducted, and we call it today a *Dowáŋpi* ceremony, is that for the first time we experienced the spirits who came into that room and talked to us. We could hear them and un-derstand what they said and we learned that there was more than we had heard throughout our lifetime in our churches, that in fact God and his powers had spoken to us, and that was the first time we had that experience.

The second issue is that we were all coping with issues of alcohol abuse, with issues of domestic violence, and issues of physical and emotional damage that comes from those particular types of abuse. In the process, we wondered, "Well, perhaps it is because we ourselves are evil people. We must be evil," we thought. We don't know how to do any-thing other than those things.

Through the Sweat Lodge, we attained a condition of what we call *wakȟáŋ*, purity. You can go into that Sweat

Lodge and become reborn, recreated in a sense, in the Sweat Lodge.

So we can understand that God did not make garbage, that we are in God's image and making and likeness. And in the Sweat Lodge we learned that from Martin that we can do that renewal through Sweat Lodge ceremony again.

The other thing that we tried to come to an understanding is "What do we do?" and "Where do we go from here?"

He would never give us that answer. So therefore, he suggested that we go to Bear Butte in the Black Hills and go on Vision Quest to find out what we should do.

And so a group of us would go there. We did that for a period of four years, and we fasted four years in a row. And those of us who did that at that time in the early 1970's, four of us are still alive. Jerry Flute, myself, Mike Selvage, and Peewee Wayne Eastman. There are two others who were a part of that and they have since passed on.

They would tell us that each time we came back from Haŋblécheya-Vision Quest. They would say "Remember, you are protected by four rings around you. There are four circles. You do not need to have hatred. Or you do not need to exact revenge on anybody. That power of the sacred Pipe is such that it will take care of you, no matter what has happened to you, what has happened to your parents, or your grandparents, or your great grandparents. You have the power provided you make the decision."

Especially those of us who have become elders, old men and old women, not having too much wisdom, owing to becoming programmed, we have made a decision that at least our children and grandchildren will not know that oppression that we grew up in. And that continues as a constant struggle for many of us is the process of being de-programmed.

And many of them don't. We have tried our best with our children, and now our grandchildren and great grandchildren – to see them experience only the traditional seven sacred rites – the Pipe ceremony, the Sweat Lodge, the Vision Quest, the Sun Dance, and so forth. And so for the first time, 30 or 50 years later, we have a first generation.

The key today, however, is in some fashion to re-institute those teaching and that legacy that was passed on by Martin High Bear. We need those seven virtues – those virtues of understanding and compassion, of bravery, and kindness and fortitude, and the basic value of kinship, *mitákuye oyás'iŋ – We are all related*. That today remains our greatest challenge.

When I look back at his method of delivery, it was in his Lakȟóta language. We speak the D [Dakȟóta] dialect here. However, now we have a significant Dakȟóta language re-vitalization program going on. And it is not so much from those of us who were programmed. We were programmed in the 1930's, 1940's, 1950's. It is coming from our own children and grandchildren who have not known the boarding schools, who are from our own school systems.

Martin always talked about this, that we need to stop go-ing to the boarding schools, so we have invested as a people in our own school system. And we have a large school sys-tem. It's getting to be larger than any public-school system in northeast South Dakota. We have over 1,500 students in our own school systems. We have three school systems that are doing very well and one of the boarding schools, the Wah-peton Boarding School, is now owned and operated by our own tribe. We take in children that are abused and neglect-ed and the Wahpeton School District is operated under a charter that is owned and operated by our own people, so it is very different today.

I can cite other examples of the teachings. I think from the *Huŋká* ceremony, that naming ceremony, we came from the darkest time of oppression that any group of people can conceivably endure into a realization that we must go be-yond that, that we have a responsibility. And the oppression here was very very severe.

Michael Selvidge, our tribal chairman, wanted a name so that the Creator would always recognize him by his own Dakȟóta name. And so an altar was put up by Martin and a name of Swift Elk, *Heȟáka*, was given to him. He had just had an accident which resulted in a condition of quadriplegic. He felt at that time that his life was going to end. And so in that altar he was given that name, and a commitment was made that he had to fulfill. And today he is a tribal chair-man. He will be an elder and so that has come about in that period of time.

Marriages were performed here. And the outcome of those marriages included Michael and his wife. They had two sons before this accident and now he has 14 grandchildren. With those 14 grandchildren, we suspect they will each have five children. So how many is that and who would have thought? It is going to be a huge number of people who came from this man and his wife. And it comes from a time and a place where there was one man and his wife inside that altar.

My youngest son in the 1970's was afflicted with asthma, untreatable. And so we had tried everything. And nothing had worked. And so we had with Martin four ceremonies. And as a result of that he was cured. He has not had asthma. And he completed recently nine years of which four years was spent with the US Navy Seals. And so he is a very strong man. He lives in Montana. But he came in a healing context from that altar of Martin during that period of time when there was no hope.

Now we are getting to be old men. We learned and each had our own spiritual experiences that have guided us since that time. It is over thirty years since we have done that and we have not left the community. We continue in the community and we all have significant roles to fulfill in the community, and that came from that vision as to what we should be doing.

As an example, when Martin came here, we had just an incident in the City of Sisseton when a police officer was chasing a young Indian man. He told the young Indian man to stop and he wouldn't. So he shot the Indian man in the back and killed him. That was our situation here, that we could be killed at any time.

And since that time, we have asserted our own jurisdiction. We have our own tribal attorneys now. We have two of our own attorneys that work full time for our own people. And we have three to five young people today who want to finish school and come back. One of them that is an attorney was the daughter of Jerry Flute and she is a practicing attorney for her people today.

And of course, today we now have Indian gaming and we have dropped to 33% unemployment. We are now the 10th largest employer in northeast South Dakota. We have over 1,700 people who work for our tribe. And you have to have people who are committed to have made that happen.

We are still alive. We are still working hard to create that self-sufficiency, a vision that we learned in those very very hard times. And so the spirituality has translated into everyday living. It isn't something that is cerebral and isn't something that we can't talk about and doesn't have any substance. In fact, it does have real substance and it who we once were when we were self-sufficient. We have a long way to go, but those teachings persist. And the way it was done here was addressing specific issues that the families had that were working with Martin. Whether it was health, psychological or physical, that is how it was approached, in the context of ceremony, in the context of outcome.

I think of so many things that have come from integrating this second commandment back into our lives. We have talked about a simple thing such as wanting our buffalo back. And again, the response is that we should do something about that. Today we have a herd of buffalo in excess of 350 head in a rather developed rural part of our reservation. We have one of the largest buffalo programs and projects in the Midwest. We are able today to provide buffalo meat to our people. We have five Sun Dances here at Sisseton-Wahpeton Reservation every summer and we are able to provide buffalo to every one of them. Our elderly program is provided buffalo meat. These are practical, from teachings that were set down many years ago.

EDDIE CROW PHILOSOPHIZES

Dakhóta Elder, Eddie Crow spoke about living from generation to generation for the Seven Generations as taught by his elders. He has dedicated himself to teaching his own son, even when it is difficult to express himself in the English language:

> I didn't have my history. I had to learn about my history. There was no one to teach us what we had to know so we had to make mistakes and find out who we were as Indian people. In order to do that we had to seek out spiritual advisors, and spiritual people and Medicine People, and my father, Martin High Bear, happened to be one of the spiritual leaders, along with Pete Catches and John Red Bear and Lone Eagle and Dark Road and Touch the Cloud. I owe a lot to Fills the Pipe and Looks Twice and Looking Eagle and Grass Robe and Landless and Tom Bad Cob and George Eagle Elk and Frank Kills Enemy. And many more of my uncles and grandfathers for their help and support. Mainly, my adopted father, Martin High Bear, my spiritual dad.

So that is what the old man is all about. That is what he did. He was a ceremonial man. He was a bundle carrier. He was a traditional historian, and he had helpers, spirit helpers. And he was what he was in every way, a spiritual man. And he passed on to the Spirit Receiving House like that with dignity, honor, humility, reverence for life.

His relatives that remain have something honorable to live with in remembrance of him. As I look in relationship to him and in regard to his life, it is something that I will cherish for as long as I am here, that I got to know all of these old ones both men and women who are no longer here. Or those who are here only in spirit and who are still helping to make good things happen in regard to the next seven generations of life.

If it wasn't for my old people, I wouldn't be here. I attended a lot of the treaty council meetings with the government and state department. And that is where my old people did a lot of that work that was necessary for young people like me to continue. And if it wasn't for people like my father, I probably would still be behind bars, or in bars, or not have a very good life.

So that is just a little bit about my feeling and who and what I am in regard to this holy man. And my old people had to do a lot of talking to me as a young hothead to get me to cool off, to get me to act right, be honorable and respect and walk in dignity and beauty and hold reverence for life.

All these old ones said, "The old is coming back." But we have to understand the reality that there is not much that we can say in regard to our loss of wisdom and knowledge. Recent history, oral history, tribal history are all seen through the eyes of the people who experienced it. And it is really difficult to give people a perspective.

There is not much that can be said for the English language in its translation, in its embarrassment, in its rudeness, in its nondescript nature. We can't always rely on hearsay and gossip in this language called English. It has various interpretations and difference of opinion and expression in its tonal quality and its root base. You can't describe kindness and generosity, caring and sharing and love in this scientific language that is only used for business and pleasure.

My Lakȟóta language is untouched by English in comparison. My Lakȟóta language comes from the heart. That is why we call it the mother tongue. The first thing a child hears is the mother's voice. The first sound that a child hears is a mother's heart. So that being said, the eagle bone whistle and the drum represent that interpretive sense of worth for us as Indian people. It is the language and music and culture and heritage, our hereditary background, our cultural upbringing and historical documentation of who and what we are as people.

When I talk like this I have to interpret in my mind, from Indian to English back to English to Indian. And so I pause a lot and I have to recall, "Did I say the right thing? Did I mean what I said?" because if I didn't, it is too late.

When I was an interpreter and an advisor and a counselor and a representative of these Indian ways, I had to be perfectly clear so as not to be misquoted or mistaken as to what I was trying to say, directly or indirectly, or justly or unjustly for the purpose of some qualified information.

It is very hard for me as a somewhat traditional man to live in a non-traditional world. I have a son and I want him to have the best of both worlds. He was blessed by my father, Martin High Bear. And all my sacred articles of prayer that I have were handed down to me by my elders, both men and women. So like I have been saying, we have to move on from this cloud of scorn and shame and ridicule to a new world, a true world for the next seven generations.

Our children are our future and this world belongs to them because they are the ones that have to live it. And as long as I am here, I am going to have my son live a good life to the fullest extent of the law, whatever that means. (laughter) And all of that history that I talk about will help him get through this life, and identify himself when people ask him who he is and how he got here and where he came from. He will be able to tell them in great detail because he will have his history.

We all have a purpose and my purpose as a history keeper, as a somewhat traditional man, as a keeper of these ways, I try not to exaggerate and interpret. In regard to interpretation, we have to be correct and precise in our information. If we are not, we are called liars and of the imagination. We make things up. But we, as Indian people, we are taught as children not to do that. What I am trying to do is to give the listener a chance to make their own inquiry or their own decision, draw their own conclusion.

We as Indian people don't think of death the same as other people. We look at death as a change of life. So as I sit here and live out my life, I look to the next seven generations. With me in my dignified way of speaking, I look at it as honorable to have lived this long and to still be in one piece. To still have my health and my reassurance, and my mental capability and be in good health. That is one of the commandments, you know, to live in health.

The history as seen through the eyes of the people who witnessed is better than the written word. History, like the Bay of Pigs, like Pearl Harbor, like Auschwitz, like the wall of China, the history of the working-class people, the peasant people of Mexico, Peru, Nicaragua, and El Salvador, or Guatemala, or Africa, or Ethiopia or Turkey or North Carolina or Afghanistan, Honduras, Corsica. You could look at these land base areas.

So there are stories of good kind people struggling to be free from their own destructive measures, dislocated lives, and ideals, the way they were brought up and instructed to do by "Lord knows who or what." We all have had to see some dastardly things, things that weren't right according to somebody. But who is to say what was wrong and what was right and what was fair and what was unfair. Fifty years have went by and we still haven't resolved nothing.

You know, it is like fulfillment of the second commandment. The people shall live from generation to generation. And we have to do that for the sake of each other and ourselves. I look at our ceremonial lives and we have very little water, very little land base. Our herbs are dwindling. Our medicine is leaving, and we are still struggling.

Whatever it is worth, I am a traditionalist. I have old ways and if I am the only one who is doing them, God bless the rest. I am just following instructions that were handed down long before my breath. Because I ran from these ways and hid from these ways and didn't want these ways. But these ways I got and they are kind of scary. I am a representative of a culture lost and I have to adhere to that because these young ones rely on me. They call me almost every other day with something and I have to be there for them. Even though I may not like it, they never said that was going to be easy. If it was, maybe there would be a lot more help than what is here.

But the old ones had always said, "It won't be easy."

It is something that I get daily. People call here and ask for interpretations and stories. People want me to interpret things, old songs, old music, old language. So I got to go deep within my memory to bring up all that is there, like the anniversary of the hanging of the 38 Santee Sioux.

I got a letter from the State Department. "You are exactly who you said you are."

And I said "Thank you. I knew that, but if you are going to compensate me, does that mean you going to give my grandfather back?"

Martin High Bear at home at SE Flavel Drive in Portland (1994).

CHAPTER 9

THE THIRD COMMANDMENT:

INÍLA

THE PEOPLE SHALL LIVE WITH QUIETNESS

*I*níla is the quietness commandment. It may contain some of the smallest number of comments, but it embodies some of Martin's most transformational wisdom. Iníla translates as "The people shall live with quietness."

It is much more than quietness, with extraordinary potential to create harmony in the lives of the people, even and especially in the midst of conflict. It emanates from a deep and firm spiritual conviction that the peoples' greatest defense comes not from themselves but from faith in the guidance and protection of Great Spirit.

It is also a part of the rich cultural values and teachings from generation after generation of ancestors who lived their lives surrounded by their rich cultural heritage and way of life. That includes spiritual qualities and cultural values such as humility, patience, tolerance, endurance, and discernment. The willingness and ability to listen is essential.

The simplicity of this conflict resolution commandment sometimes eluded those reluctant to follow its quiet footsteps along the *Čhaŋkú Lúta*, the Red Road. When people are quiet and able to humble themselves, they are able to hear the guidance from the Spirit World. Through reflection, we can discern the truth.

Martin's understanding may have been advanced beyond most people because of his relationships with his grandparents and extended family members. It deepened through his own personal experiences during the trauma experienced during his younger years and later during the decades while he served as a spiritual elder.

He taught these teachings to Native spiritual communities that stretched out from Alkali Lake, British Columbia to the Dakota Tipi Band of Dakhóta peoples around Portage La Prairie, Manitoba. Many Native people were able to learn from his lectures – from Minneapolis/St. Paul, Sisseton-Wahpeton where he was adopted into the Thompson family, urban Indians in Colorado, California, and in Anchorage, Alaska. He shared many times with Native families in recovery at Native American Rehabilitation Association, the residential alcohol and drug treatment facility in Portland, Oregon where his cousin Rufus Charger served as drug and alcohol counselor. This helped clients learn from Martin in recovery circles, and heal during spiritual ceremonies.

He eventually stretched his influence by following the instructions of his Spirit Helpers to spiritually advise people of all cultures and colors including the Pig Farm near Laytonville, California, the Two Eagle Circle in Füssen, Germany, the community of Hermann and Erika Haindl in Hofheim, Germany and over "the Wall" into Eastern Germany which had just opened to outsiders months before his 1992 trip to Europe.

Preparing to Walk the Red Road

In several of the following sections, a number of Martin's recordings were transcribed and included so his his thoughts could be shared:

> It says in the Bible, "Thou shalt not lie." "Thou shalt not steal." Forget about that hatred. There is no such thing as that in the Indian way. Jealousness; no such thing as that. People were happy.
>
> So for some of these things, we have to prepare ourselves. The main thing is quietness. It is pretty hard for some of the people, but you got to learn. These are the good educations, good experiences. You can teach yourself a lot of good things.
>
> Quit your bad habits. When we talk about bad habits, them are what I just mentioned. The jealousness, you learn that, and that's a bad habit. It's like smoking a cigarette. That's a bad habit. It is like you crave for it. You crave for the hatred, the jealousness, and these are the most important things you want to purify yourselves on because that falls on that Red Road.

This is how you use your religion in your studies. A lot of these things, we have to remember and we have to learn these.

Maybe you want to pass this along to a relative that's having a hard time. A hard time is when we talk about hard times. A lot of times we put that on ourselves. We make it that way for ourselves. We don't realize there's a better way of living, a better way of our lives that could be forming a habit.

WE SAID NOTHING WHEN THEY TOOK OUR RELIGION FROM US

Where I come from lies the Sacred White Buffalo Calf Pipe. And I had Vision Quest there at one time – four days, four nights. I respect and honor and I love the White Buffalo Calf Pipe as much as I love God, as much as I love these spirits that work with me in my everyday life.

But at one time, our religion was taken away from us. Yeah, it was taken away from us. But my ancestors never said nothing about it, because they knew the time would come when this Indian religion would be back on this island which God has placed here.

And so it did. It happened. Since 1978, the President passed the Freedom of Religion Act.

So we still have what God gave us. We never lost our religion. I know it was outlawed. One time, you got prosecuted if you used your Indian religion. They went ahead and assassinated our holy men. They went ahead and broke the Pipes up, ceremonial things, burned them up, put them in museums.

But that didn't stop our religion. So today, it's still here. This is why, when I hear people argue about the religious structure, what I think spiritually in my mind – the holiness in my mind that I think with – I've always said: "This religious structure don't belong to us. It belongs to God. He just handed it down for us to use. But we fight over it."

And when I hear they're going to court over religious structure, Supreme Court, Indian people know that it don't belong to us, that we can't go that far. We know better.

We have to ask, "Who has the true God?" We can't run down anybody's religion, 'cause it's God's creation. And we love our God a hundred per cent. We believe in Him. What is created here for us, we're thankful for.

As for the Indian people, the Red Man, we don't invent nothing. We don't create nothing. God has created everything we need here on this island, on Mother Earth, the green of Mother Earth and the fruit on the trees and the four leggeds that give themselves to live with the Red Man.

We believe in the Great Spirit, and He has created things for us on this island. What more do we have to create? What he has created is all holy. And so these are the things that we all have to understand. But most of all, believe in it.

OUR ELDERS WERE QUIET, LIKE THE ANIMALS ARE QUIET

The Third Commandment is Quietness. There was a quieting way the Indian people, back in the old days, used to live. People were quiet, just like the animals are quiet, the birds. And we are all related. Living among the wild animals, they were quiet. They traveled and acted like the animals, the great big bands, with a chief as their head man. That's the way God created us all.

Do you people realize it, that you're related to animals? Sounds silly, doesn't it, but back in the old days it wasn't silly, because we didn't know what silly was. Maybe this word "silly" is just another thing that we picked up from the other culture.

But the old Indian people, they lived happily, quietly. Even today, you take an old man or an old lady and you walk up to him thinking he's going to say something. He'll never say a word unless you ask him. He'll give you an answer but it's going to be very short.

I WAS CALLED NAMES. ... BUT I NEVER SAID A WORD

In my spiritual travels during the past 24 years, we went around all over the country, like they told me to do, to help heal illnesses and heal the spirits of the human. That was my line of work. During my travels I've been places where I was called names.

Christians called me "devil worshiper," but I never say a word. One day the mistake will show up. But if I argue back, I am just helping them prove what they think I am. And so these are the things that we often talk about.

Remember one of our commandments is quietness. Whoever says anything to you, cusses you up, don't pay no attention to them. Them are just words. Don't let it hurt your feelings. And whoever threatens you, listen to them. And when he gets through putting these words out, walk around him, for he's telling on himself on a lot of things.

Like I was telling one of my friends, these are the things that have been handed down to us, generation after generation. This is why people live in harmony. They lived with one mind, and this is why, today, we try to bring that back to the young people.

We use that word *"quietness."* This is something that is very important to you people. Face the problems. Live with quietness, 'cause the young people are the ones going to have to hit these problems. And some of us won't be here to see it happen.

MARTIN LEARNED *INÍLA* FROM HIS GRANDPARENTS

Martin spoke of *Iníla* from personal experience. His grandparents had taught him long before it was revealed to him as the Third Commandment in his vision. *Iníla* was a distinctive family gem among century-old Charger family treasures.

A glimpse into the home life of Martin's maternal great grandfather, Chief Charger, from *The Biography of Martin Charger*, illustrates his quietness under challenges by another man for his wife:

> The Chief was known by the Indians as a great humanitarian, a righteous man, never known to offend his fellow tribesmen. He was said to be generous, be possessed of patience, endurance and fortitude. A story is told of his home life: His wife went after water and Charger was in the tipi with some guests. Someone called his attention to the fact that a young buck was courting his wife and attempted to incite Charger with jealousy.
>
> Charger remained silent and when the guests had gone and his wife had returned with the water, he told her to cook some good food. When the food was ready he invited the young man who was courting his wife and when they had eaten the food and the meal was over, he got his best buffalo horse and asked his mother to pack all the clothing his wife would need. Then the Chief got together some clothing for the young man, packed it all on the horse, and told the young man he could have the wife, the horse and the clothing. Indians say this trait in Charger was unusual. He did not get jealous and beat his wife, but wanted her to be happy. He became noted for his attitude toward her in this instance.[88]

88   Martin Charger Biography by Samuel Charger, South Dakota Historical Col-

Martin also personally demonstrated *Iníla*, reflecting the slow transformation from the *hokšíla* (young boy), who once terrorized White boys on his reservation into a spiritual elder who embodied quiet patience to his community.

MARTIN HAD A HARD TIME IN SCHOOL

Martin said, "I had a hard time at school because, at the beginning, I had to learn how to speak English. I remember when I first went to school. I started talking Indian to the teacher. I'd get in trouble, and so after that, I had a hard time with school. I've always blamed that teacher, trying to tell me something with the ruler there. I always figured that teacher hated me. I used to have swelled hands. I tell that to my grandfather."

When his schoolteacher struck him on the knuckles with a ruler for speaking the Lakȟóta language in the classroom, his grandfather's stellar advice to him was to be quiet. "Don't worry about that," his grandfather said. "They will all come back. Just don't say nothing, and they'll all come back."

Martin's grampa was right. As early as 1819, Indian boarding schools and other schools on reservations throughout Indian country had inflicted multiple traumatic experiences on the younger generations as part of the government's assimilation plan.

Indian schools were placed under the jurisdiction of the U.S. War Department, which supplied financial support to religious organizations to educate Indians "for the purpose of providing against the further decline and final extinction of the Indian tribes and for introducing among them the habits and arts of civilization."

Indigenous nations from the northern great plains had such deep respect and awe at the spirit of the infant at birth that they selected midwives who could strengthen the character of the child at birth. However, the ancestral pattern of nurturing their indigenous young with unconditional love became challenged by school matrons' cold and sometimes cruel discipline patterns.

It came to the public's attention beginning in the 1990's when educators and others released research findings about the boarding school experience, exposing the violence and oppression inflicted upon the young. Cruel tactics exposed the internalized op-

lection; p. 24

pression and its traumatic impacts upon more than a century of generations of Indian families.

Young Martin suffered a rough transition into the La Plant Day School experience. It was not only the disciplinarian philosophy of the schoolmaster at the reservation school. Antics and taunting of the White children also affected him.

He'd been raised out in the country where elders respected the infant's spirit at birth. He was accustomed to that high level of behavior from the elders at his grandparents' homestead. Since he had no brothers, sisters or other children to play with, he frequently played alone or with animals that his uncle had trapped. He missed the luxury of play experiences with other children.

Once he started attending the La Plant Day School, he became mean to White children, and they began to restrict him from daily recess with the students. They devised a plan where the school's Indian janitor would escort Martin from his uncle's wagon each morning into the classroom. After a fifteen-minute delay at the end of the school day, the janitor would walk Martin back out to the waiting wagon and his Uncle Phillip.

Martin's grandfather grew concerned about him. He said, "Doing it this way, he's not learning much. He's learning to be ornery. He's learning to be mean. That's not the Indian traditional way." His granddad said to him, "You'll lose all the respect we're teaching you."

It took Martin a few years to integrate the wisdom of his grandfather's teaching and the third commandment of his vision into his own life. Reflecting back, he appreciated his grandfather's guidance. During his later years, Martin demonstrated the ability to transcend difficulties with quietness.

"He preached to me a lot," Martin told me. "He said 'One of these days, grandson, one of the best friends you'll ever have will be a White person. You're going to have to learn to get along with them because you'll have to spend the rest of your life living among them.' "Now I know what they mean by that."

Martin went on to say, "I know I was mean, but after I got older, I realized. I start getting wise to a lot of these things. And this is what my grandfather left us. When he told me these things, I never forgot them."

Whenever someone came to Martin to ask his guidance about a conflicting or painful relationship in the community or seek his protection from attacks from others, his voice of deepened experience would encourage them not to respond to vindictiveness from others.

He would expect those who became targets of gossip and slander to "brave up." He would tell them to pray about the situation and rely upon the Grandfathers to resolve the problem instead of degrading their own behavior. Emotional reactions to offenses might cause further eruptions and even physical attacks.

"Just don't pay attention to that" Martin would say, indirectly referring to the vulnerability and weakness the individual had allowed himself to inadvertently slide into.

"Today's people disappoint easy." Martin would say. "It's not like the old days. People were strong in them days! They didn't let little things get them down. They would just laugh."

Although he expected members of these communities to be strong enough to ignore others' criticism or attacks, generations of alcohol consumption and the consequent cycles of abuse that had run through too many Indian families made some vulnerable to challenges. It was hard for many who were in recovery from addictions, to ignore challenges and harsh comments of others. They appeared too much like threats to their manhood. Some had lived with oppression so long that they had internalized it and inadvertently began to use it on others. Cultural and racial conflicts had become the bedfellow of many, making them vulnerable.

Not everyone was prepared to understand or accept his sage advice that we never defend ourselves. He also asked his drivers and his friends never to defend him in the midst of conflict when they drove back to the reservation. Fewer still understood his wisdom of never taking sides in ongoing eruptions between others.

He would go on to share a few positive words of encouragement with them before dropping the subject. "You must be doing something good or they wouldn't notice you. Don't worry about it. Don't say nothing. Someday they'll see where they went wrong."

It was common for some to perpetuate conflicts and power struggles. The concept of the warrior in traditional culture as it transitioned into today's contemporary Indian world changed. Contact with European Americans changed the role of the warrior. Some went to war in service to their country. Others rose to protect their traditional way of life, such as with the American Indian Movement.

A warrior learns at an early age about the goodness of his peoples' cultural values. They develop an attachment to ancient customs for protecting their people with honor and respect, especially for the elders. Listening to elders help to enlighten their mind and stimulate their ambition. They learn at an early age to not just learn, but also narrate the legends of ancestors, the true stories of deeds done in the past by their people.

They learned to show generosity to the poor and reverence for Great Spirit. They also learned to be patient, never quarreling with others, demonstrating courage and bravery. They learned to seek skills in spite of danger and hardship. They grow accustomed to being alone, unafraid of the darkness and endure hardship without complaint, to endure privations, fasting without food and water, running without a rest, traveling a path without losing their way, day or night. They prove their courage near a hostile camp with perseverance and self-control. Nowhere was there any training to be hostile or kill and maim with a vengeance.

With a special measure of patience, Martin subtly instructed his community that if they don't speak ill feelings towards loved ones or community, or about them behind their backs, they wouldn't become a personal obstacle to the harmony they were seeking in their own lives.

He also advised them that when someone is preparing to go up on the hill on *Haŋbléčheya*, or into the Sun Dance arbor to *Wiwáŋyaŋg Wačhípi*, we don't say anything to disappoint them. We don't make them feel bad or argue with them.

Almost every member of Martin's communities was either preparing to go up on the hill for Vision Quest or into the arbor to Sun Dance. Since Vision Quest and Sun Dance commitments extend through the entire year, it seemed essential to learn not to say anything to disappoint or hurt anyone at any time. It also became important not to react to others who had not yet learned or internalized this commandment, Iníla.

Martin discouraged gossip in the community. Patterns of jealousy, judgmentalism and racism fueled cycles of anger and rage, reflecting layers of unresolved grief in the lives of some. Gossip seemed almost like an addiction to some who reacted to the sensationalism of new rumors with great excitement. Spreading it gave them the attention and recognition they seemed to crave from their community. Verbal threats, intimidation, shunning of the victim were some of the tools of this addiction.

Martin had faced a number of attacks over the years. More than once, members of his own tribe verbally abused and publicly humiliated him. They accused him of leaving the reservation to help others when his own people were in need of help.

Medicine Men of another reservation blackballed him for doctoring people off the reservation, accusing him of profiting from it. Another Medicine Man who'd previously been his friend and helper, slandered him in an attempt to take over two of his Sun Dances. A small group of misguided Lakota men conspired to shut down a Sun Dance ceremony in Oregon accusing him of allowing Whites to dance, stating that all Sun Dances needed to return to South Dakota.

The difference with him was that whenever he was criticized or abused, he would empower himself with quietness. Watching him maintain silence in the midst of trouble, others could almost feel his heartache as he lapsed into periods of silence.

He was also silent when Sun Dancers misbehaved or relapsed, causing sorrow and disappointment for their family and community.

"People don't behave" he simply said. "They don't treat each other right, but I don't say anything."

Some of Martin's biggest disappointments came from Sun Dancers who brought anger, jealousy or racism into camp and used it on one another at ceremony time. After 1988, he began sitting over by the drum during ceremony instead of with the helpers and dancers so he wouldn't hear their comments. He never personally singled out or publicly scolded any individual, but he would take time to speak to the group. He would remind them to leave their jealousy and hatred outside the gate when they came. He would talk to them about showing respect for one another.

Martin knew that *Iníla*, or quietness, does not work alone. Intertwined with other traditional qualities, this invaluable First Peoples' perspective of conflict resolution becomes the remedy for family and community harmony and eventual world unity.

INÍLA AT A DEEPER LEVEL

Before the Sun Dance ceremony in 1995, Martin spoke to a group of dancers about how spirituality grows throughout the year interconnected with the Sun Dance. He shared at a deeper level about *Iníla*:

> Leading up to Sun Dance, we walk into Sun Dance with *Iníla*. It is not just at Sun Dance that we practice our spirituality. All the preparation throughout the year that leads up to Sun Dance is not separate from Sun Dance. People separate the preparing when it is interconnected. They do their sewing and other preparation to get their spiritual items together, while they prepare themselves spiritually.

He reminded his community that it is not enough to pray. We pray, but we need to remember the other side of the equation that balances it, which is listening. We can sit in stillness or *Iníla*. Everyone thinks *Iníla* is just not arguing back and holding our tongue, but it is more about putting yourself aside and listening in quietness.

He expressed how times are hard for people and being kind is very important. To prepare for what is coming we can learn to be positive and compassionate with one another. This is not a warrior time. It is *Iníla* time. People may be tempted to take offense easily, but we can instead see where others are. Are they in pain? Are they overburdened?

He spoke of how sometimes, people want to be reactionary, but that is not okay. Everyone needs to focus on being centered and balanced. People want to fight too easily but we can find the quietness within and not be so willing to be offended. He expressed:

Even the warriors were trained when to be and not to be. They also needed to be family men. People think warriors were always a warrior but they can't survive like that. It could bring sickness to be like that all the time. So there is a time for that.

He cautioned many that it is time for us to have compassion instead of calling people on their shortcomings. It doesn't mean we feed their shortcomings. It means we have to be in a place where we have compassion so we can focus on their abilities and gifts and help them focus toward the positives.

His comments were reminiscent of David Gehue, Spiritual Counselor for the Mi'kmaq Nation who spoke with the universal voice of elders at the 1992 United Nations Cry of the Earth gathering:

> All the prophecies from other nations now coincide and complement each other. It is time for us all to stop blaming one another, heal from our wounds and move forward, for the survival of the world, as we know it, lies in our hands. We must seek out and absorb the wisdom of our elders and use it for the betterment of others.
>
> The Great Spirit left a clear and legible path in North America with petroglyphs and natural monuments. This knowledge is kept under guard by our elders and only entrusted to those ... people who abide by the natural laws of the Great Spirit: respect, honesty, sharing and caring. Without each one of these, the others do not exist.

DEAN BARLESE LEARNED QUIETNESS FROM MARTIN

Paiute Circle Dance singer Judy Trejo's nephew Dean Barlese was one of Martin's lead Sun Dance singers. From Pyramid Lake, Nevada, he met Martin in 1980 and began to learn the value of quietness from him.

He spoke of how Martin and his grandmother Louise Billy had instructed him to handle negative behavior from others:

> We started learning spiritual things once Martin came through. I didn't know about Lakȟóta ceremonies but I started learning then and we went to ceremonies with him.
>
> In 1983 we went on the hill up over Reno. Right now, there is houses all over the place there, but they put us on the hill in Martin's altar. That was in September 1983. I picked up my Pipe and went on the hill first thing. It was good. It was a good experience.
>
> Martin said, "Just use my altar. Sometimes I may not be around or I may not be able to help you guys out. But use my altar. Use my colors." And he gave directions how to set up it. So we set his altar up. So once in a while we still use it. Not too often.
>
> I remember going to Portland in November 1983 and he was staying with Judy Standing Elk. And Martin started vis-

iting with me. And he started telling me, "This is what you saw when you were on the hill.' And he said, 'This is what you need to do."

I never told people I was Two-Spirited until he started to tell me.

"You got to tell people what you are," he said. He started telling the tradition behind it. This is what you do. This is what they do.

I was still in the closet. It was really tough to come out. Martin directed me in all that.

He said, "You didn't have to go on the hill for it. It is just something that came to you. You were born with it. You weren't taught it. You didn't learn it anywhere. You were born with two spirits and that is just how it is. It is a gift from Creator."

He continued, "And very few people are truly gifted like that. Very few will follow that way because it is so tough and so hard to follow."

The quietness, like I was saying here, a lot of people say things and being two spirited, they say a lot of worse things. It gets real bad. But the quietness, it helps me out. It keeps me going.

Martin said, "Don't worry and don't pay attention to anyone else. Just keep going and doing what you got to do."

Gramma Louise Billy said "Don't listen to nobody. Just do your work. That is God's given work you are doing, so don't listen." She said, "Just do your work. The spirits will help you and they will protect you."

To me that is quietness, not to listen to nobody but to keep on doing your work. It is really difficult. As spiritual people, we are not to worry about what the people say. But if we are still learning, it will take a long time to learn to walk in quietness.

Every time you lose your temper or start saying things about other people, that is your learning too. It may take a long time for you to learn to keep your mouth shut. When you are still learning, you can get in more trouble than when you started.

They would repeat it. "Keep your mouth shut and you won't get in so much trouble."

A lot of people, I kind of laugh, because they have been walking on this path for years and years and they still get themselves in trouble. They haven't learned how to keep on going and not worry about what others do or say. Sometimes you have to say something but sometimes that spirit takes care of you so you don't have to worry about it. Just keep going.

Then I started learning our own Paiute ways and the things that you do over here in this country. I started dealing with remains and funerals. I learned how to dress bodies, and learned how to get people ready for burial, going into the mortuaries and physically dressing the bodies. How you are going to put their clothes on forever and get them ready for their burial for the last time people are going to look at them. You are going to try to get them dressed the best that you can.

And it gets tough sometimes. We find bodies that have been dead for a while and it gets tough. We have had to dress bodies when there were already maggots on the body. They have already starting to decompose and it does get tough – hard to do. But it is just the work that you do.

Like Martin was saying, it is a tough lifestyle to live. It is just the work you do and with different tribes, they have different traditions that you use to pray with. And that is just one of them. You start learning to deal with human remains and you start bringing them home and people start relying on you and you start bringing remains home that are 2,000, 3,000 and 4,000 years old and reburying them.

That is part of the two-spirited tradition. Plus praying for people. People ask you to pray for them and you have to go and wherever you are asked to go, you sing at funerals and you are sometimes the last person that looks at their physical remains. And you have to wrap them up and make sure their face isn't showing when you close the casket the last time. And it is pretty difficult to do all that.

You are gifted to cook, do beadwork, I see a lot of two spirited guys that do basket work. They do all manner of work that a woman does. Sometimes better than a woman would do. Women especially get all upset because you can cook better than them, do beadwork better than them, sing better than them.

They joke around. "Well," they say, "what do you do? Is there anything that you can't do?" They are teasing you too.

Martin is the one that first showed me that I had to come out of the closet and be who I truly was and start following that road that is set down for someone that is two-spirited. It is not sitting at the bars getting drunk. I always say "You guys want that. You can have it. It is too much work."

Martin was always joking about different things about that. He would catch me off guard sometimes and he'd look at a guy and look at me and do his pointing at him and then he would laugh. He liked to tease like that.

Then he would say to them, "Well, this guy makes the best fry-bread that I know." He was bragging about my fry-bread and cooking. And he starts joking with other women, "He makes big plate-sized ones, not a little one with a hole in it." Some would get all upset over that when he would say that.

He taught me about who I am. But the most important thing he said is, "You have to learn this on your own, from your heart. Whatever your heart feels, that is probably a good thing that they are trying to show you. As long as you are going to do this work, whatever is in your heart, they will show you and let you know that it is something that you should do. You will know. You have to experience a lot of things."

And then he said, "You will be alone all the rest of your life because you have a lot of people to take care of. You will have a lot of friends, but you will be alone."

And he said a lot of things spiritually. "Spirits will take your life." Or, "they will take your health from you and you still got to go on and do your work. That is the sacrifice you give to help people."

He said that for himself too. They took his health. If you look at a lot of Medicine People, a lot of them are sick. A lot of the real Medicine People are sick and having a tough time with their sickness, but they are still going out and helping. They understand that and they don't cry around about it. They know that is just how it is. You can't change that.

That is the other thing he said, "You are made to suffer, but that is part of your sacrifice, how to help other people." So he taught me not to feel sorry for myself and just keep going and accept whatever comes.

MARTIN WAS QUIET WHEN HE WAS ATTACKED

Dean Barlese witnessed a Medicine Man from another reservation put Martin on the blackball list for conducting ceremony to doctor people off the reservation. They had seen lighter skinned breeds dancing at his Sun Dances and thought they were White. So they accused Martin of allowing Whites to Sun Dance.

Martin had learned to accept people of all colors as supporters at Sun Dance when others preferred the dances be closed to non-Indians. But he had only accepted Indians into the Sun Dance altar. Dean shared:

> I remember when he was black-balled. There was a lot of things going on between Martin and different people. And I know there is a lot of things that happened when Martin left Mt. Hood Sun Dance and started Four Nations Sun Dance. And we stayed away.
>
> But it didn't take me long before I said, "I'm going to go and see Martin at Four Nations."
>
> So I just left. Didn't tell nobody. We went with Margaret Jackson. They had been going there for a while. People were saying things against him, but I went to that dance and I never stopped going.
>
> Martin was really happy when I showed up. We sat down in his trailer.
>
> John Brave Hawk said, "I'll have you lead sing."
>
> One morning, Martin said "Let's have breakfast." They sent runners over and Martin said "Oh, they can go without you."
>
> We talked for a long time in the trailer. Just private stuff between me and him and what was going on and what he felt. I know he was really happy I showed up. I never told anybody about what was said. I still won't talk about what was said between us. But I know he was happy when we talked.
>
> He had tears in his eyes when we talked. I don't know how many rounds they went through. It was noon time before we got done visiting. We sat there all morning. There is a lot of emotion that he let loose.
>
> Just jealousy. That is all it came to be. That is how it is, even now, especially here where I live. There is a lot of jealousy, and I say, 'Whatever.'
>
> I just keep on doing my thing. I know what he probably went through. You watch different families turn their back on you. You thought they were your friends, but you have to just keep on going and not worry about that.

WISDOM FROM ED RED OWL

The late Sisseton-Wahpeton tribal leader Ed Red Owl, who had learned *Inila* from Martin, discussed how difficult this was from his own personal experience to follow these instructions after three decades of abuse working as a grant writer and program officer with his tribe:

> Today the Sisseton-Wahpeton Tribe is, corporately at the wealthiest time in recent history because of our economic development ventures. It has been very good for us, but with it has come much envy. There has also been an increase in alcohol and chemical dependence with specific reference to methamphetamine. And so today we have much jealousy about money, and much jealousy about an alcohol and drug free way of life.
>
> The key then in following in Martin's footsteps is not to answer back and to endure those pains that are inflicted upon us. We are taught to point out, "Yes, we are not going to respond to it but we are going to continue on the road we walk on."
>
> So that is our challenge today is to not answer the hatred, not answer the jealousy, not answer the personal assaults and slander, but to continue on. We have the means to respond to that financially, police wise, in terms of political and clout, but we are choosing not to do that. We are choosing to say to groups or persons, "Well, that is your prerogative in a free society. However, we are not going to answer. We are going to continue to do good."
>
> I also recall back to the time I was putting a house together for my family, and there was a lot of jealousy about it. So at a Sweat ceremony, Martin was there.
>
> He said "Do not answer any of it. Complete your house. Do what you have to do. Don't respond to it."
>
> We have tried to live that way. So that is a part of the challenge today is to continue walking on that road. Therefore, the ageless and timeless virtues and values need to occur again. So the most that those of us who are older need to fulfill those basic teachings is to constantly reiterate it, not so much in word, but in action. That is the challenge to follow the commitment, and that is a very difficult thing to do.
>
> That, I would say, was perhaps one of the greatest attributes of Martin High Bear. In those few instances of slan-

der that would be directed towards him, he never answered back, and that is very difficult to do.

Presently I have been self-employed for many years and in the community, there is always much jealousy with regard to that. The other side of it is I have many responsibilities financially, not only for my children but also my grandchildren.

My immediate family here is 85 people. That is my immediate family. And I don't consider myself as a leader or a head of that family, but I consider myself as a provider for that family and not just financially but also moral support, always being there for them and doing what I can.

And they also bear that brunt, so I always counsel them "Don't answer back. Continue doing good. If you become preoccupied in retaliation, or meeting blow for blow, it will absorb you. It will consume you. It is more preferable for you to continue doing the things you feel you have a vocation to do in life. Just continue doing good." And I think that is a very key fact of life that we learned from Martin's third commandment.

I think from the oppression when a soldier or scout killed one's grandfather and raped the man's wife and threw the children in the fire, that is how we learned to do those things. And I think part of the deprogramming process as a civilized people under this Pipe, is we must learn not to just de-program ourselves but to be free people again, to be free as that buffalo, to be free again and live in that harmony, that kinship.

That is very hard. Not a day goes by in private or public life that we don't have that reaction to this way of life, but again the emphasis is to not answer.

One of the things I remember Martin saying was "You don't use the sacred Pipe to hit people over the head. You use the sacred Pipe to pray for them, to remember them in a good way and have that good feeling inside yourself."

And that is what I remember about that teaching. And so I think that he had a difficult time with us, but there are a number of us alive that are trying to live that way.

DR. ALFRED BIRD BEAR OBES STORY

Dr. Alfred Bird Bear Obes (Owl Ghost or *Hiŋháŋ Naǧí*) was a German trained medical doctor who lived in New Town,

North Dakota for many years with his wife Iris Bird Bear from Flandreau, South Dakota. He remembered Martin:

> I met Martin not only two, three, four times ... so many times that Martin High Bear became a fixture of my own life, an imminent fixture of my own life. Therefore, I am glad, happy and honored to have something recorded about him. I am glad that somebody took up the task to write a book about him.
>
> First and foremost, I want to say that Martin was a very eminent man. He was what American Indian people themselves would call archetypical. Skinny Medicine Man in his figure, in his behavior, in his demeanor, in his manners, and in his doings and actions he always portrayed an old-time Medicine Man. That he was what other Indian people, insiders, saw it as a doggone skinny man they saw it as a sign of a quality because many old-time Medicine Men fasted for a long time and they turned out to be just as skinny as Martin High Bear was himself.\
>
> And when he stood there with his little skimpy smile on his face saying nothing, waiting to go into a Sweat as skinny as he was, everybody knew they dealt with the real thing here. So we went happily into Sweats with him.
>
> What other people hoped for and needed to have some evidence of a spiritual presence, Martin High Bear never needed. Everybody saw it. Everybody felt it. He was the archetypical old time Indian and somewhat opposed to bells, whistles and pageantry that not only Hollywood, but modern-day Indians seem to wish and expect.
>
> He was the entire showman. He was not presenting himself. He had no ego. He had no blown up inflated ego which had to be defended at all times as we see it with so many people today, becoming a big burden and an 800-pound gorilla on their back, having to defend their ego at all times, making all kinds of difficulties for their life. Martin High Bear never had that so he did not need any pageantry. No bells and whistles. He was just there.
>
> The spiritual presence was there too, day and nighttime. It did not matter. He didn't even need a ceremony to have the evidence for it or darkened rooms or darkened closed up windows. Only then things would happen. No, that was happening daytime. Things would happen at high noon what-

ever. So we have seen him in silent effective action whenever we called upon him.

We called upon him for many different doings – Sweats, ceremonies, fastings. I myself fasted under Martin High Bear for four days and four nights. It was a very encouraging and happy fast even though it was hard and I was myself only clothed with one single skimpy little breechcloth. Otherwise I was naked and had one blanket which I gave away afterwards. And Martin watched over my fast in his non-showy way, humble, smiley, with the input of a great Medicine Man he was.

Many of my friends relied on him too. He seemed to be portraying that image to many other people too, but as so often in life, a good horse. There is a Hungarian saying, "A good horse throws up a lot of dust." And he was a very good horse throwing up a lot of dust even though he tried to hardly be noticeable.

But word gets around. So when you are good you get punished for it. That seems to be the case wherever you go around the whole world really, so this Hungarian saying means that when Martin High Bear was so good, so beloved, so cordial, so harmonious, so beneficial of a man to many people, to the various tribes too, he became a thorn in the side of mischief makers who tried to portray him as a Medicine Man who gives everything away, who gives too freely, who is a sell-out.

I have heard of some internet and e-mail messages that were negative about him, but one can forget about these messages altogether. Only apparent mischief makers who did not even identify themselves put it on, being obviously jealous about him when they had nothing to offer of themselves besides greed, meanness and despicableness, throwing poison in the pond, or trying to poison the well.

Martin was indeed a wellspring of goodwill, of true tradition and Indian spirituality. Therefore, it was very sad to see that he was such a humble man, so much non-showy, not so much against showmanship that he was targeted by a few whom we don't even know, who are clearly unidentifiable, who hid somewhere in the bushes not being identifiable by any means shape and form but he was targeted by them.

So the good saying goes, "a good horse throws up a lot of dust." They try to cast doubts on his wonderful experience not only amongst Lakota people but throughout so many Indian nations from coast to coast."

Martin High Bear at Green Grass.

CHAPTER 10

THE FOURTH COMMANDMENT:

WÓWIYUŠKIŊ

THE PEOPLE SHALL LIVE WITH HAPPINESS

With the soul of a storyteller, Martin could move listeners through time and space back to his meaningful growing-up days in LaPlante, on the Cheyenne River Indian Reservation. He frequently reminisced about his early life as a *hokšíla*, or boy, out in the country. We could almost visualize him on a childhood adventure, howling with his coyote pup on a distant hillside, picking chokecherries with his gramma, digging *thíŋpsiŋla* (wild turnips), and then watching gramma braid them together to dry for the winter.

We could see him sleeping under his gramma's chair at the New Year's Eve celebration at the church hall, acknowledging the elders who came to visit Grampa Samuel Charger, helping Uncle Phillip fill the cellar with enough potatoes and jerked meat to last the winter.

Martin's early days are in stark contrast with that of the generations since the 1920's and 1930's. He alluded in many of his talks to the difficulties today's families and communities face. He told stories to demonstrate a better way to live and happier times ahead, suggesting his Indian people choose to step onto the Red Road of Happiness.

One of those occasions was in 1995 at the Nanitch Sahalie, Grand Ronde's residential drug and alcohol treatment facility for Indian youth, located an hour south of Portland. Martin was invited by one of their cultural advisors, Mala Spotted Eagle, to speak to the group.

As we settled among the couple dozen youth and their advisors in their small lounge, his inherent capacity to awaken good feelings in the heart came alive. With his soft-spoken voice, he wove a picture of a time and place, rich with meaning, embodying a gift of hope.

The following sections are compiled from a number of similar recorded talks about living with happiness that Martin shared over many years with many groups throughout the country:

THE FOURTH COMMANDMENT IS HAPPINESS

The Fourth Commandment in our Indian religion is to make people happy, or you can say happiness. They're all happy. When I was growing up, you didn't have to have money to live. My grandparents lived about six miles out of town. They survived off of Mother Earth and so there was nothing that they had to go to town for. I never was in town. I'm always out in the country.

Back in the old days, when I was growing up, we went out to pick wild fruit. I used to go out with my grandmother and pick June berries, turnips. We would go out and pick wild turnips. She'd braid them, dry them out. She'd take dried meat, berries ...

Fall would come and they would butcher. Maybe they'd butcher two cows and they'd get two or three older families to come out and camp around. They'd jerk and dry this meat on teepee poles. They'd dry it out, put it in boxes and store it away. That's the way they'd keep their meat. Wintertime comes, they never went hungry. That's the way they survived off of Mother Earth.

So this is the way I grew up. Nobody starved. Nobody seen hard times. Everybody was happy. So this is why I honor and respect everything, because I was taught from the time I was your age, maybe smaller. I lived with it.

This is why, today, I try to get things to happen. So maybe you want to go back to the old ways again. This is why today we have to bring this up, so that the people can hear it. So the children can hear it and understand it. Somebody never told you this in the books, but these are the main important things we have to learn.

Thousands of years ago, there were as many as two, three thousand living in one big tribe, one band. The big bands were like one great big family. They are all happy. When they talked to each other, they make that sound. There's happiness in that speech. There's happiness in what they talk about. People didn't have nothing to worry about. This is the way they lived. They like to make people feel good so that they can live with this health.

So that is why they live up to this Fourth Commandment. There never was anything said among each other to make them sorrow or to make them unhappy. They never cause unhappiness among each-others. No sorrows. There is nothing there that makes them sorrowful unless a death comes to their relatives.

It isn't like today. Today, people say things to make people unhappy, criticizing somebody, but then they hate to be criticized themselves. They'll criticize others but not themselves, because they feel like they're above all people. Each one of them has the same feeling.

And so this is why today we have to bring this teaching of happiness up, so that the people can hear it, so their children can hear it and understand it. It is one of the commandments: Happiness among all the people. Happiness among all animals. Happiness among everything.

So try to be happy. The old people used to come out of the tipi and say "*Ahó, Tȟuŋkášila*. Thank you for everything! *Philámayaye ló!*" They prayed to Him right away. Meet the day with a good smile. When the darkness comes, people always say the darkness is the holiest part, especially at midnight, when they turn the day into a new day. They always say that's the holiest part of the night.

Ask a spiritual leader, Medicine Man, about a lot of these things and he will tell you what that meaning is, so that you can understand. That is the way to get the help. So it is very important today, living in our everyday lives.

THE RED ROAD AND THE BLACK ROAD

The time is here. There's a Red Road. And so this spirituality that we talk about, we talk about the Red Road. Maybe your ancestors walk on that Red Road. Generation after generation, they walk that Red Road.

But today's people live on promises and don't live on trust anymore. And a lot of these things that's going on today don't want to be claimed. It's not the way of the Pipe. It's not the Red Road, and so there's a lot of things. People walk the Red Road hard. There's sorrow – a lot of sorrow.

God created all four colors of people, all Black, Red, Yellow and White. He created them all to live in harmony together. It never happened. Something went wrong somewheres after that was all put in order. Somebody broke the laws of God.

So there's another road over here. The Black Trail. *Čhaŋkú SápA*, they call it, the Black Road. It's not the blacktop you travel on every day, but they call it the Trail of Darkness, the Black Road of Darkness. There's nothing good in there. There's no spirituality in that trail. All we see there is people who think about what they want. It is the trail of seeing nothing.

That's the trail of the people in alcohol that steal, lie – all these. People walk in darkness. They live without spiritual guidance using the alcohol, hurting people, not respecting others. It's all bad. There's nothing good that comes to them. They walk that Black Road.

The only way you can ever find out about these two trails is from the behavior of a person himself who does ungodly things and doesn't mind God. He does things wrong. He hurts people. With his bad talk, he has taken like the devil. When he does all these, into our believing, then he is a living hell, because nobody will respect him. He has lost all good faith from other people. He shall live with not one friend. That's when you can consider yourself living in hell. All these – they are all decisions to walk on the Black Trail.

And so this is why, today, this hatred, this jealousness, has been created and has been going on. Just like we say, we hate jealousy. We hate hatred. But a lot of time, if you notice that, that's in the air. That's the pressure that we live with today when we should be living with harmony.

COME BACK TO WALK THE RED ROAD OF HAPPINESS

Like I have always told people, the Red Road and the Black Trail is there. Which one do you prefer to walk on? That is up to you to make your own suggestion. You want to walk the Red Road, fine. You want to walk the Black Trail, it's up to you. We're not trying to convert you. It's up to you to make your own decisions. It's up to you to use your own mind.

We're trying to teach what is good to benefit you people and to put it down with respect. There's a lot of happiness that you can show to each other. So help each other with what you want to do.

This is why some of them have made up their minds to start coming over and walking the Red Road of Happiness. So on this Red Road, there's a lot of good things. You can pick it up. You can pray for what you get. You start recognizing other people that are walking with you on the Red Trail. These are the things we have to understand.

So, be good to each-others. Try to live happily. Help one another. If anybody needs help, share it with people. That's one of the biggest studies, one of the biggest learnings, not with words but by feeling compassion. That's very important.

Keep up the good work 'cause there's something down the line. Somebody has put this in your mind and I know that you have worked forward, because we're under spiritual guidance. Every day, twenty-four hours a day, the spirit's guiding you to what you do. So let's live the way God wanted us to live and we'll all be happy and respect and honor each other.

THANK GOD YOU WERE BORN

So today, I hope that God will bless every one of you. Remember, we are all God's children and make sure you know that we're all no different because God created us all alike. We all belong to one family. As you sit here, you are just like brothers and sisters, so live in harmony with one another. Pray together because one of these days, with them prayers, you are all going to have a nice family and you will be happy together.

But learn. Get your education. Behave and be yourself. Don't be imitating others. Don't live that way, because it is very important not imitating others. The whole world is in problems today. Everybody is having problems, having a hard time because they're imitating one to the other. They all imitate and they forgot how God taught them to live.

So as I leave I will only leave one word: Behave and be happy. If you are not happy, nothing works for you. If you don't behave, nothing works for you. But if you're happy and behave, everything will work for you, because everybody talks today about *Čhaŋkú lúta*. Everybody wants to follow the Red Road and you kids can follow that Red Road.

So I am glad to be here with you kids. We will all get together again one of these days. So today, enjoy yourself. The main thing is enjoy yourselves. We can always, most of all, enjoy and thank God that we were born.

Humor is a Lakota Cultural Value

Martin sprinkled life with humor. People would sometimes come to him, serious and nervous, fearful of meeting someone who might know the dark recesses of their past. It seemed the weight of the world was on their shoulders, so after speaking a while, he would sometimes help them relax a little with his mischievous teasing or a little joke.

In May of 1995, close to the end of Dr. Zeff's class at the National College of Naturopathic Medicine, a student asked Martin, "How does one clear their sins before a ceremony?"

Martin hesitated and looked around the room of college students. A coy smile began to form on his face. Then he said, "This is something. There is no medicine made that clears your sins."

The students, who had been listening intensely for the past hour, burst into laughter. After a moment of brevity, he went on to share:

> You put that sin on yourself. This is why we say "behave." You can pray for it, pray for help for what you have done. You have to do something there to have this sin. You can't pick it up in a schoolroom here, or in a beer joint, or dancing class, or anything. You have to do something to perform and to sin. This is why you pray for help and they will give you help. It will let up a lot of your grief and a lot of things. But as far as taking sins away, they can help you, but they can't take sins away.
>
> So study hard, don't overwork yourselves and learn what you can. Give yourself a little time. Pat yourself on the back. Be happy. Leave all sorrows, madness behind. If you carry them with you, nothing of your studies – nothing happens. The only thing that will happen is you will be frustrated – you'll be bored and have a hard time.
>
> So don't have a hard time. Have a good time. Be happy. Be friends to one another. Work together. That's the old traditional way. Help one another, because, like I say, you're all brothers and sisters. No matter what color, what race, you

are all God's children. And we shall live happily with our spirit power.

HE WAS HAPPY

Rufus Charger was Martin's cousin on the Charger side of the family. He recorded his memories the day after Martin's memorial in September 1996. Rufus spoke of the happiness that he experienced in his relationship with Martin that they enjoyed during their growing up years. Their relationship extended through the decades of the 1970's, 1980's and 1990's as they shared ceremony and celebrated life and sorrows together:

> The person that befriended Martin was a guy they called Papasan, Devere Eastman, Brave Buffalo. I met him on skid road row Denver. We became friends and we rode the rails to Salt Lake City, to Elko, Nevada, Sacramento, Nevada into Portland, and Papasan got off there. I went on to Seattle, Spokane, Canada.
>
> When I came back to Portland, "Papasan" [Brave Buffalo] was still there, but he was sick. We were both sick from alcoholism, so he checked into the hospital and I sobered up through AA.
>
> We helped form NARA (Native American Rehabilitation Association). It was struggling those days. We kept that going. A lot of people don't believe Papasan was there, but he came out of the tuberculosis hospital, and he was a van driver at NARA.
>
> He was with us for a year and then he formed his own group, ANPO. For that first year ANPO was in existence, NARA administered the funds and made their checks for everything. After a year we cut them loose, and they survived as a spiritual group and grew stronger.
>
> Martin, in the meantime, came into the picture to doctor Frank White Buffalo Man, and he befriended Papasan. When Martin first came to Portland and started to help out in the Indian community, not too many people had Pipes or Sweat Lodges. There were no Sun Dances in the area. The closest Sun Dance was in Nevada.
>
> He shared a lot of the Sweat Lodge songs, Sun Dance songs, *Haŋbléčheya* songs, prayer songs we use. I was a culture supervisor at NARA so we incorporated a lot of that into our recovery program.

We would get different elders from throughout the region. We weren't just a Lakȟóta group. People from all nations came to recovery. We would pay their mileage.

Martin talked to them too. He would come every time we asked him to help in any way, dedications, ceremonies. There were a lot of them because he was my cousin and he would always come when some of the others wouldn't come.

A lot of them lost their cultural ways. They didn't know about their names, traditional dancing, songs. It was good. There a lot of people helped by having something to believe in. AA would call it a "higher power." It was the Great Spirit and people have to be awakened. They were away from it too long and if they were aware of it, they were ashamed of it, because of Christianity.

He didn't turn people away from Christianity. It patterned another chapter of your life that they could believe in. It gave them hope.

We always talked about respect for each other. Indians were always being governed, so we were taught to respect authority. Most people don't, but respect for each other as human beings, respect for our beliefs, our Pipe, and the ceremony songs, respect for elders, respect for children. These were some of his teachings. I agreed with him wholeheartedly. I incorporated that into my teachings.

I had two visions at Bear Butte. The first one was how to build a treatment program for Native Americans, spiritual-wise. I had trouble with the board and some of the people who believe in AA alone. I couldn't quite convince them that it is all one. But overall, they came to see things as we did, so NARA grew strong, spiritually, with a spiritual face. We kept the face of AA because they were an established spiritual group that was successful, but we put a lot of our Lakȟóta spiritual beliefs in there like the Pipe and talking circle and we encouraged some of the people to go to the sweat lodges and stuff like that.

These were things that Martin helped us with. We were one of the most successful NA (Narcotics Anonymous) programs for recovery. In 1980, Sidney Stone Brown and others, and myself, we went to Louisiana and accepted a national award for the best program geared toward NA recovery. They gave us a plaque and I am proud of it.

But as we grew older and stronger in spirituality, we began to think of Vision Quest. I always kept in touch with

Martin, so when it was time to go, we always picked June 1-10 and made reservations at Bear Butte. We talked to the head park ranger, Tony, and requested the first two weeks of June. Then we could convey cars and go up there and meet Martin there. We would go up on the hill. He would put us on the hill.

Charlie Fast Horse's mom would always cook us a big meal and we would have a big feast and come back to Portland. I would always take a day off and beat it to Eagle Butte to be with relations. That was good.

I was organizing groups to come back to the Sun Dance here at Green Grass. At that time, in the early 70's, it was the only Sun Dance in the nation. So that's where I sun danced. There was only one.

And I think my third year, Chief Frank Fools Crow got sick, so Martin ran the Sun Dance. I forget what year that was. But I helped out at Sun Dance since then, and that has been 16 years as a Buffalo Dancer.

Those were good days. All people from all over. There was an Arizona camp, an Oregon Camp and a Denver camp and a Chicago camp. There were about 200 dancers. They would kill probably about 15 head of beef to feed those people. It was always a good time to be with relations. After that, there were a lot of sun dances that started up.

I attended and witnessed the results of some of his ceremonies. I saw some of what would happen at ceremonies, how people were helped. I seen the spirits and I heard them.

He was always poor. When he traveled around, sometimes he would need money. He was stranded, so I would wire him money so he could get to Portland.

He was always a happy guy when he was at my place. We would sit and talk, and visit and talk, about long time ago when things were happening. We would always laugh about our drinking days and Martin's brother, Joe High Bear.

I used to get a kick out of that, how Martin would travel all the way to South Dakota, and nobody would let him drive. When he would want to go somewhere, and two or three people would drive him, like he was helpless.

They didn't know he was one of the best heavy equipment operators. He was also a pretty fair saddle bronc rider. He was a little guy, but he was never helpless. But he would never argue with people if they wanted to do something.

When he would stay with me, we would sneak away. We would tell Ann and whoever he was with that we had to go out. We would sneak away to wrestling matches in North Portland. We would sneak in there and when we got back to the house, an hour later they would show it on TV. So he knew blow for blow what would happen. A lot of people thought it was amazing that he knew what was going to happen. They didn't know we were there earlier. So we had some good times together.

Sun Dance Intercessor Michael Two Feathers Remembered Martin's humor

"Live Happy" was the next one. For some people who were not Indians, they will think, "Oh, those Indians ... they are standoffish. They are stuck up." But that is not true. When you get around Indian people, we laugh a lot. We love to laugh. Once they become comfortable to you. You are laughing all the time.

And for me, that one is probably one of the most powerful. Not that being quiet isn't. They are all equally powerful. But I tell people that humor is a medicine that you can administer any time without having a formal ceremony or ritual. You can uplift their spirit.

Us Indians, we do that all the time. We are always kidding one another. And I truly believe that humor or laughter is a powerful medicine. That was so powerful that the old man brought that off the mountain- that humans are to live life in a better way. Even the White Man learned from their science and beliefs that people heal quicker if there is humor or happiness. So I always try to keep people laughing or tell a joke.

Martin used humor a lot. People ... it would startle them. People go to a Medicine Person and he would say something funny and they wouldn't know what to think.

One time we were sitting there at Sun Dance camp. We had those porta potties ... and a lot of people ... and they weren't pumped enough! That is just part of it, and he says 'I am getting kind of nervous going in those now, because they are so full and because I am kind of like this...' [made a gesture]. And there were men there and a couple of women and they turned bright red because we just carried on.

Martin said, "we can get a rubber boot and people can push it down to make room."

That blew my mind when he said that! For men that is one thing. But you know, he didn't laugh big, but then he laughed and made that big smile that he had. That just blew my mind.

There would be other ways to say it and get the same point across but to use that kind of a physical motion, and you imagine in your own mind all this and it was just startling and hilarious.

And then we were sitting there at your place [speaking to Rose] and some people had come in there and I always brought A&W Root Beer and I can't remember if he said it first or if I said it.

"Hey Martin, do you want a beer?"

"Yes, bring me a beer."

So I bring out two A&W Root Beers. I hear the stoic Indian Medicine Man and he asks for a beer! He laughs. I haven't drank alcohol in almost a quarter century, but I make that joke all the time. I like to play with peoples' minds ... play with words.

The humor, when you make a joke. The red phone; the old Indian going to talk to the pope, whatever it is, it makes people think. They are using their own mind putting two and two together and figuring it out. That is good.

MARTIN SHARED A JOKE FROM A GERMAN FAMILY

Did you ever hear the story of this little beautiful bird that talks – the parrot? Did you ever hear that story? Well, I'll give you a little story about that little parrot. You know, the parrots – they talk.

This family had this little parrot. He wasn't in the cage anymore. He was a pretty nice parrot and so they let him loose in the house. He sees everything that's happening around; when the kids are gone to school and the mother works and the father works, and they're gone during the day. But evenings, they all meet back home.

So, he thought, "Well, ain't nobody here so I'll make a phone call." So he knocked the receiver off. And he picked up this number that they used. He memorized phone numbers. With his claw, he knew what the number was, so he dialed it. Somebody answered.

"Could you bring up 200 pounds of potatoes?" So he told them the numbers.

"Okay."

And so when the two kids come back, the mother and father came back from work, and they had supper. They was eating supper and somebody knocked on the door. The mister got up and went over. Here was that storekeeper, the guy that goes around delivering groceries.

He said, "I brought you that 200 pounds of potatoes you ordered."'

He looked at him and said, "I never ordered potatoes."

"Well, somebody did. They made a phone call, ordered 200 pounds of potatoes."

So he asked his wife, "Did you order 200 pounds of potatoes?" She said, "No, I didn't."

"How 'bout you kids here?" and they said no. "I guess nobody ordered them."

So the delivery man got mad and went home. He took his 200 pounds of potatoes and went home. And so after supper, the mister started asking questions. "Are you sure you didn't order? Did anybody order potatoes?"

He looked at this parrot. "Did you order any potatoes?" The parrot shook his head no.(laughter) "You sure?" (laughter) "I'm going to choke you if you're lying."

Finally, he got mad and he knocked that parrot around. It was laying down and he said, "You sure???" Parrot said, "Uhhuh." So he got mad at him and took the nails and pinned his feathers to the wall. He was hanging up there by his wings. [Martin made a silly expression on his face and put out his arms to demonstrate the parrot's plight, causing everyone to laugh.] So he was hanging there, and looked around, and the door was open. Down the hallway was Jesus on the wall, nailed to this cross.

And so he hollered across the room at Jesus, "Did you order potatoes, too?"'

MEMORIES FROM ED RED OWL

Ed Red Owl talked extensively about how Martin exemplified his seven commandments. He also spoke about the teaching "The people shall live with happiness," remembering how Martin loved to fill their house with happiness and humor:

Martin was very unassuming when he came to our homes in those years. A very unassuming person. And he would become like a family member. We always gave him his own room where he stayed. Very quiet.

And a good part of everyday conversation was always filled with humor and he would always tell stories. He told about a family from Cheyenne River who were new to the tribal council. They went to Washington [DC]. And he said when they got uptown and they were walking that evening after arriving on the train, he said, they saw a stop light. They had never seen such a thing. Anyway, he said that the sign flashed where it said "Do not walk." So these council men pulled down their hats and started running. And they were dodging the cars. And so it said "Don't walk" and so they ran!

He would tell stories like that with the happiness. At no time do I ever recall that happiness ever involved anything in pornography. It was always wholesome. It was very wholesome humor that he had.

Happiness did not rest on having material possessions or money. That was not the point. Happiness was the social interaction. And most of all happiness came from the extent that we tried as hard as we could to have positive feelings for one another. And I think it pertained to what we talk about a lot here. And that is what are the requirements of kinship.

He often would insist that we relate to each other in terms of kinship.

"This is my brother; This is my sister." "This is my *thuŋwíŋ*, my aunt. This is my *dekší*, my uncle." The feelings that would come from treating each other as we are related, he said "All of it will go back."

And he swiped his arm like this ... [made a motion]. The power that comes from the arm that goes back to your mother, that goes all the way back to the Sacred Buffalo Calf Pipe Woman.

We all have happiness. If we don't have happiness, what is the point of all this? We think we all need to be hermits and wander off and become a mountain man or a mountain woman living all by ourselves, but we are not intended to be this way.

We have this kinship that can sustain itself only to the extent that we treat each other well. That we treat each other with respect and that we do not abuse each other or put each other down. We can treat each other, sure, especially our in-laws we can tease, but it is in a good way that everyone has a function and a role to fulfill in the sacred circle.

Wó-Lakȟota. What he meant by that is the sacred circle is always in the process of being healed. And so brother and sister and nephew and parents and all, even down to those who are first born and they are all a part of the circle and so it makes no difference what has happened.

If someone has lost a family member, then it is not the end of that person's life. We have to have a *huŋká* and have an adoption ceremony and bring someone in to replace that person.

And if someone has fallen by the wayside, someone has committed a crime, we must have reconciliation and bring that person back into the harmony of the circle of the family, the circle of the extended family and take a look at what has happened. And let's forget that and not to allow this to happen again, and restore *Wó-Lakȟota*, that harmony that is here.

That is our understanding. And there are many. We have had family members who have fallen, but we do not forever exclude them. They are family members first and foremost. And what we have learned is that if a person has sugar diabetes, or cancer or some other illness, the ultimate goal is to restore that person to the condition of the act of creation when that person was whole. And that is what I think he was all about. And that is the extent of the happiness that that person has.

Happiness as opposed to the current trend of being very wealthy financially or having material possessions, or being consider as a "gooderati," being glamorous, that those values are in ones' family to the extent that we relate to one another and treat each other well. Everybody has shortcomings, but those are the things we have sweats for. That is why we have reconciliation over and over again. That is how I understand it.

And often Martin and Felix would talk about a time that we came from. A time in that *thiyóšpaye*, in that extended family, living in circle wherein the sacredness was so powerful that it was euphoric, that there were structures in that camp life that were so powerful.

We were reminded of that time and time again when the state highway department would encounter a burial ground and the remains have to be removed, or those remains placed in museums were brought back. And often here our custom was that very few of us have worthiness to handle those remains because we, in a sense, have not de-programmed ourselves sufficiently.

And so we asked two groups of people to do that. One is the mothers or grandmothers and those who are virgins. And the second is the young children. We ask them to take care of the remains, because that group has *wówakȟáŋ* – holiness, and are worthy to handle them, because these remains have come from a time that we have heard of where our ancestors lived in holiness. And that is where our teachings are going.

As I look at the times today, we were programmed to think that that particular condition is an eschatological condition that will happen not after death but after the final times. No, our people lived in *"paradiso,"* a condition of paradise, the paradiso man. And that is what we talked about. We can achieve that if we make a decision to achieve that.

And they talked about that over and over again. They talked about it during the ceremony of the Sweat Lodge. They talked about it in the ceremony of Vision Quest. They talked about it during the healing ceremonies. These were common ceremonies that were being held, whether the ceremony was being held here at Sisseton, or Cherry Creek or Green Grass or Parmilee or Rosebud.

Often, we would sit and marvel at the conversations that were being held with each other and with their peers. So that is what I remember.

Martin High Bear in Minneapolis, MN with friends at Four Winds School, July 1995.

THE FIFTH COMMANDMENT:

ÓKIČHIYA PO[89]

THE PEOPLE SHALL HELP ONE ANOTHER

HELPING ONE ANOTHER IS THE WAY OF THE RED ROAD

Now we come to the Fifth Commandment: The people shall help one another. People in them olden days used to help each-others day in and day out. That's a very important thing. Anybody need help, they all help 'em. So they helped each-others with food, or any kind of help they can. They all pitched in and helped each-others. Whatever anyone has to do, they all share. If one was sick and in need of help, or somebody getting hurt, they was all one big happy family. So that's why they looked up to these Seven Commandments. That's the way they lived.

So I say to everybody, think about the people, your friends, your relatives, before you think about yourself. Think about them. No matter what color, we are supposed to be here on this island to help one another. Anybody need help, they all share and help them. That's the main important thing.

But today, the world over, people live thinking about themselves but not others. A helping hand, this helping hand.... Today, that's gone. Instead, they make it miserable. Someone can struggle with doing something here and they'll all go by 'em. They won't even try to stop to help the guy out. They're not sure how to help, so instead, they live in their little world with a fence around them. They don't let nobody in. They can go out, but don't let nobody in. I'm thinking that is a poor system.

No one else can make it miserable for you. Just yourself makes life miserable. And so all these ways, today, it's too modern. We

---

89   *ókičhiyA* "-po" indicates a man speaking. Women use "- pi" and "-pe."

are His children, but a lot of us don't behave. And I think a lot of people don't respect others. We forgot a lot of good things. A lot of good things have passed by us. So that is one of the things we have to study up on – what things have happened.

THE MOST IMPORTANT TRADITIONAL WAY

Help one another. Share and help one another. Respect them. This is one of the things that was taught really heavy to us Medicine People and to everybody. And so these are the things we often talk about when we spiritually advise people. It isn't what we are. We're not supposed to be proud of what we are as Medicine People. But we are supposed to be humble, live in harmony, respect, honor, and share. The most important one is to share and help one another.

It's not that we're trying to make it good for you. It's you that has to make it good for yourself. Time has come for us to behave, before it gets too late. Time has come when we have to help one another, especially in prayers. We can pray for them. They can change their minds a little bit. And so these are the things that we have to understand and believe within ourselves.

One of the first things we want to learn is not to hate people. That's not the way God put us down here. That's the reasons why they help. If anybody tries, you have a minute to think. You can make things happen in the right way instead of the wrong way.

But most of all, the help comes from our Great Spirit, Grandfather. This is why He has put out laws to his people, the four colors in this world. He has given each one their religion of these four colors, the Black, Red, Yellow and White. He wants us to live in harmony among each other. And this is why we have to understand each other. That way, everything will work fine for us because God will help us.

Help one another is the most important traditional way. People lived with that and this is why, today, we have to teach that. Help one another. Show your respect to one another and have the pitiness. Pity each other. Happiness is the most important thing in there. People never did live with sorrow. Today, people live with that. They kind of form a habit. They will have to get rid of that.

So help one another. It's the old traditional way. Respect one another. Be happy, and everything good will happen. Because the spirits will make it happen, because every one of us has spiritual guidance. That is the old and that is coming back.

So if you use your spiritual power that God gave you, you can do miracles with it because we're a walking miracle. I know a lot of people live happily by negotiating and enjoy life together because life is only once.

HELPING ONE ANOTHER AT *HAŊBLÉČHEYA* CAMP

Some of Martin's happier times are in the reunion atmosphere of his *Haŋbléčheya* camps just before Sun Dance. In early June every year, he travels three hundred miles south to Butte Falls, Oregon to *Haŋbléčheya* (Vision Quest) camp, where as each day brings friends and relatives back together again, the atmosphere becomes recharged with laughter and activity.

In his camp talks, Martin frequently speaks about *ÓkičhiyA po*, the Fifth Commandment: The people shall help one another. Some in the community travel over a thousand miles, and a few travel close to two thousand miles in their annual journey to camp, sometimes arriving in the middle of the night. He encouraged everyone to greet arriving friends with a welcome and help them get firewood and whatever they needed to set up camp. Usually weary after long hours of road travel, Martin would remind camp neighbors to offer a cup of coffee and maybe something to eat.

Every day, hungry to learn more about the ways of the *Čhaŋkú Lúta* – the Red Road, and the Seven Commandments, friends walk from their hillside camps over to Martin's camp in the meadow. They circle around and listen to him advise the ones getting ready for the Vision Quest ceremony. Sometimes he prepares their eagle feathers or prays to bless a new Pipe. He gives instruction and permission to the Sun Dancers who come to camp early to purify and prepare for the ceremonies.

Most of the friends take a full year preparing to go up on the hill for a Vision Quest ceremony and in June they arrive at the camp prepared. However, some don't always have everything they need for the ceremony, so Martin takes time with them. In those talks, he always includes the Fifth Commandment. "It is the Medicine Man's job to help the people," he says. "You can help one another too."

He reminds his community about the importance of treating each other with respect and cautions them to put aside any conflicts while they're at camp or in ceremony. He says, "Leave your hatreds and jealousness outside the gate. We don't need them in here." Then he teases them, "If you still need that when you leave, you can pick it back up again on your way out."

SISSETON-WAHPETON BROTHER JAKE THOMPSON

Jake Thompson was Martin's adopted brother. Later in life he would become the Vice Chairman at Sisseton-Wahpeton Oyáte. Back in 2005, he recorded his memories of Martin, telling stories of the healings from the ceremonies he ran and about the wisdom he shared:

> The systematic teachings of the government and the boarding school systems was to take the Indian out of the Indian and make them think like a non-Indian. Forget your Native ways and your language, your culture, everything. This had a very detrimental impact on our people.
>
> When you're sick as a baby and those songs got sung to you by the grandmother, it can heal you. But we were deprived of the family and it did extensive damage to our people. You see through the addictions today that are rampant throughout the states and into Canada with our people.
>
> The sexual abuse, physical abuse, mental abuse, the anguish kids went through, and all probably not counseled.
>
> There were people who realized the importance and the value of God, the Creator in our lives.
>
> There was an *Inípi*. My brother Nathan who was and is, was at that time an international fancy dancer, world renown international, he beat everybody that danced that style. Nobody beat him. For years, he never took second, always taking first. And it was through the help of Martin and Felix at that time.
>
> Nathan said, "We're going in."
>
> There was Jerry Flute. There was Ed Red Owl. There was Elijah Black Thunder, and Norbert Jones. I was living down in Kansas at Haskell Indian Institute, and came back home. I was anxious to go in.
>
> And my brother, he's seven years younger. "It's good. It's good. Go in, Bro."

"What's in it?"

"You'll like it."

"Is it hot?"

"It's good."

That's all they said.

Ed and those other guys, they all worked at the tribe. Jerry was Chairman. My brother was tribal Planning Director, and they were all going in there.

There was this guy smoking a cigarette down there. Coffee in one hand and cigarette in the other, cowboy hat on. I went down there with my brother, looking around. Each of those individuals, they all had a Sweat Lodge up there on their property. I was just being so happy to come home and see what they had all been talking about.

Unbelievable, it was. He couldn't have been a better person at that time to run that Sweat Lodge, that Inípi. They sat there and told the proper etiquette as you address the fire. You don't throw your cigarette butts on the ground. You don't throw them into the fire. You keep your language clean.

You prepare before you go there for two days. You get your mind ready, and your heart ready. You should always have respect when that Pipe comes in. Everything, the vices and addictions and etc., you leave them over there and you come in and pray. You give everything to the Creator. All of that was a whole new onslaught of information of how to carry yourself as an individual.

Lakȟóta had Medicine Peoples in their families for years. It was outlawed to have Sun Dances until 1978 and the Indian Religious Freedom Act. Prior to that, you had to hide your Indianness, your participation in the Sun Dance, as a singer or a helper, or an intercessor, whatever the calling was for.

People in the boarding school years were hesitant to go. Families that were split on the belief systems, but these people having ceremonies realizing that our health is very important. Well, gradually, there was an advancement of education, and I like to call it renaissance, in the way that the Red Nation people were able to openly and publicly announce that they were Native, returning to the old ways. They ensured the survival of their families and their community through songs, through the language.

When these elders came, Martin High Bear and Felix, we could go in the Sweats. I would come home and get the

Sweat ready, get home by five-thirty, get the Sweat ready and go in by eight o'clock. Come out by ten, ten-thirty. And it was only a small group of those two elders, middle-aged men, my brother and Jerry, etc., some other fellows, and younger of guys like me – twenty-one, twenty-two years old.

What they brought with them was a wealth of information, treasure chest of things that were told to them, and realizing that just doing the Sweat Lodge and then the ceremonies would take place at midnight. So that's æholy hour.æ To him, midnight was the holy hour. That's when these ceremonies started. It was often in Mom's basement and people would come, but not that many, maybe ten people in those days.

Then you're going to have to have something to eat. It might go until three, have something to eat, then you might be visiting until five. Then you're going to sleep for an hour or two and go right back to work. And then you're doing that for four days straight, and then sometimes eight days straight. So between supper break and setting up the fire, you might just go to sleep for a little bit.

From my brother, you could find out how exactly, because I wasn't really here then, and he of course was, he'd just returned from the monastery. He would have been the first Catholic Indian priest in the United States, but he saw and felt the lacking of the spiritual experience, so he took a sabbatical and he took a year of absence to get in touch. This is late '60s, early '70s. He quit.

Those days, the gentleness of the words, the wisdom that you felt from an elder who was, I would say, not afraid to be who he was. Martin explained to us that's the way it was in those old days. You had to hide, and here they were in Dakhóta country, of all places. They were in our home, my momma's home, in our land and nobody could come and penetrate or come and chew you out or you'd didn't have to go to jail for anything.

It was real positive in that way that all the proper etiquette prior to being told by them setting up the Sun Dance, setting up the Sweat Lodge. Getting ready for it was an act all by itself and equal to that ceremony itself because you are preparing yesterday, the day before, the day before, for this day. It was just a beginning, a door opening, and an enlightenment.

To this day, they talk about my brother, "Nate the Great." That's my brother. Nate, nationwide they know just by one name, like Elvis or something. Don't even say their last name. They know. That's the impression that was left with him of how he advanced himself. And my sisters, they don't drink, don't smoke, and haven't for years.

I would say just for myself that if it wasn't for those individuals I probably wouldn't be alive today. I didn't like the boarding school systems, with its repressive policies and people. I didn't like how we got treated, and I didn't really understand the dominant society. And I didn't understand being abused, put down when I didn't do anything to anybody.

In the '50s, we were just bombarded with about fifty or sixty westerns. They were black and white and we always wanted to be there, with a cowboy hat, and a stick horse and everything. But Indians were portrayed in that narrow negative fashion. You know, even today...

I felt personally that we weren't able to express who we really were because we were Natives and never allowed to understand and appreciate the beauty of who we were. So it was really more than a breath of fresh air being educated by someone like those two individuals, something that you just thought would never happen, and there it was here in our home.

I feel so inferior, inadequate, the language barrier and etc., but I'm checking this out. Five, six-year old kid is what I felt like in those days, being surrounded by more knowledgeable family who had positions within the tribe, and Felix and Martin being the elders.

Through all of that, you'd see miracles taking place. People were being doctored. The fellowship was exchanged. Ideas, teamwork, everything that you could write about or talk about from the pulpit, wherever, they were living. People were helped through their visits, just sitting around the table.

When you can sit there from nine o'clock at night until six in the morning, just visiting, you knew that vast amount of knowledge that you was talking to somebody who knew that. For once in your life, somebody knew. It was so valuable to the people.

And you realize, "This is real. They're real."

You have to be on that Red Road, they call it, or the Good Road. It's a lifestyle. It's a way of life when you realize that you are all the time ready to help somebody with these ways. You're in that position to pass the teachings on in your everyday lifestyle.

In the 70's, my brother Ed was put up on the hill [Vision Quest] by Martin and Felix at Bear Butte. My younger brother Nathan was put up on the hill by Martin and Felix. I think Jerry Flute was there.

Through my brother's efforts there, he Sun Danced later. Well, he followed through everything that he was taught, and they put him on the hill out there. And he Danced a few months later in Montana. I think he was at Fort Peck, and he changed.

He later said, "My brothers, they're going to college. They're going into the service. They're doing stuff with the tribe. My sisters are in college and nursing. They're social workers. They're doing these things. Why are we teachers? Why are we nurses? Why are we social workers? We are a family oriented community. It's for the *oyáte* – the people."

The ones who were in prison liked what they saw when they got out. The ones in the wheel chairs, all dressed in black because their husband had died, it brought inspiration to them. They were able to give to the people an appreciation of who they were. "I'm Indian." That come from Martin. That come from Felix.

Martin would say, "I used to be a drunk, and I was a good one. I staggered them streets and I'd go to back alleys and I learned to panhandle. Everything you could possibly talk about, I seen that. That was me."

And you looked at him. I still see him. And Felix would nod in agreement.

That was him, as opposed to Felix, who at eleven or twelve years old, his family knew and how they partnered up. "I know all about," if he would name a certain direction, a certain way, "I know all them songs."

God had really sent him. He was really chosen, and when he sits at that table and he's smoking his eighteenth cigarette looking at you, wondering where these other ones were or whatever, smoking one after another, that guy. He says, "Anybody can be a Medicine Man."

And you'd give him a double look. You kind of shake your head in disbelief, and then you really understand later. This

individual, any individual, can go through all kinds of walks
of life and downtrodden trails, desperateness, loneliness,
possibly without compassion, without a will to live, down
and out. They could rise above all of that, knowing that person is chosen.

You talk about hereditary ways, how altars are passed
down through the family to a selected individual, how it's
earned on the hill. The fifth, sixth, seventh, eighth, ninth,
tenth time.

"Okay, he's for real."

... And you realize the beauty of it because it was something so different every night. And it was an ample supply of
energy that they held – unbelievable energy. Just sit there,
and just go elaborately talk. Ask him a question and it would
be one hour, hour and a half like that. Then he'll tell you the
answer. That was so cool.

At the time it was frustrating. "Oh, I'm tired, I've got to get
up in the morning."

And he'd say nothing ... I cannot say the exact words
how he would then say it, but he was saying, imparting to
you.

"It's okay. It's okay. I don't have all the answers either, but
you can pray about it."

And it might not be that night or that morning. It might
be six months, or a year or two later.... There is the commitment. It is like no other commitment you'll ever have. You
can never figure out that respect and that love, the bigness,
the mysterious part of all that. And you don't need to. You
just accept it.

Jake paused.

We went up to Green Grass and the Pipe that come out.
There was twenty people. It was nighttime and there was no
lights. We were way out there. And there was Felix. There
was Martin. Stanley Looking Horse, Arvol's father. Fools
Crow, John Lame Deer Fire. And there I was.

Dakotas talk fast so they were all kind of sitting on cars,
two, three, four cars. The Sun Dance was going to be over
here. They all talked. They were going to have a Sun Dance
over there, so I helped build it. I said, "I'll help."

And my brother Red Owl would talk fast to me.

"This is what they said."

227

He would probably remember the conversation word for word. He'd tell me and then he'd go back and listen some more. They were all talking about this medicine stuff, healing stuff. And it was still in the infancy stage. It wasn't really public yet.

Then we went into the Sweat Lodge as soon as they brought that Pipe out. They had a big buffalo robe around the Pipe, that sacred White Buffalo Pipe. They brought that in. I think Martin had run that Sweat Lodge. So I was the second to the last one in.

He said, "Bring this in, before you close the door!"

And it came through the door and it closed and there it was. sitting like this, sitting there, and I looked to my right, and it's all dark.

It landed right on my leg and it was so heavy, and I couldn't move. It filled up the whole door space in the Inípi .

And well, I thought, "I'll hang in there. Somehow, I'll work my legs and get one of them out."

I didn't want my legs to cramp up. And later it dawned on me. That's the buffalo robe that the Pipe is wrapped in.

But being amongst all these folks, it was so spiritual. To me that was such a marvel. I'm living through this time and I knew it. I knew it right then and there that down the road, I would be able to look back and talk about it to anybody. It was history being made, like Wounded Knee or something, and I was there. You value and treasure that experience, and realize that through their efforts and their love for the people, their love for these ways, that they had truly helped families.

It was not only here, but the advancement to other races. As they talked, we understood that we're all the same: The Black Man, the White Man, the Yellow Man, and the Red Man. Knowing that wholeheartedly, embracing that way, we're different colors, but we all have the spirit inside of us.

We're spiritual beings through all of these God given miracles. It just brought forth a way of life and thinking, the humbleness and the beauty and the mysterious ways of the Creator, if a person was open to pray and to talk.

LESSONS LEARNED FROM THE MARTIN CHARGER BIOGRAPHY

Martin's great grandfather, Chief Martin Charger was noted for his neutrality in conflict and acts of generosity to advance peace among conflicting bands during the mid- to late-nineteenth century. He also exemplified how past generations lived to help others during the early treaty days. The chief's son, Sam Charger, offered a glimpse in his father's biography:

> *At the age of nineteen, Charger married a Yankton Sioux girl, named Walking Hail. It was in the same year the treaty was signed at Ft. Laramie, 1851, and Walking Hail with her parents was going to the Fort. They had to turn back on account of sickness in the family, and after they reached the Sioux camp, Walking Hail's mother died. According to the Indian custom Walking Hail was given to Charger when she became an orphan, and the young Indian was so impressed with the new responsibility given him, that he recalled his father's lecture on generosity and after he had been married a year the Crow Indians joined with the Sioux for the first time in History. Charger then became noted for giving feasts. He made great feasts and invited the Crows while they were in the Sioux camp, and all the older Indians sang praises of Charger. He not only gave feasts for the Indians but gave horses also.*
>
> *During these years, there were many War parties raging among the Rees[90] but Charger, busy with other matters, did not take part in the fighting. Then in the year 1855, General Harney attacked and surprised Chief Little Thunder at Ash Hollow and came to old Fort Pierre.*
>
> *Charger resumed his warlike activities and became very active in getting search parties to go north to the hostile bands and get them to come to the Fort to negotiate with General Harney. This undertaking with the hostile Indians was successful and in the spring of 1856, a majority of the hostile bands came to Fort Pierre where a treaty was made to discourage war parties which were going on among the Sioux, Crows and Rees. During the treaty, Chief [Bear] Ribs came to the Fort with two rascal Indians who had killed a team of oxen on the Ft. Laramie Train in 1853, and then fled into the hostile country.*
>
> *While General Harney was attending the Treaty, he made ten chiefs from every band to watch the conduct of the warriors, their warring against the white people and the carrying off of white women and children. Many Indians were for violations of these orders from the Chiefs and Charger, seeking to stop the violations, became a friend to Chief Bear Ribs. He was very much attached to the Chief and made feasts to the hostile bands, winning their friendship, but was not successful in this undertaking for peace among the tribes of the Crows and the Sioux. In 1857 the Sioux and the Crow Indians were at war again, and ten Crow Indians were killed.*

---

90 (Arikara or Arika-ree)

Charger's advances for peace was all there was done to discourage war parties between the Crows and the Sioux, and that being of no avail, Chief Big Crow was killed by the Crows in 1860 and in the next year, 1861, the noted Crow Feather, Chief of the Sans Arc band, was killed.

Charger and the non-hostile bands were camped in the vicinity of Ft. Pierre, when news was brought to them that the hostile Hunkpapa bands of the north were coming to old Ft. Pierre to do some trading. It was this same year that a young warrior about the same age of Charger had a remarkable dream. The young Indian, whose name was Kills Game and Come Back, told his dream to Charger. It was: that he had seen ten stags in his dream, all black and as he advanced toward them, one in the lead spoke to him. It said: 'This vision is to be fulfilled by you and to be complied with by all who are members. You and every member is to be respected and feared and you must be united in your undertakings.' As the dreamer looked closer, he said he identified himself as the one who was speaking.

When he met Charger, he told him what he had seen in the dream, and in secret told Charger he would like him to help him and interpret the meaning of the dream. Since new great deeds were to materialize as a result of the vision, Charger suggested that it would take more than two heads to come to a logical conclusion as to what it meant.

The next night a council was held at Charger's tipi. Kills Game repeated the dream. Attending the council were Swift bird, a mixed blood Indian and Four Bear who heard the vision related, and Kills Game afterward interpreted it to mean that the membership should be ten in number and that to be respected by the tribe, they should be generous, not only with food but with their property. Charger agreed as did all the others. "In order to be feared," said Kills Game, "we must be united, and if anyone should steal the wife of any member, or kills a pony, strikes or kills a member, the other members will take revenge"

To this latter Charger did not agree. His argument was that dreams were contrary in their interpretation and should do good for humanity. Kills Game did not agree to Charger's interpretation. As he was a medicine man, considered a hard character, the council went on with the argument throughout the night without coming to a conclusion on the matter.

Another council meeting was held the next night at Charger's tipi, to which Charging Dog was invited, a man of the same char-

*acter as Kills Game, also a medicine man of fame throughout the
tribe. The dream was again related but Charging Dog had nothing
to offer as to the conclusion of the matter. When supper was served,
the council smoked the pipe of peace, and Charging Dog told them
he had given the matter serious thought. He recalled the teachings
of the Indians, that bravery and generosity have broad meanings
and few Indians accomplish their objective – to be recognized as
Chiefs in their tribe. Although the Indian's life was a proud one,
Charging Dog said, at times it ends in a sad plight. 'As a medicine
man, I do not always get riches, but the good I do my fellow tribesmen is something to strive for' said Charging Dog. "'We may be
brave in battle, but as everybody knows we do not live long and to
do each other harm in our camp is very bad. I have seen a lot of it
during my life. I believe the hardest thing for anybody to do is to do
good to others, but it makes their hearts rejoice."*

*Charging Dog commended the younger Indians for their good
intentions, and told them he "could see that your hearts are good
and that for some nights you have gathered to solve this vision. I
have had a similar experience, and I will not do or say anything
that will make you feel bad. Both of you, Kills Game and Charger
have presented your arguments, and life is before you. It is what
you make of your life that counts and I agree with what Charger
says, that we should be generous."'*

*After that speech, the Society was organized, rulings made and
thus five became members.*

*Their Society, the Fool Soldier Band or Foolish Soldiers, was
organized under this agreement:*

*"When the Society is to do some good deed, one member shall
go from tipi to tipi and take anything that is needed, and their
wives shall cooperate with their husbands to the fullest extent.
They (the women) will do all the cooking. Property and food will
be generously given at all times, the old and indigent will be cared
for and in the buffalo chase, one member will go and bring in the
meat to the less fortunate Indians so they shall not go hungry."[91]*

IT WAS IN 1860 WHEN THIS SOCIETY WAS ORGANIZED ...

*While in this camp, the noted Hunkpapa Chief Bear Ribs
was visiting with some relatives, when word was brought
by a traveler that the hostile Hunkpapa band were to come to Ft.
Pierre to do their winter trading and that the society known as*

the Artichoke Eaters had threatened the life of Chief Bear Ribs. The Chief was advised by them not to return, but to stay with the non-hostile band and they would see that no harm came to him.

Early in the fall of that year a messenger brought word that the hostile Hunkpapa band were on their way and would be at Ft. Pierre within the next three days. Charger and his partner, Kills Game, immediately broke camp and went to the old Fort, but left their wives in the main camp, fearing that trouble might arise. They took Chief Bear Ribs along with them for safety.

A band of Foolish Soldiers also pitched their tent outside the Fort to Guard the Fort, as they had also heard that the Indians had threatened the traders. One morning while the [Indian] soldiers were in the tipi eating, they heard someone call Chief Bear Ribs outside. They did not suspect danger as they thought his son had reached the fort and was to meet his father there. They did not hear the conversation with the other party, but they heard Chief Bear Ribs say: "It has happened before, but it will not happen again." About this time, they heard two shots fired in succession. The Foolish soldiers ran out, but they were too late. Their friend, Chief Bear Ribs lay on the ground dead. The other two Indians, Lame Legs and Mouse were seen running toward the hostile band who were on the bench to the north and west of Ft. Pierre. The [Fool] soldier band fired at the fleeing Indians. Four Bear, who was considered a good shot, missed several times. Charging Dog came up with his gun and struck his gun on the ground. He fell, the only remaining Indian they had thought would escape.

The Lower Yanktonai Band was in camp on the east side of the river and tried to cross. Soon as they heard the firing of guns, they commenced to fire at the Fort from across the river. The gun fire aroused the main band of the Sioux who were camped a short distance from the river on the Bad River, and soon all of the warriors from the main camp were charging toward the Fort. About this time, the Hunkpapa Band reached the Fort.[92]

At the death of his friend, Crow Chief Bear Ribs in 1861, by a hostile society among a neighboring band, Chief Charger gave a feast to honor his fallen friend and reasoned with them to stop their plans to retaliate and seek further bloodshed.

The warriors were singing, some were crying and the excitement was high. Bear Ribs was taken inside the Fort for safekeeping. His son was the only person allowed inside the Fort and when he saw his father was dead he was very much grieved. When he came out, his relatives and friends gathered around him as though they were planning a revenge on the members of the Artichoke Eaters who had planned the killing of Chief Bear Ribs.

The charging warriors from the main camp now reached the Fort. When they learned what had happened, they surrounded the Soldier Band and found out what they intended to do. Charger suggested that a feast be made and accordingly food was given the [mourning] band by the officers at the Fort. The Indians all helped in preparation of the food for the feast and before it began, Charger gave a talk, with emphasis on the Indian lecture his father had made, that it was a disgrace to fight among themselves and shed blood.

Charger told the Indians they would mourn the loss of their friend Chief Bear Ribs, but there was a lesson in this death because he had delivered the two fugitives, but had paid with his life. The Indians also recalled a similar incident when Broken Bow Band had a fight in their own camp, and many Indians were slain. The tribes were all related, with the same ancestors and friends, Charger said, and before they partook of the food, they called upon the son of Bear Ribs to come forward and take the horse which Charger presented to him.

At this point several Indians from the Hunkpapa Band spoke, assuring Charger that all would be well and they would not mourn the loss of those who had violated the law of their society. The next day, the Hunkpapa Band traded as though nothing had happened and the two Indians were buried where they fell.

Charger, after this affair, became noted throughout the country for his good deeds, not only among his own tribe but the northern tribes who knew him well. During that winter (1861) Charger and his band, the Sans Arcs went to the Black Hills country where the game was plentiful and made a winter camp. They returned to the Fort in the summer of 1862 and were in camp on the Bad River in the vicinity of Ft. Pierre, when they heard the Santee had an outbreak in Minnesota. Chief Angry Eyes of the Two Kettle Band was with a small band of Indians out on the east side of the river, hunting, when word was brought to them that General Sibley was on a campaign and that all Indians who were not Santees were ordered to get back on the west side of the river. Chief Angry Eyes, with his small band, crossed the river and camped at Ft. Randall. He stayed in camp several weeks, and when his supply of meat was getting short, he asked the officer at the Fort for permission to go out and get a supply of venison as antelope were plentiful in the flat country.

The officer gave them permission and they went up the Creek from the Fort, stopping for dinner. Much to their surprise, a detachment of soldiers from the Fort overtook them. Chief Angry Eyes immediately informed the officers that he had permission to hunt and then return to the Fort. He presented his papers which were given to him by General Harney. He was recognized as a Chief from the Two Kettle Band, but the Captain would not be persuaded to give permission.

Late in the afternoon, the Chief and his party were fired upon without notice, and Chief Angry Eyes was killed. The members of the party then fled, and made their escape, returning to camp on the Bad River. Charger was in this camp, as they got their winter's supply of provisions there and intended to have their winter camp within the vicinity of Old Fort Pierre. The survivors of the party told their story of the death of Angry Eyes, and a council was held.

Chief Tall Mandan wanted revenge for the act committed by the soldiers, but Charger and members of the Fool Soldier band held contrary views on the killing. In spite of this, the Tall Mandan sent some messengers to the hostile bands asking that the Sioux Nation be united once more to make war against the whites. Members of the Fool Soldiers remained neutral. They realized that the situation was serious, coming at a time when the Indians would be incited to hostility, and all that they had accomplished was in vain. With the hostile Santee outbreak in Minnesota, the killing of Chief Angry Eyes, the Chief appointed by General Harney in 1856, the Indians in camp were much agitated. The warriors from the camp went north to the hostile bands and brought back word that Tall Mandan's attitude was favorable and had been accepted. Charger had his hands full, but he still advocated that his Indians remain neutral.

Councils were held frequently by the Fool Soldier band. They made their plea, knowing what their plight would be if they took sides with the hostile bands. But Chief Tall Mandan was not convinced. He had his followers who were determined to make war against the white men.[93]

THE INCIDENT THAT MADE THE FOOL SOLDIERS FAMOUS

While Charger and his band were in this camp, a white man brought word that the hostile Santees, under Chief White

Lodge had camped at the timber opposite the mouth of the Grand River on the east side of the river and with him were some white captives.

The Fool Soldier Band held a secret meeting that night, Charger advocated the organization should unite in their convictions and all the captives should be liberated at all costs, thus putting into practice all that their organization stood for. With the danger confronting their Sioux tribe and their faith in Charger to find a way out of the situation, the Indians agreed to take Charger's advice.

Putting their plan into action, a sergeant at arms, Two Tails, (a Yankton Sioux Indian) and Charging Dog were detailed to collect the food and pelts that could be traded at the Post for sugar and coffee and other commodities to talk with them. Tall Mandan made a strong plea in behalf of the relatives of Chief Angry Eyes. But Charger, determined to rescue the captives at all costs, ignored the plea, and early one morning in November the Indians crossed the river (with the help of the officers from the Fort,) swimming with their ponies.

They were followed to the river bank by more Indians, singing and crying. They thought the "boys" as they called them, would not come back alive and the undertaking was foolish. There would be the sacrifice of their lives for the enemy but Charger told the crowd that "there is only one life and that is short, hence we should do what we think is good."

After the band landed safely on the east side of the river, they slowly climbed Snake Butte, singing the War song as they went, with the crowd watching them. When they reached the top of the Butte, they sat down to rest and signaled "good bye" with a mirror, and then disappeared on the other side.

As they traveled on, they met a band of Indians from the lower Yankton tribe known as Yanktonai Wiciyela, and some of them joined with the "boys" hoping to see what these young Indians could do in war with the savage Santees.

Upon reaching their destination, the camp was visited by a few Indians from the camps nearby, who told them their mission would be fruitless as the Santees were stubborn fighters. But Charger encouraged his men to put their courage to the test and after they had rested for a time, a feast was made, as they knew the hostile Santees fled through a country where the game was scarce. If they were hungry and the feast was set, the hungry Santees would be filled. In this, Charger sounded the keynote of their mission with the Indian tradition: "The skies are red with the blood of the white people and you have fled into our country with some of the white captives. You have done wrong. The Teton

Sioux from the west will not take sides with you and we are here to get the captives."

Chief White Lodge was not willing to give up the captives and each was bent on making the best bargain for his captive. The Foolish Soldier band insisted, however, on their bargain and towards the evening, the mission was ended.

The rescue party started for home, but a blizzard was coming from the north, and the captives were not clothed for winter weather. One of the elder women was without shoes, and Charger took off his moccasins, put them on the woman and went barefoot the remainder of the day, until they reached the Yanktonai camp. Before they reached this camp, White Lodge overtook the party, but he was bluffed and each had to stand guard during the night, fearing that the captives might be stolen.

At last they reached their camp where there was much rejoicing. They were a pitiful sight. The captives were not only dirty, but their clothes were in rags. The moccasins they wore were ill fitting and the savages were much grieved especially for the children. Wives of the Fool Soldier band came out and took the children in their arms and wept. A collection of robes and other commodities was again made and exchanged at the Post for clothing. The wives of LaPlante, Dupree and the Fool Soldiers Band assisted in bathing and dressing the captives in the best that they had. The captives were taken to the fort and after they had rested a few days, they left for Ft. Randall with LaPlante and Dupree, giving thanks for their rescue. They knew that some of their relatives were at Fort Randall and would take further charge of them.

In 1863, Charger went north to visit his uncle One Ghost, his mother's brother, and while there he found that other bands of Indians were much agitated over the killing of Angry Eyes. He told his uncle what had happened and told him of the rescue of the white captives. One Ghost was in sympathy with his nephew's activities and it was not hard to convince him that he should return with Charger to the non-hostile bands.

Charger then heard about his friend's capture of Chief Big Head who was held a captive at Ft. Randall. He went to intercede for the prisoners who were later released. Charger's second wife was also in the prison camp. He found her safe and a girl baby had been born to her at the Fort. Charger stayed on at the Yankton camp during the winter and came back to the Teton Sioux country in the spring of 1864. There he was in camp on the Bad River with other Indians and it was while they were here in the Slim Butte *country that they heard of the battle at Kill Deer Mountain. They at once made haste to get back to their band and the fleeing bands scattered to the four winds. Thus the plan of Chief Tall Mandan to make war against the Whites, took effect and part of the hostile band from the north came back to join the hostile camp.*[94]

CHIEF CHARGER HELPED THE PEOPLE

Martin's Grandfather Shared Other Stories of Chief Charger's Efforts to Help the People and Offers a Reflection of His Cultural Values:

It was the summer of 1864 when Charger and part of the Sans Arc Band went into the Black Hills country to hunt. They came back to the Bad River, crossed the river and camped on the east side in the vicinity of Ft. Sully. That winter the snow was deep and he heard that a small party of Sioux Indians were in winter camp at Medicine Knoll on Medicine Creek. They were facing starvation. Men and women with the children were in destitute condition and Charger with other members of the Fool Soldier band went to the Fort and traded robes for some food. With some pack ponies, they set out as a relief party and every day for more than a week they faced storms. They reached their destination in time, and upon their arrival they found the few families were in dire need. They had had nothing to eat for several days, children were crying for bread, and a few who had left on a hunting expedition looking for game to eat, had never returned.

Charger distributed the food, then he with Charging Dog and Kills Game went to look for the lost hunting party. They found them, (one of whom had a badly frozen foot) and stayed with them until the weather modulated. Then he brought the band back to the Fort where they camped until the spring of 1865. While in this camp, they heard that Chief Spotted Tail was agitated over the routes which were being established through the Sioux country. Charger did not take any part in the matter, and this led the Sioux into battle at the Lodge Pole where 100 Whites were killed. Charger, who always remained in the vicinity of the forts and advocated peace, was often consulted by the hostile Chiefs and their bands which were roaming in the north. They asked his advice as to the conduct of the white men, their aims and other matters.

In 1868, Charger was one of the delegates to visit Washington, D.C. for the purpose of defining the country known as the

---

94 *The Biography of Martin Charger*, South Dakota Historical Collections, Vol XXII, 1946 p. 11-14

Great Sioux Reservation. The president told them that "the Indians were like a fish — nobody knows where they are. They are migrating and the Government wishes to know what country they claim." The Government, he said, would make a plan for the Indians whereby they can be established, and much money had been spent by the government on the Indians in past campaigns.

The Chiefs then told the president what country they claimed and the Government sent a commission with the Sioux that summer. Although Charger was in the Sioux country at that time, he did not go to the Treaty. He was mourning the death of his partner, Kills Game and Comes Back, who was killed by a Santee Indian named Gray Face at Ft. Rice in the spring of 1867, as revenge for the rescue of the white captives in 1862. Charger's friends advised him that since there would be some Santee Indians at the Treaty he should remain at home.

Kills Game had been brought to Fort Rice and died enroute. They buried him in the vicinity of the place where the Pierre Indian School now stands. According to the Indian tradition, when an Indian makes a friend and one dies, they both must die, and Charger was carefully guarded fearing he might commit suicide. But Charger was not of that nature, and although he grieved deeply for his friend his life was spent in doing more noble deeds.

The Fort Bennett Agency had been established at that time and Charger and his band camped near this Agency. In 1869 when the hostile band stole some horses from the non-hostile bands, Charger once more established his reputation for good deeds and went in quest of the stolen horses. He found them in a camp on the Little Missouri and with the assistance of his uncles, the horses were delivered to their owners, while Charger went north to the hostile bands and learned, much to his disappointment that the Sans Arc band has gone to War against the Crow Indians. In this battle 15 of his fellow tribesmen were slain. There was sorrow and grief among his relatives and while he heard them singing and crying, he talked with them about moving back to the reservation which had been set aside for them. He convinced some of the tribe that was the thing to do.

In 1870 Charger was again sorrowed by the death of one of the leaders in the Sans Arc band, Crow Feather, who died that year. The next year, the slaughtering of buffalo and the wild game so plentiful in the Indian country, gave him much trouble, for Government hunters would kill the buffalo for the hide only, throw the dead carcasses away, and there seemed nothing could be done about it. Charger realized only too well, that the buffalo was their chief sustenance and that with this exhausted, the Indians would be subdued. Small parties were making their raids on each other as usual, but Charger did not encourage it. He knew that in time all would stop.

With his band of Indians, Charger crossed the river to the east side in 1872, and established a camp on what is known as Little Bend across from Fort Bennett. There he was instrumental in the building of Log Houses with chimneys and was the first to cultivate the soil. Indians gradually crossed to the east side of the river and followed his example. They helped each other in the building of log houses, tilling the land, raising corn and vegetables, and in the course of time, the community became organized in compliance with the stipulations of the 1868 Treaty.

This new camp was at Little Bend and was the first Indian community in the country. It was a self- help project where some of the Indians settled down to learn the ways of the white man. The Rees were still making raids on the Sioux. Two Ree warriors were slain that year and Charger, being busy making contacts with officers in charge of Fort Bennett Agency interceding for his fellow tribesmen, knew that some perplexing problems were yet to confront him.

In 1875 Charger was one of the delegates sent to Washington for the purpose of negotiation for cession of the Black Hills. While in Washington, every bluff was used to intimidate the Chiefs. They were taken out in the sea at times and held until they signed the treaty. But they would not give up. It was Charger who thought of a scheme. He told the Commission that they were not the only head men of the Sioux nation, but that the majority of the tribe was still in the buffalo country and when they had returned to the Reservation the question of the Treaty would be discussed upon a basis of a three fourths majority. The plan was considered by the authorities and it was finally agreed that Charger was right.

The chiefs returned from the eastern trip and called a Council to be held between the Red Cloud and Spotted Tail Agencies that summer. But due to the three fourths majority rule, the council did not accomplish the mission. However, a lengthy report was made.

In May of the next year, 1876, Charger was informed that General George Custer was stationed at Ft. Lincoln, and the purpose was to launch a campaign against the Sioux nation. The Indians heard this with much distress and Charger called a meeting of a group of Indians composed of the headmen and Chiefs who were requested to intercede on behalf of the hostile bands who were roaming in the Buffalo country. This group met with Custer, a feast was made and the Indians discussed their mission. Custer

*told them that his mission was to discourage the War parties go-
ing on in the Sioux country. After the discussion was over Custer
and the Indians danced. The different tribes took part in the dance
and the Peace pipe was smoked. Short Leg performed the ceremony and Custer smoked the pipe. The Sioux delegation returned to
their reservation, glad that they had accomplished their mission.
However, within a month, the Sioux tribe heard that Custer did
not keep his pledge and they were wiped out.*[95]

ADAPTING TO NEW WAYS

The Martin Charger biography showed how Chief Charger continued to hold councils through difficult times and difficult gov-
ernmental decisions as his people learned to adapt to new ways:

*While at the camp at Little Bend, Charger heard of the Sioux
campaign in the north which was in progress after the Custer affair. He also heard that Military authorities were coming down
the river and in retaliation planned to confiscate Arms and ponies
from the friendly Indians at Little Bend, Charger called some of
the head men and discussed the matter with them. To avoid trouble, they decided that a meeting should be held when the soldiers
arrived, so that whatever action the soldiers took would be understood by the Indians. Word was delivered that the soldiers were
then arriving and Charger, with some of his followers met them
with a white flag. They decided at this conference to allow each
family two ponies. All arms were to be confiscated and it was also
agreed that the Indians deliver the guns and ponies.*

*Charger's troubles were not over. Soon after all their ponies
and guns had been taken, a Commission came to the Agency and
renewed the effort to take the Black Hills from the Indians. The
Indians were told that the Government wanted a lease on the
Black Hills area for the purpose of mining gold and other minerals
on a fifty-fifty basis.*

*The Indians held a council during the night. They knew some-
thing must be done as they saw the guns and cannons were set
toward the Council House ready for an emergency. To the un-
educated Indian the situation was baffling but they proceeded to
negotiate with the Government.*

*Several days were spent in the negotiations for a lease of the
Black Hills. Finally through threats and intimidations the Chiefs*

---

95   *The Biography of Martin Charger*, South Dakota Historical Collections, Vol XXII,
1946 p. 14-18

and head men signed the Treaty because they did not want to be moved to the state of Oklahoma.

Charger then moved to the west side of the river in 1877 with his band and established a camp opposite Little Bend. The Mincanowoju band, under Chief Swan established a camp above the Cheyenne River above the mouth the camp Charger established was known as Kitto honoring one of the first missionary workers who was also stationed there. The band was mixed with Sans Arcs, Black Feet and Two Kettle. Since they were practically on foot and with no means to support themselves, many new dances originated at this camp, among them The Badger Society, Night Dance, The Night Eaters and the Grass Dances. These societies were busy with their dances every night and the Mnicanwoju were invited to join them.

Charger knew they could not continue this for all time. Cows were issued to them in 1878 and it was necessary for the Indians to find range land. The Chiefs held a meeting and decided that Chief Swan should occupy the Cheyenne River and Cherry Creek area. Charger and his band moved to a place on the Cheyenne River where the Agency was located in 1880.

The stock issued to the Indians in 1878 was moved to the new location in 1879 and Chief Four Bear came to that camp that year and established a community known as Four Bear camp. Swift Bird came and his camp was named Swift Bird's camp and Chief No Heart moved to the mouth of the Moreau River with his Black Feet Band.

With his 18 families and their gardens, Charger was busy with the community building. Log houses were built and a herder selected to look after the stock while the other families were putting up the hay. Charger was one of the first Indians to own a Mower and each family helped with the haying. Since the Indians had come from such long distances to the Agency Charger suggested that they receive their rations every two weeks. But this kept them busy traveling back and forth and finally the rations were issued only once each month.[96]

THE CHIEFS FACED THE DAWES ACT

In 1887 Chief Charger with all the other Chiefs from the Sioux reservations was called to Washington to discuss what was called the General Allotment, or the Dawes Act. Since 1880, the

96   *The Biography of Martin Charger*, South Dakota Historical Collections, Vol XXII, 1946 p. 18-20

Chiefs had been engaged in absorbing the hostile bands as they were brought to the main agency in steam boats, taking them into their respective bands and teaching them the ways of the White Man. The Indians did not fully agree with the Allotment Act. The tracts of land which were to be allotted to them were small and as the Indians were engaged in raising livestock, the reservation was more satisfactory for this industry.

The delegation returned from Washington very much dissatisfied. They had at least suggested to the Government what they wanted, and the Commission came to the Sioux reservations in the summer of 1889 and advised by the Indian Rights Association, signed the Treaty of 1889 for the opening of all the country that lay between the Cheyenne River and the White River.

The Indians were to get an allotment of 640 acres for each family head, and persons of 18 years or over would receive 320 acres. Minors drew 160 acres each. Heads of families were to receive farm implements and stock and when a child reached 18 years he would also be entitled to implements and stock.

Chief Charger continued his work for the welfare of the tribe without discouragement. The tribe at times grew despondent, but Charger always cheered them with the assurance that they would soon be on their feet, that he could see they were making progress.

These and other excerpts from Chief Charger's life were shared by his son, Sam Charger, in the eulogy published by the South Dakota State Historical Society in 1946. This eulogy revealed a man rich in qualities that have been demonstrated in many other great Lakȟóta people – dependability, bravery and generosity. Martin was raised with these ancestral qualities. They are interrelated to his teachings of ÓkičhiyA po, that the people shall help one another.

ED RED OWL TELLS ABOUT THE TEACHING

We had a number of people who took that up. I can remember a community member. It was an old man. And he would come to our ceremonies with his wife. His name was Willie King. He and his wife would come. And after they came they gave him this name "He will help the people."

And what the spirits told Martin is that when he was a boy his vocation was to do what Martin did. And this man started coming in his 70's. He has been gone now, but for 5 or 6 years, he took care of the altar.

Myself and Mike and his sons and grandsons have taken care of our Buffalo Lake Sun Dance. They have taken care of that altar for ten years now. They have done that to make sure that the Sun Dance arena and all the materials are provided for the community when they have that enactment of the Sun Dance. It is one of the Sun Dances we hold here.

But *wawókiyA* is the life here. It is what we have dedicated ourselves to. I would say if we receive a payment of $100, we will keep $20 and the rest goes out for what we call our responsibilities for our families and that is the way we live. But yet we always have more than what we need. We have never gone without and it seems to be that to the extent we help others to that extent, we are taken care of.

And the other thing with regard to that is we were told that we should not worry about the means to support ourselves, but if we do *wawókiyA*, we will always have sustenance for our basic needs. And that has been the case. We have had the know-how and in the course, we are compensated for those services. And then in turn our compensation is shared with our families who depend upon us to do that.

It is moving closer to that traditional circle that we once came from. I don't know how much longer. I don't think I will see it in my lifetime, but in due time, I think it will happen again where our people will come back to those camps and begin living that way of life that was once as we say "Paradiso."

We have many stories here and from oral traditions and that is what Martin and Felix and others taught. There is a whole group of people. They are all gone now, but I recall times at Green Grass when they were all camped together there, either for the bringing out of the Pipe or for the Green Grass Sun Dance. I remember Frank Fools Crow, Pete Catches, and John Fire and they would be talking and teaching. And they would never exclude us. Although we spoke a different dialect we understand what they were saying. And they talked about those things and they all had a part to play in these types of discussions and what was going on and what was happening and they were very much a part of those circles."

Martin High Bear traditional dancing at powwow in Coos Bay, Oregon.

CHAPTER 12

THE SIXTH COMMANDMENT:

WÓWAŠ'AKE

THE PEOPLE SHALL LIVE WITH POWER

Martin invariably starts his work and begins his talks with a prayer in his Lakȟóta language to the Great Spirit, his source of spiritual power. This afternoon he translates his prayer into English for those who do not speak the Lakȟóta language. He sometimes has trouble expressing the depth of his feelings and thoughts in his second language, the English language, but his love and reverence for the Great Spirit and the power of the teachings invariably shine through.

PRAYER OF THE SEVEN COMMANDMENTS

Martin usually gave permission to others to audio or video record his talks. This 1984 recording was made in Willits, California and kept by the Clem Wilkes and Yuwach Gleisner families for over a decade. The speech that was recorded includes a prayer about the Seven Commandments:

> Whenever we want to make a spiritual speech or hold a ceremony, we always like to start out first with a prayer to the Great Spirit. Then we come down between heaven and earth and pray to the four men and animals that watch the Four Directions. And so, tonight, we pray to the Great Spirit and these spirits that have worked with me throughout the day and the night. We call the night the "holy night," the "spiritual night that appears."
>
> So I shall say the prayers of the Seven Commandments that have been laid down:
>
> *"Oh Great Spirit, look down upon your children that you have created on this spiritual island, that their prayers shall be heard,*

that their minds will be straightened like You wanted them to be, to walk the Red Road, the road that you have laid down for them.

Oh, Great Spirit, we know we are suffering on this island for some reasons and we are going to straighten them out. But first of all, we never forget about You, by our prayers to You first.

Great Spirit, we always thank and honor You for the Sacred Pipe that You have honored us with and handed down to Your children here on this island. Through this, we have the power, the guidance.

Great Spirit, tonight I want to tape a little verse and also talk about the Seven Commandments that was handed down to us Indian people here on this spiritual island, what the White Man calls North America.

Great Spirit, look down upon our Indian people and I will say the Seven Commandments so that nothing shall happen to our Indian people here on this spiritual island. That there shall be health; that the people be populated; that there shall be quietness; happiness; the help; the power and kindness. So there is the Seven Commandments that was taught to me from my spirits that work with me.

And bring Your Indian people back together with kindness, and see that the Indian people, Great Spirit, that they will be kind, with quietness, among each-others so that they won't have to live in groups like they are today. That our Indian people shall always be kind to each-others in these Commandments.

Great Spirit, guide over us. Watch over the children. Help them in any way with their needs. Help them with good luck, so they can always have good luck on this island.

Oh, Great Spirit, listen to your interpreter, your Medicine Man, as I pray tonight, so that I shall see better days coming for my Indian people. Look down upon us, Great Spirit, so that nothing shall happen to the Indian people here on this spiritual island, that there will be no bad luck, no disasters of any kind.

Now, Great Spirit, You have heard my prayers. Listen to my prayers. And I thank You for praying to You, Great Spirit. Háu! Mitákuye Oyás'iŋ."'

WE GET THE POWER FROM GREAT SPIRIT AND THE SACRED PIPE

Martin's friend, Devere Eastman, also known as Brave Buffalo, traveled with Martin on this 1984 trip and introduced him to the college audience in Willits, California. Brave Buffalo refers to the spiritual power Martin lived with as he introduces him:

He is a Medicine Man, which runs in the blood of his family. For generations, his people have been Medicine People. And I've helped him many, many times in ceremony.

And I've seen ... I know of this awesome power. We have probably never experienced the power of the Great Spirit in that world beyond on the other side. And it's too awesome to comprehend for an ordinary person how awesome this power is. And these people, they talk with God, Great Spirit and their helpers and get instruction.

Brave Buffalo (Lakota) also known as Devere Eastman or Papasan, Sun .

At another lecture on the same tour, this time at the University of North Dakota in Grand Forks, Martin refers to the spiritual powers that are a part of the Red Road and how his people are beginning to return to their "holy and spiritual" ways. More than three hundred students at this university were Native American. A number of them sit in the audience that evening to learn more about their own traditional spiritual ways. Indian religion was declared illegal until the late 1970's, so these ways had been previously unavailable to many of them:

So then came the Power, the Sixth Commandment: The people shall live with power. They had the spirit power in them at all times, day and night. This is what the Great Spirit handed down to the Indian people.

Our ancestors were powerful people because they were healthy. Jump back to the First Commandment. They lived with health. They were strong. They had good water. They had good food, nice fresh air.

They were on the move all the time, running with the good nice winds. And they got their power from God. They have a good standing with God because they prayed to Him. Like I always said, God's power has no beginning and it has no end.

We always say today that when our ancestors were living, they lived a beautiful life compared to what we are living today. And so you know, our ways are different. In the old days when our ancestors lived, they were all together living in a big band. They had all the tipis. Always, in the center is where the chief is and that's where they all have the council fires.

Everything that was said was memorized in their minds, so people never forget. What they talk about, they listen. What they have heard, they go home with it and study it to see what they meant by these words. We haven't got no books with no pages. There was no pencils.

So they studied the great powers that God handed them. It took them many years. They had to search for it. And then they found the power. And they lived with this power, but not the full power. Some of it. So this was what they worked with. That's the way our ancestors lived in a big family under the Seven Commandments that God has given us.

They were pretty powerful. They were holy and spiritual people. They had everything they wanted and they thanked the Grandfathers for everything.

And also they had the power through the Pipe that was handed down to them from the Great Spirit. You know, the way the Indian religion is put together among the Lakȟóta, it is the Sacred Pipe. It was handed down to us from a Spirit Woman. They call her the White Buffalo Calf Pipe Woman, the Maid.

And the Buffalo Nation gave us the White Buffalo Calf Pipe which we still have to this day. So we still have our God-given Pipe on our reservation. That's where the Pipe is. And the boy that's taking care of it is the nineteenth generation to take care of the Pipe. But She never told nothing about how to use this religion. So our ancestors had to dream and vision. This was the way our ancestors lived. That's the way this religion was put together. So this is where we get the power – the Pipe.

And some of the old elderlies, at their age, are now just telling what it really means on this earth. Our elderlies at one time used to change themselves into anything they wanted to. They can change themselves into animals.

In them days, everybody was afoot. Everybody traveled by foot, and so they used to go out here.... There used to be an old lady when I was a little boy. They called her Deer Woman. She used to come out of there with a bundle on her back. She would come out of the house, any hour of the night. They trailed her – her foot prints. She turned herself into a deer and loped all the way where she was going. When she was pretty near there, she turned herself back and walked into the village.

That's the way people traveled. Or they would make themselves into a bird and fly. They could turn themselves into anything they want to, because there were no horses. Later, years later, then the horse came. Spaniards brought the horses into the country. Then horses were in big demand.

But today, we can't. That ... we've forgotten that. We've lost that. 'Cause there are a lot of things that interfere with us today. This is why today our young people are still going up on the hill for Vision Quest. So we thank them for the religious structure which they are bringing back.

Those mistakes, a lot of mistakes have been made. But sometimes they overlook those mistakes. They study those mistakes out and make sure they don't happen again. So these are the things that go into the purification, when you want to go into a Sweat Lodge to purify yourself and get prepared to walk the Red Road. So this is why people go in the Sweat Lodge today in groups. They stick together and make their preparations to do different things – to pray to God, to pray to the Four Directions; up and down – the six powers. And sometimes they pray to go up on the hill.

So it's up to the elderlies to back these young generations who are now picking up the religion and culture. A lot of prayers have been said and a lot of help from spirit power has been given to them. And a lot of these young generations today are living with these spirit power. They see it happening. So do yourself good and do yourself right. It's the only way and that's the way God would tell you to do if He was here tonight. He would recite to you a lot of good things to follow up on, to be a good two-legged and to be God's children.

LIVING WITHOUT SPIRITUAL POWER

Martin explains that the concept of power in indigenous culture is not the aggressive, dominating force frequently demonstrated in today's contemporary world. Instead, it is the endowment of spiritual qualities, gifted by *Wakȟáŋ Taŋka*, the Great Spirit, to empower them during their life of service to the people.

During his travels between the mid-1970's and until mid-1995, Martin crisscrossed the country innumerable times; speaking at colleges and universities, spiritual camps and prisons – teaching the Seven Commandments. Martin also visited many alcohol and drug rehabilitation centers during his years on the road. Some of them were for youth and some were for adults and their families.

With his soft-spoken voice, gentle mannerisms, and fragile frame, Martin captivated the hearts and minds of many as he brilliantly reflected the Lakȟóta quality of power.

One afternoon, we drove to a halfway house located in a brick apartment building in Portland's eastside downtown at LeAnne LeBarr's request. Martin spoke with a couple dozen women who were transitioning back into their community after completing prison time. Drug and alcohol addiction had played a role in their original offense and so they were working on their recovery with a twelve-step program.

They form a circle with the chairs in their recreation room, and he sits down to speak with them, taking off his cowboy hat to say a prayer. Like a father counseling his children, he reminds them why they are in hardship and advises them to think of God. He tells them that no matter where they are on Turtle Island, the Great Spirit will hear them if they take a few minutes out of their day to pray. Their own prayer might bring them the spiritual power they need to turn their lives around.

Martin spoke:

> So today, we're having a lot of problems because we're not using our spiritual powers. So these are the things that are happening today all over the world.... Lack of this spirituality.
>
> I tell them "You have the spirit power, but you don't use it. You don't exercise it. You live the White Man's ways. You try to be a White Man but look at your skin... You're still an Indian."
>
> And this is why, today, this younger generation is going up on the mountain to Vision Quest, to fulfill a dream that they have dreamed of. So these are the ways today the young generations are bringing back the spiritual power that the elderlies once forgot about. They're bringing it back and they're teaching the older ones what they have lost. They was lost and they're still lost until they come back to their own Indian culture and way to live.
>
> So it's up to the elderlies to back these young generations who are now picking up the religion and culture.

A lot of prayers have been said and a lot of help from spirit power has been given to them. And a lot of these young generations today are living with these spirit powers. They see it happening.

So do yourself good and do yourself right. It's the only way and that's the way God would tell you to do if He was here tonight. He would recite to you a lot of good things to follow up on, to be a good two-legged and to be God's children.

SOME OF GOD'S CHILDREN FORGOT GREAT SPIRIT

It's nice to be God's children. And so when you are living and learning about this spiritual work, don't take no 'cut-across' trails, 'cause you're not going to make it. You're not going to learn it. So don't cheat yourself.

Some of them think they can make it without spiritual power. They forgot Great Spirit. But they find out they can't make it. Some of them don't make it. And when they come into disaster and it shocks, they ask: "How I'm going to get help?" It's the only time they think of Great Spirit or God. Beyond that, they don't even think of Him. So then the hardship returns.

Here we come up and say, "Oh, I had a terrible night. Oh, God!"

I imagine that Spirit just kind of laughs at you people when you yawn around, innocent, thinking you never did anything bad. Remember, you may have done something bad. I know you aren't all perfect. We all did something bad at one time down the line in our lifetime. If we didn't do it, we're going to do it. It's coming yet so remember that.

You are under spiritual guidance twenty-four hours a day, so don't try to hide and do things thinking nobody is around. There's someone out there watching you. You're going to fool yourself, really fool yourself. So don't be sneaky, because somebody's watching you! [Everyone laughs]. Don't think you can go into the darkness and do this and whisper around. Somebody's watching you – saying that and doing wrong.

Today you can live with this supernatural power, the miracle, the mystery. People who do live the spiritual way of your ancestors, walk the Red Path, the spiritual path. You can help one another, respect one another. It's the old traditional way.

Every one of us has spiritual guidance. If we didn't have spiritual guidance, when you tried to walk out that door, we'd run right into it [the door]. But the spiritual guidance will open that door and we will walk out. The same way down the street when the red light comes on, you have to stop. Somebody there, a spirit, stopped you. Without that spiritual guidance, you'd walk right out and the car would hit you and knock you over.

And this is why, today, I know people want spiritual advice, spiritual ways of doing things. Every one of you has a spirit through your body and that spirit has a power, so pray to God and tell Him you need help. That spiritual power in your spirit can help you.

Be happy, and everything good will happen because the spirits will make it happen. That way, you live a happy life. You have the spiritual power with you at all times.

All Great Spirit Asks of Us is a Beautiful Prayer

And so today, everything is happening. So we pray to God, the Creator. We call him Grandfather, Great Spirit. He's our Grandfather, *Thuŋkášila*. He is older than all prayers, because He created everything. And He has put out everything on earth here for us to live with. And it means a lot to us.

So today, this is why I always tell people, "The only thing that God ever asked from you and the only gift you can offer him, and he enjoys that gift, is a nice beautiful prayer." That's the only gift we can give Him. He appreciates that. This is what I teach people about.

I've always told the people, "Whatever you are doing during the day, set things aside. Give God a few minutes, two or three minutes of your time. Thank him. That will be the biggest gift you can give to God." So always remember that.

This is why I always said we can't give gifts or anything to our Grandfather, the Great Spirit, God. He doesn't want anything from us. All He asks of us is a beautiful prayer.

Pray to Me and I shall help you

That would be the biggest gift you could ever give to God – a beautiful prayer. So those are some of the things. Back in the old days, they never created nothing.

He created everything for them to live with and to survive with. And so that's the way they lived for many years. Today, things are changing, but still we're living with the old. So we do a lot of praying in order to make things happen. We need to pray to God. We need the prayers really bad.

Think of the Creator, your Grandfather, Great Spirit, in your everyday working conditions. Always stop and give at least two, three minutes and speak to Him. He's listening. He'll help you for what your needs will be. This is why the Lakȟóta people pray seven days a week. We don't have to wait until Sunday to pray. We always say the whole world, Mother Earth, is our altar. We can pray anyplace and we shall be heard.

Right now, maybe there's three, four different places that the Medicine People are holding ceremonies back home in the Dakotas. They're praying for all people of the four colors. And so, every night, they say prayers, praying to Great Spirit for help and guidance.

This is why I say we all have to pray. We have to think of God so we can get on the good side of Him, and He'll help you. Just like when He brought the Pipe to the People: "Pray with the Pipe through Me and I shall help you." Pray to Him and tell Him you need help. Just like He said, "Pray to Me and I shall help you, because you are my children."

This is the most important thing, because we are all related people. He created everything in six days. And so everything He created is holy. Everything he created for you. He handed it down so we can use it. We can work with it. He created us to live and walk with health. We live with it during our time.

You don't have to go to church to do that. You can be out here in the old altar. This whole North America, at one time, was an altar. You can go up on the hill. Go on the flats, underneath the trees, along the edges of the water, anyplace. Stop and pray to God because he's always listening and He will hear you.

I often wonder if God was here and walked around the streets of Portland, walked around the streets of Seattle, I wonder what people would think about it? They'd probably all go out and hide to show their sins. Run like heck! [laughter]. Try to get out of His way. Stumble, bruise a knee or two, skin your face. It would probably never hurt because you're still scared, running [chuckles]. Yeah, these are the things we have to think about.

So this is why today I'd like to make that announcement: If you give two, three minutes of your time to the Grandfather, Great Spirit, that would be the biggest offering you can ever give to Him.

Like we say, everything that God created has spirits. These spirits that work with us – we call them Grandfathers. And if you need help, tobacco is one of the most important things as the offering to the spirits, because what God created, they all have spirits.

Whenever you walk down the street or around the house, you walk with balance. You learn that when you started walking when you were a baby. We walk with time, every step we take. This is what's very important to you. If we didn't have that time, balance, we'd be falling all over. But these spirits that are with us have given that to us and helped us to walk in balance, live in balance. And so when you live, live in peace and harmony among all people.

Some of the people might be having a hard time. Really having a hard time with nobody there to help them spiritually. Someone might say "You're going to make it alright," and then walk off. It is from temporary minds that those words have been said. They are not really spiritual words. It might make you feel good for maybe a few minutes, but then it comes back down on you.

So if you have that kind of problem that you can't depend on anybody to help you, go to a tree. Hug that tree and tell it you are needing its help, and it will help you. You don't have to all pray together. You go by yourself somewhere. These are the things that people think that we're not in our right mind when we talk this way, but it's a big meaning to you.

Hold that tree and pray to it. Pray to it for guidance and health and power. Tell it that you need help. Then tell the tree why you need that help, maybe some of these subjects you can't get very clearly. That tree standing there. It's got a lot of power. It can help you do what you want to do.

The spirit of that tree will help you. That's unbelievable! That's a miracle! For that tree stands there ever since it grew up there with no sins. So it is powerful. And so these are the things we have to understand.

It is the same with the water. If you have problems with no one around to help you, get some tobacco and offer it to the water. Go along any of these rivers, a lake. Offer a little tobacco. Drop tobacco on top of the water and speak to the water. Pray to it.

When you tell them you are having problems, the spirit of that water will contact your own spirit and help you. The spirit of water will follow you and help you. It can travel a long way. The same with the spirit of that tree. That can help you. Even a rock. Pray to it, the spirit of that rock will help you.

Do you know why we're talking this way? Because that tree and water have no sin. We have lots of sin. We can sit here and talk and look at each other and we are maybe full of sins. But the tree, the water, the rocks, the fire – they have no sin so they can help us in our needs.

Now when we start asking questions, how many people have no sins? That's a hard question, isn't it?

And so this is why, sometimes, they come when I have a ceremony. It is quiet in there. Pretty soon, it sounds like someone dropped a bunch of rocks – like marbles. It looks like everybody is going to get a rock, a little stone, or something. After the ceremony, we turn the lights on and everybody looks for one ... *nothing*. It is just that they want to see what people have in mind at the present time. This is why I say we go according to these powers that go from one generation to another.

Some of them use it wrong. Some of them use it right. But it's a lot of power. And so these are some of the things that some people are scared of Medicine People, because some of them use it wrong. And so they think we all use it wrong. When I was up on the hill and came back down into the Sweat Lodge, Grandfather spoke to me. And he said, "We have given you a power that any time you want to use it for good or bad, it's yours." I've used it for good, to heal people with. I never use it for bad.

So this is why we always say, "Live and walk with balance upon our Grandmother, Granmother Earth." She, too, is our Great Grandmother. The time comes, she takes us. We cover up with her blanket. We go to her in peace and harmony.

BEHIND ALL THIS IS A BIG POWER

We want to talk about some of the things we had in mind. One of the things that, today, people start thinking about is Vision Quest. Some people are thinking about going into Sweat Lodges. They ask what going into the Sweat Lodges really means and what it really means going up on the hill – Vision Quest. And these are some of the things that we are supposed to be here to give instructions.

But before all that, why do people want to learn all this? Behind all this is a big power. They are doing all this, getting people back to where they are bringing the religion back. So from there on, a lot of people started to know about the Sweat Lodges. People started to know about the Vision Quest. And a lot of them are thinking about their first time in a Sweat Lodge. A lot of them are thinking "When am I going to go into the Sweat Lodge?"

Some of them say, "Well, it isn't time for me to do that." And some say, "Well, it isn't my time to go up on the hill Vision Quest. It isn't time for me to do that." These are the things that people say and think about. They are not really thinking about what they're saying. They are fighting themselves over it. They want to do it, but No, it isn't time.

Nobody taught them to do that. They taught themselves. And this is why, when the Pipe came up in this country, it had a lot of messages with it. There were seven commands that came with it. God created the Seven Commandments – seven laws – so everybody would be inside the seven. These Commandments was related out so that every walking person on earth is a walking Seven Commandments. Your ancestors lived the same way because they were taught that same way. And so people all over the world of the Four Colors should live within these Commandments. So when we pray, we always pray for that power. That is what we need is the power.

We know people lived with health, but today, there aren't too many of them that live with health. There are a lot of interferences – chemicals, polluted water and the food that we eat is polluted, and the air is polluted. And so there aren't hardly anybody that is really good and healthy. But back in the old days, they had no interference of that kind, so the people were healthy. If there were any illnesses, there was a Medicine Man to heal them.

Sometimes we pray for forgiveness and help so we can live a better life. And so when we want to live a better life, we will have to start thinking about the Red Road and start learning what is in that Red Road that people talk about.

To us, we say, *Čhaŋkú Lúta*, the Red Road. Today there are a lot of boys and girls that are thinking about that. So we talk about the power. All this consists of power from our Grandfather, Great Spirit. So we always pray for power.

FAMILY MEMBERS REMEMBER THE SIXTH COMMANDMENT

Jake Thompson, Martin's adopted brother from *Sisíthuŋwaŋ Waȟpéthuŋwaŋ* (Sisseton-Wahpeton), shared thoughts about Martin's Sixth Commandment and related the power commandment with the beginning of the Red Power Movement and the spirituality of the American Indian Movement:

Martin was able to get into the system and talk about the spirit of who we were. People don't know that story, but when they picked up on this spiritual world and went for it, here came Red Power. They were saying Red Power because Black Power was already out there. Brown power was already out there in L.A., San Francisco, Oakland, all of that.

They stood up for our people there in Minneapolis because people got beat up when they got out. The American Indian Movement was born and they filmed them all the way. That's what my older brother did [referring to Martin], encouraging them, and when all this was going on, the spiritual part was coming about. When these individuals came here and helped out, we got to witness that.

On a personal level, we had endured the onslaught of obstacles, negative talk. We all know the negative publicity that they all received. People might be drinking and they see you and talking that way, with the same last name – Thompson – and getting put down. We ride down the street, boy they got them "stares" on us.

"Trying to be a big Indian?"

"No, we don't go to church anymore."

It's not like we didn't feel rejected before, but we felt the rejection. We felt isolated and hurt. It was painful because

257

in a real big way we were being true to the value of love, family, ceremonies, and the healing.

That spiritual movement inspired a nation. They were not afraid. They were not intimidated. Matter of fact they were radical. They were saying, "I'm not taking this anymore. I did my Service time, and we deserve better than this." And "We gave up our land, so you need to honor our treaties."

The power comes from confidence. And it comes from our belief. I believe in these ways. I believe in this Sacred Pipe. I believe in this cause, but I don't need to get angry and upset anymore. I don't have to demonstrate now. I don't hitchhike any more. I can't be a weapon any more.

The quieter things, it doesn't get any attention, but I don't care. This is how Martin played, his being alive. To see it on his face and to feel all he was, let's say "saved." That's what I saw. It's not jumping up and down. It's just graceful, gentle wisdom coming from him and from the Creator.

We all saw the beginnings, fabulous and unforgettable, in him. It'll change a person's life forever. You realize you are being blessed, feeling fortunate for a person like that to walk in your life.

Ed Red Owl shares

I remember going to Bear Butte and Martin and Felix talking about it. And we told them we tried alcohol. Some of us have been millionaires. Some of us have attained college degrees. Some of us have been in the clergy. Some of us have been in gangs and were the head of that. Some of us were in groups that stole and robbed. Some were in organizations that took life. Some of us were in the service and were taught to kill and be killed. And we fought to do those things that provided us power.

Actually, in fact, we felt nothing. There was a depression. There was a feeling of disappointment. There was a feeling of failure that anything had been acquired other than an extreme sense of disappointment, an extreme sense of shame, and what we would say today as negative self-perception.

And so therefore, we were told to go to Bear Butte to enact that ceremony for ourselves. And I use my own experience that first year (to share about living with power).

Being placed in that altar that first night, I almost froze to death. And nothing happened. I had been forewarned that the elements of the forces of nature will cleanse you of everything. They will take out all the negativity and the disease that is in your mind and body. And they said, beginning on that second day, maybe the spirits will talk to you.

Before sunset on that second day, there appeared a man standing in front of me with his back to me, and all he had on was a loin cloth. And he had long hair. And he kept looking to the west and occasionally he would look back at me. But he didn't say anything. And he was praying. He was a very handsome man. He was not an adolescent and he was not a young man, but he looked like he was an adult man standing there.

I prayed with my Pipe and he was gone. And that is all that happened. And so when I came down I told Felix and Martin this is what I seen:

He was standing facing the west. He didn't say nothing, but yet he stood there and prayed.

And so they told me, "Who you have seen does not live here anymore. You have seen Crazy Horse. You have seen Sitting Bull. You have seen a holy man. But today there is no holy man. The happiness that you are looking for, that type of happiness you are looking for does not exist anymore. But nevertheless, know that there were such men and women who lived in that ultimate condition of happiness and you are to embark on a road. You are to walk on a road to make those conditions happen at some time during your lifetime.

"That is what you have to do with regard to this traditional Dakhóta way of life. We will all get there at some time so that perhaps that future generation can stand there as did those men of long ago and they will see that time of power. But presently, we have come through a horrible time."

I went down the second year to Bear Butte, and I saw again on the second night up on Bear Butte. I was taken up. This huge man picked me up.

And he said "Look to the west." and I saw planets flying.

And he took me to the north and this man was standing there with an old-time suit and a hat, and he said, "Look to the north." And he said "What do you see?"

And I saw things. And likewise to the east and the south.

And they said "What you are living through today is not what is. What they showed you is what real reality is. There are powers that are spiritual in nature and these powers do not pertain to everything that you have endured in your lifetime. The powers of the money. The powers of sex. The powers of materialism. The powers of political leverage and clout. That is not the powers that they show you. Spiritual powers that are greater than any of us."

This man stood 25 stories high and his dress was black and his face was in the shape of a sun flower. "That is the man from the west. He has power. That is where power is at and that is the nation and the family of power which you belong to. Listen to that and realize that is where power is at." That is the way I learned it. I think that power comes from the west and the north and that is the power.

The last time I saw Martin, that is in 1982, my mother had passed away and she was a great friend of Martin. And we asked him to help at that funeral. And so we entered that cemetery and he had that committal ceremony of her spirit. And so he put the flags up and prayed with his Pipe and then he went to the four directions and pointed it to the south like that.

And without saying anything, everyone who was standing at the south side parted. And he pointed that Pipe south. And her spirit we felt. It was like the wind. It was a wind that came and we knew that her spirit had left.

And we didn't cry. We didn't fall down. We were happy for her because when we looked up we saw a young woman in the distance going and that was our mother that we had seen pictures of when she was young, and she had gone.

And that, we knew, was power. And we felt no grief. Our mother had laid in bed for a period of three months dying of cancer and she knew it was her time. Ten years previous she had been at Green Grass and she asked for ten years to live and she was granted ten years.

Martin High Bear had that Sweat at Green Grass, and her ten years had come and she said. "That's it. I want to go home now."

And that is power. That is how we understand power.

I have no fear of death. I have no fear of disease. I think I know where I am going, so we do it as we say, one day at a time.

CHARLES FAST HORSE REMEMBERS

The late Oglala Lakȟóta Medicine Man, Charles Fast Horse also worked with Martin and the power that comes from Great Spirit through him. He sat with his wife, Hazel and he remembered his favorite memories of Martin:

Remember if a man gets powers, if you mind them, they'll mind you. Pray with that Pipe, they said. Because if you mind them, they'll mind you. But it's tough to be a Medicine Man these days. If he accepts the tobacco, he has to do it, because he accepted it. You are born a descendant from that line, that DNA, that lineage. I come from a Medicine Man in my ancestry, and the power jumped generations so I had no one to teach me.

Then I understand that if a man goes on the mountain, he has to walk with that Pipe with two hands. Don't look to this side or that. You got one way. Walk to the center and then go home.

I was told if a man goes and misuses that Pipe and sells it, and goes on and people hear about him, he loses that power.

These are some of the things Martin told me. It was just like listening to my grandfather all over again down at Pine Ridge.

All these things mean a lot. These commandments that he talked about. All the commandments, they have a lot of meaning to them. I understand when he names the Seven Commandments in Lakȟóta. He says 'These Seven Commandments, this land, these hills, this North American continent, it was all given to us to walk with health, generosity, respect, power.' So he told me about those commandments.

"*Wašté*" I said, "that's good."

He had to mind his vision so he went all over. A lot of people didn't understand that, but I did. He always talked about the man from the west with the black shawl, and the thunderbird, and the others. "'But,' he says, 'Remember, you don't just become a Medicine Man. You have to earn it. Like me, you come from a Medicine family. This is why I was sent to you. So you have to learn this oral history and all these things."

"So when you want to do something for yourself, you have to first go in a Sweat and wash your body. That don't mean the outside. That means the inside so your body and soul can become one. In the Sweat Lodge the spirits come, they wash you inside and out.

"And when they come in, they come in not to hurt you but to prepare you. They come in not to scare you. They come to help you. They take out what is bad and they put in what is good.

"And when you come out of this, you stand up and walk and do this. But you must mind them and then they'll mind you."

He says, "There's a lot of people that cry for a vision. But you have to be careful because they pick up the Pipe and bypass the Vision Quest. They are going to go in the Sweat, but they're going to start running it.

"If someone wants to have prayers recited and interpreted, this guy will take up what you recite and interpret. Those are imitators and plastics, born yesterday. So be careful, Charlie. This Pipe is dangerous. It is nothing to play around with. Pretty powerful. So remember that."

"Ahó!"

He said to me, "No man controls the powers of the sky, the four directions, or the earth. If a man has a vision, and he performs it, and he dies, the powers that were shown him die too. He can't pass that power on to anybody. That goes on with him. The stories," he said. "they mean a lot.

"The story comes with your mind. So in the morning, when the sun comes, get up and walk with life and all the generations toward where the sun sets.

"We go inside the Sweat to get our body and soul as one, so we can come out and face the world. It is a tough world, Charlie."

I remember what Martin said. I remember what old man Spotted Bear said. "This Pipe is ours. It is a symbol of a belief, of a culture, of a practice, of a language that was given to us, all the seven Sioux nations. The Western Teton Sioux share this culture."

So I remember. "You're right, Martin. You're exactly right."

Martin was a powerful man. In his own way, he was powerful, because the breath of life was in him. And when it came out, it grew flowers. It grew grass. Trees would grow. Martin had that power, the breath of life in him. He talked it.

He was like a cocoon. When he traveled and slept, it closed. And when he got to where he was at, the cocoon opened and a butterfly came out and nourished. It nourished people with the health; the generations; with the quietness; with the peace; with the sharing; generosity; strength and pitiness to one another.

Martin High Bear at Mahto Tipi, also known as Devil's Tower (1992).

CHAPTER 13

THE SEVENTH COMMANDMENT:

YUÓNIHAŊYAŊ NA WAÚŊŠILA

THE PEOPLE SHALL LIVE WITH HONOR AND RESPECT

Dressed in his black Wrangler jeans and white pearl buttons on his blue striped cowboy shirt, Martin sits on the edge of the bed, a slight smile forming around the edges of his mustache. Chief lays resting at his feet, cowboy boots off to the side. Oxygen tube in his nose, he is forced to sit still these days. Unaccustomed to his new sedentary life, he drums long fingers on the nightstand next to the bed and leans forward, elbows on his knees to take pressure off two fused vertebrae in his back.

He looks around at the circle of friends who have gathered this evening to hear him speak about spiritual matters and life on the Red Road. Eyes twinkling, he searches for someone to tease while he waits for me to start the tape recorder and for friends to settle into spots around the living room.

He has spoken of the Seven Commandments countless times over the years, always sharing that the most important is the seventh one: Respect and honor and pitiness. Fluent in Lakȟóta but with a third-grade public education, his use of English is limited, so this word to him actually translates as empathy and compassion, not pity.

He shares that some people of today's mixed culture may have forgotten how to respect one another, a practice that once was natural and common among his grandparents and ancestors in their daily lives. The people lived to honor one another through feasts and giveaways, and publicly acknowledge the worth and work of the members of their *thiyóšpaye*, or extended families.

Martin learned respect since his boyhood from his grandparents, Sam Charger and Rosa Red Weasel, who taught him to respect his elders and the other grandparents who traveled to their home to visit Chief Charger's son.

RESPECT ONE ANOTHER AND YOU'LL BE RESPECTED

The last one: Respect and honor. The people, they respect one another. That's the seventh one. The Indian people in them days, they were kind to each other, like brothers and sisters. It is one of the big traditional ways that God showed the people to live. So today, we're here to kind of speak out a little about these things, to tell about the Seven Commandments, how people lived back in the old days.

The richest person that's walking on Mother Earth today is the one that has friends and lives with harmony with others, with respect and pitiness for others. That's the richest person that is living today. This is why I say we all honor one another, just like the spirits that brought the Calf Pipe to us back home in South Dakota.

This commandment meant kindness. People pity each other and show their respect to one another. They honor. That's the way the old people lived thousands of years ago. They all lived in the same method. All the people, maybe we can go clear back ten thousand years, they all lived the same way. Because God created everything here on earth, the people shared alike, so this is one of the big traditional ways that God showed the people to live.

Today people live without no respect or honor each other. They think about themselves, not others, so these are all in the commandments. This is why we say – "Show your respect to one another." This is why we say "Help one another. Respect and honor one another."

These are the things that today we have to teach the kids – to behave. I was taught to behave. You didn't have to take no strap or something to beat me up to make me behave. This word – kind, respectable words – explaining. You get that and you feel happy. You live with it and someday you can speak about that. That's why the Great Spirit wanted the Indian people that He created on this spiritual island to live under the Seven Commandments.

We have to learn how. We have to teach ourselves to respect, not only toward relatives, toward humans, but respect toward animals, four leggeds, also the feathered ones that fly the air. We always say feathered ones, that means the birds. They're holy, the same as the animals. Everything – the trees ... Nature. Respect nature. You do that and you are going to be respected. You'll be honored. It is from God. It is not from a human being. It was created for you. That's the seventh one. That is the last commandment. That's you and it belongs to you."

Respect Your Elderlies

This is one of the things I was taught growing up: Respect and honor my elderlies. The most important thing I've always told people is that they respect their elderlies. Show them your respect. Help them. If it wasn't for them, we wouldn't be here. Today I still speak about it and teach people. Respect your elders, because that's where we were raised from. Help them if they need help because they are back to their childhood again. We have to recite that a few more times, and maybe things will work right.

I'll tell you a little bit of my life. When I was growing up, my grandparents took me in. They took me from my mother and dad. They took me out to the country and raised me. When I was growing up, I remember some of the things my grandfather said. "When my grandson grows up, maybe he is going to be married and have kids of his own. These are the times that he is going to need teachings."

And Grampa was a spiritual advisor. He knew what was going on. He used to tell the people. He'd get the elderlies together. He'd tell them what is going to be in the future. I remember my grandfather always teaching to me about different things. The respect, my grandparents taught me that. The one thing he always taught me, "*Tȟakóža* (oldest grandson), I'm not your only grampa. There's a lot of grandfathers here. No matter whose gramma it is, any elderly, man or woman, he is your gramma and grampa."

My grandmother used to say, "No matter who it is, if it's an elderly, always respect and call them Gramma and Grampa, even though you're not related to them." Maybe it isn't yours but it's got to be somebody's. So respect them and honor them, no matter who it is. You get that respect and you feel happy.

Our Indian word for grandmother is *Uŋčí* and grandfather in our language is *Tȟuŋkášila* or *Lalá* for a boy. For a boy, that means grandfather. So that was the way I was taught. That's one of the things I never forget.

Grampa said, "They come up and you better shake hands with them. Honor them, grandfather and grandmother. Show your respect. They'll love you for that." That was always mentioned, illustrating, "See how they respect you. Because you show that you have respect for them, they show it back to you." And every time they come, they bring a little gift to me. "Here, I brought a gift for grandson here. *Tȟakóža*, a gift for you."

And so I keep telling the people "Honor your elderlies. Honor and respect them because that's where you come from."

And today they need the help. Respect and honor them. Help them. Talk to them. I don't care who I see. I don't know their names, but I know they're a grandmother. So I ask, "How's *Uŋčí*?" They'll look, because they know they're a grandmother. They'll look.

You know, when I go back, or when I visit one of my elderlies, I listen. By rights, they live through half of their lives through this and they, too, are still studying up until the time that they go back to the Land of the Fathers. Even though I know some of the things that he knows, I listen out of respect and honor and piteness because there's always some new things coming up that we never heard before.

RESPECT ALL RELIGIONS OF GOD

Respect and honor is the way our ancestors lived, so this is why I have always spoken to the people – that we respect the creation of God, what God has given to us.

God has handed down to us a religion. And this is a true religion we have here today – the Indian religion. This religion we have belongs here and this is what we work with so this is why we respect this religious structure. It never was changed. Nothing was ever changed.

As long as I was growing up, I never hear my Grandparents ever argue about the religion. They respected and honored, I presume, because it was created from God. They believe in God. Everybody had respect. This is more important today because we need it. See what is going on today. People should pray together. We need God's help because we never created nothing and we never destroy what He created. We honor and we respect our Great Grandfather, Great Spirit. We honor Him. We pray to Him every day. That's how much we love Him, our Grandfather.

Religion is different in different parts of the world. The other religions have come in here and we have to respect it because it's part of God's work. But some people never listened up or kept up with their religious structure and so the Christianity power has kind of vanished away again. They forgot the ten laws of God that has been laid down in that Bible.

I'm not running Christianity down, because I love Christianity, because it is God's creation. I have respect for it so I don't talk against the religious structure. Only thing I've always said, "I hope people would behave and try to live under these commandments. Maybe things would change in this world."

We have to pray for them like you would pray for your relatives, your friends. We had a big conference and we were all there. Some were Indian Medicine Men. Some were preachers, Christian ministers. They had a Bible out and the Pipe. When we started talking about the scriptures in the Bible, they asked us, "What does that mean in your language?" And so we recited to them.

At the same time we had a fire going – sacred fire. People were giving the fire tobacco and praying to God. They had some Sweat Lodges. People were going in there to Sweat. Every time we had a speaking engagement, after we get through, we take our minister friends into the Sweat Lodge to pray. We talk our own language and these ministers talked our language – the Lakȟóta language. And so we had a nice two-day meeting – spiritual meeting.

We have to honor it and respect what God has given to us. This is why we honor the ministers. We respect them. The only thing that is different between them is they have to go to school. They have to go to school and graduate to be a minister. We don't have to go to school to be a Medicine Man. We go up on the hill and we stay up on the hill and suffer ourselves, come back down.

Respect and Compassion

As far as doctoring and healing people, and talking to the spirits, these are the things that us Medicine People do. We work with people, their problems, relating things out to them, how to relax. One of the main things in our commandments is respect and pitiness to everybody. Have the pity to everybody because we are all pitiful.

But one thing I'm going to say, and I spoke about this to different ones back home to make them understand about our religious structure: We don't say it's stronger. We don't say it's better. We say it is the same.

We treat all people alike. We don't condemn them because they don't see things the way we do. So, you see, that's the way people, back in the old days, depended upon that. A lot of that we have lost. We have had a lot of interference.

But still today, back home, I think the Teton Sioux Nation has about 35 or maybe 40 Medicine People in our Indian ways. And we can say we are not trying to talk over anybody. We don't brag or anything about what we are, but as we look around to our neighbors, our Medicine People have been passed down from generation to generation.

And to our Indian people of the seven vows, the Seven Commandments of the Indian religion, automatically each individual person was created under the Seven Commandments. They used to live with the Seven Commandments, the old Indian way of Seven Commandments that was given to them from God. They're the walking seven, each person.

Back in our ancestors' days, each individual person, grandmothers and grandfathers, mothers and fathers, they walked with that seven. They walked with that health, the quietness, happiness, and power. They pitied the people. They honored and respected. Today, different ones say, 'Where is that seven?'

I've always said, "With all these Seven Commandments that have been given to us, live the life." So that's the way God created us, the common people. So that's the way we have to teach. So that's the way our ancestors lived, many moons ago, even before White people were here in this country where the buffalo roamed. People believe in it. They had a lot of respect. It was the way God gave them to do it. It was the way God wanted them to be so they really honored that.

So that's the reason why they didn't have to learn it. They grew up with it ever since they came out of the darkness.

In them days, your parents, your ancestors, lived the same way, no matter what color they were. That's the way God created all people to be. Not only the common people, but the other colors of people included.

Just like I say, God gave Christianity Ten Commandments. There are ten laws of God in Christianity. "Thou shalt not this" and "Thou shalt not that." But how many people in this world obey them laws? How many?"

HONOR YOUR *ČHAŊNÚŊPA WAKȞÁŊ*, YOUR SACRED PIPE

God sent us the Pipe when people were traveling and starving. They were hungry, so this Medicine Man sent out scouts to look for and track any deer or buffalo nearby. That's when they met the Indian Maiden. That's why God handed the Pipe to the people. It was given to them in case they're in need of help.

By rights, you're supposed to walk the Red Road first and think yourself over – whether you're eligible to carry a Pipe. I know some people said that they weren't. "I'm not eligible. I'm not strong enough to carry a Pipe yet, but when I do, I'll make me a Pipe."

I bring these things up so people can understand what life is all about and what the *Čhaŋkú Lúta*, the Red Road, is all about. Because that is what God has given us to work with. The Sacred Calf Pipe, it's still here with us. It is in South Dakota where our Sun Dance comes from. It is still protected.

So if you own a *Čhaŋnúŋpa Wakȟáŋ*, a sacred Pipe, respect and honor it. And take care of it so it can take care of you, so you can live with health. So these are the things we have to know. Listen to them and make a prayer offering for them. They mind. You mind them. They'll mind you.

So whenever people have Pipes and are saying that they're Pipe carriers, some of these people smoke marijuana in these Pipes. That don't call for that. And some of the people carry a Pipe are on drugs and alcohol. That don't call for that. I've heard that some of these Sun Dancers go into a bar, drunk, unbutton their shirts in the front and show the scars, Sun Dance piercing scars, drunk, telling people "I'm a Sun Dancer!" Then, some of them lie, steal, and they say they're Pipe carriers. Some run off with other people's wives. Things like that. They don't understand right from wrong. That's not walking the Red Road.

So when we go in the Sweat Lodge, we pray for respect. We come in there to honor Great Spirit. We come in there to respect, so you can't go in the Sweat Lodge and pray and come out of there and act like you just came out of a bar. We didn't just come out of a beer parlor, yelling around. I've told different ones. I've said, 'Don't do that.' They respected you while you were in there, so have the respect out here when you walk Mother Earth.

Today all this mishap that's going on for the ones that are walking the Red Road and all that are suffering is because there's a group that is misusing the Pipe. I guess that's one of the reasons that this is all happening to a Pipe carrier.

The ones that are walking the Red Road and carries a nice Pipe, honors it. We call them the innocent ones. They are the ones who really truly walking the Red Road. It's through that Pipe you're calling the spirits.

So like I say: 'Don't use this Pipe as a weapon.' Use it to pray with. Tell God in words, ask for health and guidance and the power. These are the things that we have to talk about.

And when you go up on the hill, you pray for yourself before you go up. When you get locked in there with the Four Directions, you have the time to give a prayer offering. When the spirits are here, we tell them to go up there, be with them. Care and see what they have to say for themselves.

This is why we always say, "Behave. Behave yourselves." That's why we always talk, "Help one another. Respect and honor one another." So the message I would like to bring-Respect and honor each other. We all need that. God wants you to behave so honor one another. That's why God handed the Pipe to the people.

RESPECT GOD'S CREATION

We are all related so these are some of the things we have to study. Even the animals, the birds are all related. So it's been brought up here by using the words, *Mitákuye Oyás'iŋ*, meaning *"All my relatives,"* because we are all related. When God created everything, everything was related.

This is where that word, "*all my relatives,*" come in. Maybe you start that out with a prayer, or end your prayer with, "all my relatives," or *Mitákuye Oyás'iŋ*. Today, some of them don't understand these things. They use that word because others used it, but there's a big meaning to it, so these are things that are nice to talk about.

Back in the old days, they had a lot of respect for each other. As many as two, three thousand lived in a band.

Back in them days, when a young couple gets married, the parents of this young couple will talk. This young girl wants the boy so the girl's parents ask for this young boy to be a son. Sometimes, this boy wants the girl to be his wife, so the boy's parents will go and talk with the parents of this girl, asking for her to be their daughter-in-law. Back in those days, the people knew each other. They honored and they respected. They have a place built up – a thípi – for them, and they have a ceremony when they get married and different ones give them gifts and have the young couple into this tipi to start their life out.

After that happens, they have their own ruling of respect and honor. The girl respects her in-laws. She may talk to her mother-in-law, but she never says anything to the father. They don't go out here and speak to someone else's wife. The mother-in-law never talked to her son-in-law and the father-in-law never talked to the daughter-in-law. When a woman wants to bring a message or something to a man, she goes over to this man's wife to tell her the message, and his wife will carry the message to her husband. The same way with the boy. Sometimes they talk with the father-in-law, but they never once will look at or say anything to the mother-in-law.

My grandparents, when they raised me, they talked about how people relate to each other. How much respect they have for one another! And so that went strong by the people back in the old days. That's how much respect they had. These are the rules that they had and this is the way they lived. These are the things that we have to understand.

TIMES HAVE CHANGED IN OUR FAMILIES

I remember back in the late 70s between three of us Medicine People. We went to a ceremony and we came up with different messages from the Grandfathers. They told us a lot of things in ceremony. We heard them talking to us. We sat there and listened, just like you people are sitting here listening to me.

"There shall be a change in people when there shouldn't be a change in the people. They should be what they should be."

Now, they say, "you'll see a sign.... And later on in the years, you're going to see again a change. The young people are going to take over. They're going to be involved with the family." So these are the things that we always mention to the people when we have a gathering like this, so then people can understand what this meaning is.

No wonder, like the Grandfather said back in the late 70s. He told me, "People are going to live in fear and they're going to be scared." And that is the stage we are in now. People are scared of one another. Fear! From the time they get up, they're scared, 'til they go to bed again. It's not the good, happy life people used to live.

So, in a great big band of them living, they are all related. They are all happy. So there's no jealousness. There is no hatred in the band. They lived in a big encampment.

Boys don't go out around chasing women. The girls don't sneak around in a tipi in order to meet a boy because they have to respect one another. And there's no way that you can say, in them days, they didn't have respect. That's the way they lived.

Today, it's all different. The world has changed and these are the things that our grandparents and Medicine People told back in the turning of the century from the eighteen-hundreds. Today some people live without respect or honor for each other. They live with jealousness. They live with that hatred. They think about themselves and not others. They learn that from another class of people.

And so this is partly what we teach. This is why we always like to mention it. Not that we say that you people live that way. We have to say it to show how our ancestors lived their everyday life.

TIBETAN MEDICINE WHEEL AND PROPHESY

In 1988, I was surprised when people came to the Mt. Hood Sun Dance from Tibet. Three people came. There was two men and one had his wife with him. They wanted to talk to me and so I went over and shook hands and talked with them. They saw all them six colors, mostly the four colors on that Sacred Tree, and they were really surprised.

They said, "We use the same colors back home in our spiritual work. Same colors! We're using it the same way. Only we have a Medicine Wheel that we turn when we hold ceremonies."

They told us the prophecy. And their prophecy was nearly the same as the prophecy of the Indian nations in America. What they said was what was said back in the old days.

So this is the prophecy: "People are walking the Black Trail, the Black Trail of Darkness. They don't understand the religious structure. They don't understand humanity. They don't understand the respect and the honor. All they're thinking of is themselves and not others."

And I was surprised to hear that. I visited with them for a while. Then they were on their way home back over where they were from.

This is the stage we're in. When we pass this stage, there's difficulties. It's happening today. The world, people of the Four Colors, don't get along together when they're supposed to be living in harmony together.

Now you people are doing good and great by saying you walk the Red Road. You people are bringing back the old traditions of your ancestors. This is why your spiritual work, all these, the religions, you're walking the Red Road. But how many are there out there that are walking the Red Road? Today, they're not. And we are crossing the Trail of Difficulties, darkness, the bad luck, all these.

The time's coming when people will live together in harmony and be like brothers and sisters the way God created us to be. That's coming. But today, this world is going bad – from good to worse. And so this is why, today, we have to talk about a lot of these things. A lot of things that the human has created, God didn't create these so it never works. We can see it – the destruction.

But one thing I can say, it didn't take people like you, or like us, to make these things happen. I know people are against it, people that realize. They have very good strong minds, they have one track minds. They stand together and they share one thought, one feeling.

The teachings, we have to listen to them. And what we know, we have to send these messages out. Some of the people call it Good Medicine.

You people are the ones with the answers, so use the answers in a spiritually healthy way, the old Indian traditional way. It takes people to do things the right way. It takes people with a spiritual power, with one mind. It takes people to change things the way it's supposed to be, the spiritual way. That's the way our ancestors lived. And so today, we have to bring that all back before it gets too late.

THEY NEVER USED TO CRITICIZE

There is no such thing in our religion as hell or the devil. Some believe if you sin, you are not going to go to heaven. You are going to go to hell. To us, we believe that our spirits shall go to heaven or the Spirit World, and our bodies shall go back to Mother Earth. Our bodies will be covered up with Mother Earth's blanket. The same thing, as you go to bed at night when you cover yourself up with a quilt, Mother Earth, Grandmother, will take care of you. And she is our only Grandmother that we have. She will take care of us.

Back in the old days they never used to criticize. They all have respect so they don't criticize. They believe in this respect. But today, you're going to be criticized for what kind of a person you are.

If you use that word, "You're lying," you know yourself that you have been disrespectful. So that word "criticize," our ancestors don't use that word, because they don't criticize. They have respect. So show your respect. Pity one another. Respect one another. Then you'll be respected.

If you want to convert yourself to the Red Trail, you can do so. You are all God's children. The Red Trail is a place where we pray to God when we need His help. The good things – the happiness and the forgiveness – are all on the Red Trail.

We talk to the spirits because we are under spiritual guidance twenty-four hours a day. We always say, "Pray and be heard. It will be answered." You want this and you want that, pray for it and when the answer is given to you, you have gotten what you prayed about.

And so you see, we believe in the ways God has told us. And I presume that this is the same way that all mankind, all persons living, shall obey alike if you live in harmony among each other.

IT'S TIME TO SHOW THE GREAT SPIRIT RESPECT

They told us back home that you people are going to suffer. That's the same way when Black Elk cried for his people. And he told them what was going to fall on "my Indian people." So today, we see it.

Then he cried for the White people and they asked him why he cried for the White people. He said, "because of what they are doing." And that was the answer the old man gave when he cried for these two nations.

That was some of the old ways of telling people. And some of these things we talk about is the true meaning of things that has happened and the things that we'll be seeing in the future. These are the prophecies a way back when our Indian people were still populated pretty heavily.

We noticed, and some of the old Medicine People back home noticed it. It says in the prophecy that there shall be some people that will be spiritually advising the way God has put things and spiritually advising people of right from wrong. Someday, that's going to happen and maybe it's happening.

This is why we often talk about spirituality. Sometimes I get with some Medicine Man or some elderly. They sit down and when I talk with them, they all call me *hokšíla* (boy). I don't know why, but they all call me "boy." "You're doing something great for the people, *hokšíla*. Keep it up, but always behave."

That was always the last word. Whatever they're telling me, the last word was "behave." "Mind the Grandfathers." "Do what they tell you to do and they'll do what you want them to do." And this is the way I lived with the Grandfather – the six great powers – the Four Directions, Up and Down.

WE HAVE TO GO THROUGH THESE HARDSHIPS

These are the things that they have told us in the prophecies. These prophecies haven't come from earth people that are walking on Mother Earth. They came from something more spiritual, more holy than anything that we've ever seen. These are the things that we often talk about, and these are the things that should be mentioned.

You can see how far this spiritual power has gone among the Red Man. You can see how much they love and respect the Great Spirit, our Grandfather. We believe in His Creation. We believe in God. We believe in the spirits that He has sent down to watch these Four Directions as if it was their own – the four corners of this universe, the sacred hoop, the Turtle Island – what they call North America.

Now we have to go through all these hardships. The time is here now to pray. Everybody has to think of God, because there's a lot of things that's happening.

When we get through these hardships, we're going to see better times. When we get through these difficulties of life, we're going to see good things happen. We're going to see the beauty of Mother Earth. We're going to see the beauty among people and how people are going to meet and live in harmony together. Just like I said, all people will live in harmony together as one big nation. The time is here for that. By showing our respect, we can show the Great Spirit that we have a lot of love for God. They can bring that back!

THE PEOPLE WERE A WALKING SEVEN COMMANDMENTS

These are the Seven Commandments that our old Indian people used to live by. The Seven Commandments are on the stem of this White Buffalo Calf Pipe. The seven eagle feathers, representing the Seven Commandments, are on the stem with holy herbs. They are tied in there with rawhide that the Great Spirit has handed down to the Indian people. That was all done by spirits.

Our ancestors lived with these Seven Commandments back when they were going up on the hill, praying with their Pipes. Any place that they have stopped, they filled their Pipes and prayed with their altar. They called the spirits down. They prayed and asked them what they shall do. They mind their spirits and their spirits mind them.

So we have Seven Commandments we go by. In our Seven, we pray and study them to heal people. To bring herbs more strength, more health, we have to use these Seven Commandments. Everybody used to live with health. They were healthy people, generation after generation. The whole population of people, everybody was quiet. And they lived the fourth one: "Help one another." So this is why today, tonight, one of the most important ones that we have to walk with is the fifth commandment: "Be happy and love one another." What they'd say, they'd say in a way to bring the happiness. Whatever we need, we pray and we get it. We have the power.

They're easy to live with, the Seven Commandments – the old Indian way of Seven Commandments given to them from God. Christianity said, 'Thou shalt not.' Christianity had ten. In our Indian religion, there's no place in there where he said 'Thou shalt not,' but it still means the same.

So that's one of the things we were taught to learn.... To have patience. All the Indian people here on this spiritual island, we never could bring the culture back to the way our ancestors used to live, but we can bring it back to a certain amount and we can live happy with our spirit power.

So one of our sayings is – what we want to say is, "Behave." And like the old people back in the old days, one of the main things they lived with, and they taught their children was to behave. And this is why today we use the same word again, "Behave." That means a lot. Not only one way but in a lot of different ways.

If you want to remember the Seven Laws – if you don't remember how many there was and forgot about it – look to the Northwest and count the stars on the Big Dipper. There are three on the handle and four on the bowl. At one time in this century, I was told, the last star on the dipper handle came down to earth and then went back up. This is the same as when Christ was born. That star guided the Wise Men to where He was laying, where He was born. That star is the same as the star – the last star on the end of the dipper handle. It also came down to the Indian people and then went back up.

Now these Seven Laws God gave to us, if you study that out, each individual person that walks Mother Earth is a self-fulfilling Seven Commandments. So everything they'd say about those Seven Commandments consists of respect and honor from the beginning of the First Commandment to the Seventh. So they all lived like a walking Seven Commandments. That's what people were when there was nothing to worry about.

But we don't try to make you an Indian. These are the laws that everybody, Indian and non-Indian, should know. And I presume it`s no difference between the Black people out there across the spiritual water, and also across the spiritual water to the Yellow race of people.

And so today we're here to kind of speak out a little about these things, about the Seven Commandments, how people lived back in the old days. So to answer that question about these Seven Commandments, it can be included to everybody. That's the way our ancestors lived. The Seven Commandments was with every person. Individual persons back in their days, even back up to you in this day, can be a walking Seven Commandments. You can carry that in you.

MEMORIES OF FRIENDS

Chuck Benson, one of Martin's drivers, had memories to share about him and his teachings about respect:

It's been many years since I last saw Martin High Bear, but my memories of him are very vivid. I had the privilege of working as his helper in South Dakota where I was raised. I spent almost a month with him at *Pahá Mathó* (Bear Butte), a mountain sacred to the Lakhóta people on the eastern edge of the Black Hills. We were conducting *Inípi* and *Haŋbléčheya* ceremonies and I was Martin's helper, tending the fires and stones or singing and helping him put people on the hill.

I remember several things about Martin. The first thing that comes to mind is *wówayuonihaŋ*, respect. Martin showed respect to all people, regardless of race, age or religion. He did not flaunt his position as a well-known Lakhóta spiritual leader, nor the fact that he was an elder.

Even in correcting us, he did it in a way that did not belittle us or rob our dignity. He respected all of God's creation, whether two-legged, four-legged, winged or plant life. He explained that the Lakhóta phrase *Mitákuye Oyás'iŋ* (all my relatives) is not just the *"amen"* at the end of a prayer, but rather reflected our relationship and interconnectedness with God's creation, and- by extension – with God Himself.

He taught us the traditional way to gather sage, again showing respect. We were gathering sage for the various ceremonies and, as we needed quite a bit, we were just yanking it up from the roots. He approached me and said, '*Hokšíla* (young man – usually used in a fatherly way) we don't kill our sage. We want it to come back to help us next year. Break it off, don't pull it out by the roots.'

He never seemed prejudiced, but accepted all who came to him, whether full-blood, mixed-blood like myself, or non-Indian. As long as one was respectful and did not exploit what they were learning, they were allowed to take part.

I remember one *inípi* where Martin had me sit by the door to help him. He passed me his personal hand drum and asked me (he did not "tell" me, he asked) if I would sing for the ceremony. I'm not "full blood" and am not the greatest singer, but I do speak Lakȟóta and have a heart for the *Lakȟól-wičhóȟ'aŋ*, so he honored me by this act. It was encouraging and humbling all at the same time and it's something I've never forgotten.

Another thing I remember was his sense of humor. He was very quick to laugh and share in the joy of others. He took his work very seriously, but was able to balance that with simply enjoying life and the people he was with.

He related a story about some young non-Indian men who wanted to climb *Pahá Matȟó* – Bear Butte, while people were praying. There were some young Indian men keeping people from passing through a certain trail so as not to disturb those who were praying. These other young men were intoxicated and insisting on passing, and one of them tried to say he was part Kickakpoo Indian.

Our young men were trying to be patient, but one finally said, "Well, my Kickapoo brother, you're welcome to visit our camp down below and share a meal if you like, but if you try to pass this point I 'm afraid I'll have to kick-your-poo all the way down the hill!"

Martin cracked up every time he told that story. He'd say, "They were afraid to hit the guy because they didn't want him to bleed out all his Kickapoo blood!" Then he'd laugh again. This was not said in a racist or unkind way at all, because knowing Martin he would've fed them if they came by the camp.

Martin was typical of traditional Lakȟóta people from another time. As I said, even in the way he corrected us was done with dignity and respect. In the old days elders very seldom came out with hard or direct rebukes, but rather would hint and then let you decide.

As Ella C. Deloria put it, they would simply say something like, "Well, nobody does that" or, "That's not our way." They would seldom say "Don't do that!" They would let you decide, because you were the one that would have to live with the results.

I had been involved with a ceremony from another tribe from another area and was curious as to what Martin thought. So I related to him what had happened. He looked at the ground as he spoke, which in a traditional way was showing respect to me.

He said, "Well, I've been to a few of those myself. I respect them and don't have anything against them." Then looking up at me he said, "but that's not our way." It wasn't a rebuke. It wasn't an order from my spiritual leader. But it was enough. I never did it again.

Remembering that side of Martin reminds me in many respects of my *Thuŋkášila* grandfather, "Little Finger," in Oglala, South Dakota. They are men that have balance, a complete understanding.

In other words, there are those who practice the *Lakȟól-wičȟóȟ'aŋ*, the Lakȟóta ceremonies or "doings." But they don't always practice the *Lakȟól-wóopȟe* or *wóahopȟe*. These are the "laws" or "values" of the traditional people. It's like those who go to pow wows or ceremonies or church, then turn around and drink or use drugs or abuse their families. They don't live the lifestyle that supposed to accompany these ways. This is hypocrisy and only serves to further perpetuate the negative stereotypes of Native American people or spirituality.

Of course, Grampa would never use such strong language. He'd simply say, "They're trying to be traditional, but they're missing it." He's never told me "You don't be like that," or "Don't do that." He simply lives the life from day to day and teaches those who want to learn with humility, dignity and respect. He remembers the mistakes of his own youth, so he does not harshly judge others. He simply lives the life and leads by example. Grampa has always been one of the most influential people in my life.

These kinds of men among us are very rare these days. Martin High Bear was such a man.

JUDY TREJO REMEMBERED

The late Pyramid Lake Paiute elder and song carrier, Judy Trejo had rich memories of Martin and understood his teaching of respect, especially to support the growing two-spirited community:

The mainstream society in which we live, they have mental hospitals, where way back among our ancestors, if a child was born and they were what people now call "retarded" or "bipolar," they were considered gifted by the Creator, because they were forever innocent and the Creator likes innocence. There is nothing more sacred than a newborn baby because they came fresh from the world of Creator, but their minds remained innocent. They were close to the Creator so they were pampered and cared for and respected.

Natives did not have mental institutions and they did not have nursing homes. In mainstream society, what do they do with old folks when they can no longer care for themselves any longer? They put them in nursing homes. They send them there to die, because essentially this is what happens. People get busy and go about on their own, and forget the old folks they put away in a nursing home. We didn't have that a long time ago. It was youth that loved and respected, and took care of elders and elders took care of the very young the same way.

Martin had the teachings of how to treat women and the importance of their place in Native society. He was well aware that men and women were food providers. They worked side by side. This was equal rights. Where people got this idea that a woman should walk 10 paces behind her husband, I didn't hear about this until women's lib. And the women were saying "What about the women?" I was in college when women's lib came about and I could not understand what they were talking about – because we always had equal rights. There was always respect between man and woman. Native women were not subservient to men.

Something I noticed about Martin's spiritual camps was the beginning of keeping Mother Earth clean. You don't dirty the face of Mother Earth with your cigarette butts, etc. You respect her. I had been to many sacred gatherings and really never saw a butt can until I started going to sacred gatherings among people that Martin taught. They all had a butt can. If you smoked non-filter cigarettes and tossed your cigarette any old place, then the filter does not go back to the earth. It is not biodegradable so it was important to dispose of your cigarettes in a cleaner manner. Therefore, they used the butt can.

He was also aware of the fact that man can learn very much from a two-spirited person. They learned beauty and compassion from a Two-Spirited. Realizing that a two-spirited was a natural born healer, because they were at the right hand of many Medicine Men. A Two Spirited could teach men how not to treat a woman, how not to mistreat them. And there are subtle ways to mistreat, but the masculine side of a woman could teach men how not to treat women, make them aware of the little hurts that compound and become big.

Martin and I talked about respect for their role in the sacred way of life. It was a discussion we had many times. He was interested in what my people thought. I have a relative he recognized immediately as two-spirited, yet sacred, a healer. He was the one who told my nephew "You'll have to tell people who you are." And my nephew did not know where to start, but he began to tell people a little bit at a time and he was worried about their reaction., But when he finally decided to tell me, he said "I don't want to make you angry. I don't want to hurt your feelings. And maybe the only word everybody understands is the word *gay*."

I said, "Well, you got your work cut out for you and it is very important work." At the time I said that, I had no idea what I was talking about. All I know is he had been chosen to do very important work.

He is now a very important person among my people because women are forbidden. It is not allowed for women to handle the bones of our ancestors. Many graves have been desecrated, but Paiute women cannot handle the bones of ancestors. Yet, the men are not sensitive enough to do the work because the bones of our ancestors need to be handled gently. There is the need to talk to them and promise them and acknowledge the wrong that was done to them. It is the two spirited that do that work.

By working with non-natives, Martin made "the list" – the blackball list. Natives laugh and say to each other, "Oh, guess what! Someone else got caught doing something good. They made the list." So technically it's considered the blackball list as negative. But most natives looked at it as "Hey, somebody's doing something right so they made the list!"

My point of view is that the list is conjured up by jealousy, by envy, by malcontent people with minor knowledge. The blackballing was due to a lot of misconception and misunderstanding, but according to a lot of Native people, he would have been doing something good. This is where the blackballing came from. This is where the jealousy and envy came in. For many people, it was quite a big deal. People that wound up on the blackball list were congratulated by a lot of Native people.

I always hesitate to use the word "power." The word "power" is kind of pretentious, but Martin was a teacher and he would tell you himself, "I'm just a go-between. I'm just your teacher." This is not minimizing his ideas and his role here among the people. His vision and other of his friends that talked about their visions, their interpretations of things was basically that they were ecology-oriented, like preserving the land, preserving good water, healthy water.

Martin's basic philosophy when he talked about working among non-natives, and when was asked to take his teachings to Germany and places like that – was to bring them words of peace and encouragement. Germans were interested because they dug back in their history and found out they had ceremonies similar to Sun Dances. Their culture had similar things and Martin's way of teaching, even Natives not of his tribe, he would say, "I'm just showing our way, the Lakȟóta way, so eventually, you make relations with your own way and you go back to your own way of teaching."

I know of Apache, Paiutes, other tribes that passed through Martin's way, learned Martin's teaching and eventually found their way back to their tribal ways, their old ways. They became interested in their own culture and talked with their own elders and more or less revived their tribal ways. They were not discarding anything they learned from Martin, but it was a beginning for them to go back to their ways of respect.

One thing that stood out in my mind about Martin and his friends who were also leaders, teachers of the Lakȟóta ways, is if we teach other people, other leaders, our way, this kind and gentle way of life, and if the word could get to the world leaders, there wouldn't be any more wars. Basically, people like Martin and some of his close friends like Stanley Looking Horse, they were not selling their religion. They were world peace advocates and very strong ecologists.

And if people will look at it closely and say our spiritual leaders and teachers could teach other tribes other nations these things and the world leaders learned these ways, like taking care of your own, having respect for your elders and taking care of your elders, there wouldn't be the strife, there wouldn't be different world wars.

Martin and Rose at Mahto Tipi or Devil's Tower in Wyoming (1992).

CHAPTER 14

JOURNEY TO MIRACLE

"Miracle was born in the Moon that the Chokecherries turn Black," Martin said, still caught up in a state of awe, a few months after the birth of the white buffalo. "This is the moon that the White Buffalo Calf Maiden came, the month of August," he explains to our guest, William Ward who helped video-record our local elder gatherings. He hesitated as the oxygen concentrator clattered and chuckled in the background.

He straightened his stooped back for a moment, long brown fingers stretching over his black Wrangler jeans. They were wearing thin above the knees from the rubbing of impatient hands as he sat, day following day in a slow steady progression toward summer. He picked up his coffee cup to take a sip of weakened coffee that was cooling to room temperature.

Sentimental pride for his dog, Chief, shone from the photograph of the Shih Tzu on his porcelain coffee cup. He waited for his coffee to cool and then took another drink. It was cooling faster than the late winter sun moving across the sky.

From his bedside vantage post, he showed William the newest photographs of Miracle. Jan and I had just mounted them into frames the past night, and hammered them into place on a couple of walls in his room.

Martin's cousin, Rufus Charger, had just brought his daughter out to Portland to run in a high school track and field event, and stopped in for a visit.

Arvol Looking Horse had traveled to Portland with them. He, Martin and Rufus are all from the Sans Arc Band of the Teton Sioux Nation, the band chosen by the Buffalo Calf Maiden to watch over the Sacred Calf Pipe Bundle.

Arvol asked Martin what he thought about the white buffalo calf. He mentioned that many of their people have questioned her authenticity, especially since she was born on a ranch owned by non-Indians. "We wonder if she is true," he said.

Martin reflected, almost as though he was speaking to himself. "And now she has been born during my lifetime. You know, this little white buffalo calf is not an ordinary buffalo. She has been born during the Moon that the Chokecherries turn Black," Martin says to Arvol in response to his question. "The same moon that the White Buffalo Calf Woman first came to the people."

Miracle's birth had become the highlight of Martin's year and his life. Fully realizing this signified the return of the female prophet of the Lakhóta People, (the Sacred Buffalo Calf Maiden). Martin said: "This is the long-awaited fulfillment of our ancestors' prophesy."

He had decided that we would take a summer trip with Jan Meyer to see the white buffalo calf with his own eyes. Katie Sterbick and Robert Ito had offered to caravan with us. Katie, who is like a spunky cheerful robin bounding into the spring season, was a source of emotional reassurance for both of us. Our Japanese friend, Robert, had spent the winter months cooking for Martin during his recovery from hyperthyroidism. His offer to be the driver of Martin's 26-foot-long RV was a blessing.

Katie reminded me, "Rose, we don't restrict our loved ones from living life when it might be life threatening to them. We are simply there to provide the love and support they need to move through it." I swallowed and looked down, trying to stretch my understanding. I admired her for the wisdom she had gained from 22 years of caring for her disabled son, Mikey, who had just recently crossed over to the Spirit World.

Inside, I heard myself chanting a silent mantra inside my head: "Martin still has another year of Sun Dance to complete. The Grandfathers aren't ready to take him yet." To break the silence, I forced a flat joke: "Martin loves to rush me. Sometimes, he lives to rush me."

Katie was kind enough to laugh. "He's so good at it, and all without words too," she said. "Just a glance and you know."

"Martin always tells everyone else never to rush," I told her, laughingly. "'Take your time,' he always says to them, but not me! He loves to tease busy people. He'll say 'You people have clocks on the walls in every room, clocks in your cars, clocks on your wrists, and yet you never have enough time.' He laughs with them and then he tells them to slow down. But he always rushes me."

I thanked Katie for the good laugh. Growing serious again, I told her I was still exhausted from Vision Quest camp and Sun Dance and all the company that comes at this time of year, and from all the travel this spring when his dad was in the hospital. "Martin has been very quiet since he lost his dad, and now since Sun Dance he's been even quieter" I shared.

Pouring a Sweat that late June, I was surprised to hear the urgency in my prayers, as though I was crying for Martin's life. I didn't think his condition was life-threatening, but now my spirit was speaking for me, saying it was so. I thought it was curious that my spirit could speak through my lips what my mind didn't yet comprehend. Running errands that week before leaving town, my sense of urgency intensified in the middle of my tasks and I rushed home to him. He was fine.

Trip Through the Plains

The Great Plains, with its persistent history of hot summers and deadly winters, can weary the soul of pioneer and newcomer. To them life on the prairie is not a mysterious and sacred dance, but an incessant struggle with the ruthless world of nature. Almost constant drought, violent dust storms, destructive prairie fires, heaps of dead grasshoppers clattering in the wind add to the picture. Settlers' towns had become ghost towns and railroads had long closed because of economic downturns, crop failures and farm foreclosures.

But to the Lakȟóta, it is home. It is the home of the sacred, the burial grounds of the ancestors who help preserve its sacredness. Martin is returning home. As we departed, I prayed for mild weather and that my premonitions were incorrect.

It's 1,200 miles to Rapid City. Martin's youngest son, Leonard, joined us there to travel with us to Eagle Butte. A jockey and ranch hand, Leonard is the spitting image of his dad, and a very slender five-foot seven, and like Martin, he wore cowboy shirts, cowboy boots, slender Wrangler jeans and often had a serious expression just like his dad. His straight dark hair drawn back into a ponytail with sunglasses framed a jutting nose.

We caravaned alongside *Pahá-Sápa*, the Black Hills, leaving behind Rapid City and its heat wave, exaggerated by urban life. Outside Sturgis, we approached Bear Butte, sacred Vision Quest hill teeming with spiritual power. We're acknowledged by the powers of Bear Butte, this old spirit that reaches out to encompass travelers venturing past its earth and sky dwelling. At our first glimpse of *mathó* the bear, (laying upon its mother the earth), the spirits inhabiting this ancient holy place worked through our minds and hearts as they prepared us to approach the outer edges of its sacredness.

For Martin, Bear Butte held countless memories of the past. This was where Felix Green took him for Vision Quest ceremony when he himself became a Medicine Man in the late '60's. For years, he had traveled there to put people up on the hill so they could pray and fast. On this day we had already asked the caretakers and our ancestors to bless our prayer flags, and our path east.

As we pulled up to the visitor's parking lot at Bear Butte, Martin began to grow restless, concerned that the heat might affect his breathing as it had at Devil's Tower two days earlier. I absorbed his uneasiness and checked to make sure he had enough spring water and coffee, and then I lightly touched his hand as I prepared to step outside.

"I won't be long, honey" I reassured him as I walked up to the front of the RV by the driver's seat and turned to look back. "I don't want to keep you waiting."

"That's good." Martin looked warily at me as I slipped over the seat at the driver's door, prayer flags in hand. "We still have a-ways to go" he said.

"Okay, I'll make sure the others know," I responded over my shoulder. "Leonard's going to stay here with you."

Martin remained anxious, remembering Elkhorn Butte (known by some as Devil's Tower). Two days earlier, we'd looked forward to our arrival there but the heat's intensity had prevented him from leaving the air-conditioned RV. Feeling trapped inside his 77-degree cocoon, he grew anxious and dangerously short of breath.

As his struggle to breathe began to mount, it was as though the sacred landscape was pulling strength from him. It replicated the days of old, when Medicine Men and Spiritual Elders would travel to the sacred places, give offerings in ceremony to help the people, sacrificing themselves in the process. It felt as though he was offering up his life for us to be there.

I couldn't reach around him to fan his face, so I put my hands on his back covering the lung area beneath his shoulder blades. Almost immediately, as if by a miracle, his breath recovered. He caught his breath and his shoulders dropped in relaxation. Katie was standing behind us when it happened.

He said to her, "She really helped me. I couldn't breathe. And when she touched my back, I could breathe again."

He said nothing to me, but after that, his eyes were different. When he looked at me, they reflected fresh gratitude. He took time to hold my hands in his, gently running his thumb along my knuckles. Martin was a cowboy, a man of few words when it came to expressions of love or appreciation. This time, in front of Katie, he talked about how much it had helped him. Unaccustomed to it, I got embarrassed.

LEAVING BEAR BUTTE

Driving away from the base of Elkhorn Butte, I reflected on the words of Kiowa author, N. Scott Momaday, which I had just transcribed from the U.N.'s "Cry of the Earth Gathering":

"Sacred ground is in some way earned. It is consecrated, made holy with offerings, song and ceremony, joy and sorrow, the dedication of the mind and heart, offerings of life and death. The word sacred and sacrifice are related, and acts of sacrifice make sacred the earth." Momaday's words resonated as I witnessed Martin suffering during our journey.

At Bear Butte, I walked up the winding path from the gravel parking lot, prayer flags in hand. I wanted to honor Martin's request to be brief, but I knew I must linger a few extra minutes among the Íŋyaŋ – the rocks, the sage, the wild roses and other medicines. The insect nations were singing. Countless spirits who inhabit this consecrated spot, circled as though playing with me, checking out my thoughts, my prayers, my past, my future. Others' prayer flags surrounded the path from the four directions. Lakȟóta colors, all colors, calico prints, tobacco ties lined the path and covered the trees on all sides as I travel. Leaving the path to find a spot to pray and hang my flags, I swerved to avoid a prayer altar still closed up with a sizable quartz crystal inside, half encased in leather, placed upright.

Stopping toward a western point just above the base of Bear Butte, the midday sun seared my forehead as I began my prayer. I thanked them. I then ask for help. I ask the Grandparents to guide us and protect this fragile elder along his journey to Miracle. I felt hopefulness and then released the anxieties and fears. I felt gratitude, releasing the sense of urgency. I felt love and released the frustrations of our journey. I felt acceptance and let go of as many nagging doubts as I could assemble in one spot. I felt their presence as they read my prayers and accepted the tobacco I'd offered. "Hurry up, Rose!" then "Slow down, granddaughter!" I returned to Martin, each step down the hill a prayer placed to the breast of the Mother, each footstep sounding like the rhythmic heartbeat of the turtle.

While I was gone, Leonard had stepped outside the RV to stretch his legs in the visitor's parking lot and have a cigarette. Chuck Rambow, the Park Ranger, an old friend of Martin's, spotted Leonard and walked over.

He said to Leonard, "You know, you look just like Martin High Bear."

"That's my dad," Leonard says proudly.

Chuck introduced himself to Leonard, extending his hand for a handshake. "Well, I'm happy to meet you. I'm Chuck Rambow, Park Ranger here at Bear Butte State Park. Martin and I have been friends for twenty years, but I haven't seen him lately."

Chuck wore the familiar green uniform of the South Dakota Fish and Game Department and had a large, colorful beaded

Chuck Rambo, S. Dakota State Park Ranger, Bear Butte, S. Dakota.

watch band on his right forearm, a gift given years ago by Grampa Frank Fools Crow, Chief of the Lakhóta Medicine Men. As steward of this spot for many years, he was relaxed and outgoing, reaching out to both Indians and tourists.

Leonard pointed toward the RV. "He's over there in that beige RV. You can go see him if you want to." Chuck shook his hand again and then sauntered over in Martin's direction. Leonard added, "You have to climb in the driver's side because the other door is a hydraulic lift for his electric cart."

Chuck mounted the step at the driver's door and stepped in for a surprise visit. He afterwards shared with me about how much he'd missed Martin. I know Martin had missed being at Bear Butte. His commitment to the spiritual camp in southern Oregon had conflicted with the period of time he'd usually taken for almost two decades at Bear Butte, being the first ten days in June.

Chuck later shared with me some of his memories of the early days when Martin came to Bear Butte. "It was before today's tourist platforms and walking bridges," Chuck said, "when it was still closer to its natural state."

He hesitated as he looked over toward Vision Quest camp. "Did Martin ever tell you the story about the Sweat Lodge that he built over there?" Chuck pointed to a spot to the east of the campground.

"I don't know, Chuck. What was it?"

"Well," Chuck started, "that summer, he gathered some red willow branches from Bear Butte Creek. Then he used them to put up the Sweat Lodge for ceremony. They used it for Sweat Lodge ceremony in there all during camp that year." Chuck went on, "Later, after Martin left camp, I looked over and that Sweat Lodge was in bloom. Fresh leaves and blossoms had sprouted out all over it."

Martin's sons and grandchildren would frequently meet Martin at Bear Butte every year in early June. They would hear the news from their Uncle Rufus Charger that he'd arrived.

Darlene spoke softly, her eyelids growing slightly red from the memories of those days as she said: "So the entire family would head over to spend time with him, 'cause he was nowadays constantly on the road."

His grandson, Laurence, loved to speak of his granddad and told me about the time he went to Bear Butte as a young boy.

Laurence said: "Mom used to take our whole family over there in June when we heard Grampa Martin was coming, 'cause we missed seeing him. One time we were there, I wanted to go up and explore the hillside, so I started to head up the trail."

Martin said, "Grandson, stop. Don't play up there."

"Just then," said Laurence, "a rattlesnake crossed the trail where I was headed. I stayed in camp after that." He smiled, thinking back about the memory, shuffling his feet at his Uncle Eddie's doorstep as he remembered.

I walked back to the RV, happy to see Katie walking, almost skipping down the path behind me. Robert and Jan had also returned and were standing by the RV waiting for us.

"Hi, honey." I said with a simple lilt in my usual tone of voice as I climbed back in the front door of the RV.

"Háu!" he said, a little more enthusiastically than usual (bolstered from the warm conversation with his old friend). He straightened his back for a moment and shot a smile at me.

Before we left Bear Butte, Martin said to me, "Rose, I don't know how much longer I am going to hold on."

Numbly, I stared at him.

Katie said to me, "Rose, did you hear what he said?" I looked at her and turned away confused and silent.

Leaving Bear Butte, I jump into Katie's van on this leg of the journey to Cheyenne River Reservation. I wanted to give Leonard time to visit with his dad. Jan decided to stay in the back of the RV so she could do some letter writing and share her first memories of Bear Butte with friends back home. We stayed connected via portable CB radios with Robert, who was driving the RV.

Katie had just lost her son, Mikey. She'd experienced 21 years of life and death situations and had grown accustomed to moving, as though flowing, through trauma. A couple of days back, Katie and I had taken time at Elkhorn Butte. Robert had found a shady spot to park the RV in a grove of trees several miles from Elkhorn Butte so Martin could recover from the intensity at the base of the tower. He had a bite to eat and decided to take a nap.

Robert and Jan had agreed to stay nearby, while Katie and I took a few minutes to drive over to a private meadow Martin and I had discovered back in 1993. In the nearness of the butte, we made a red prayer flag and tied it to a tree bordering the meadow to pray.

There we raised our voices in prayer for protection on our journey. We always included prayers for the spirit of Katie's son who had recently journeyed home to the Land of the Grandfathers. As we prayed, a field of crickets joined us in a deafening vibration of song. When my prayer ended, the crickets stopped too.

Katie and I continued driving toward Cheyenne River Reservation along Highway 212 just outside Faith, and I spotted a turtle slowly walking across the highway up ahead.

I said to Katie, "Oh, my gosh, we've gotta get that turtle off the road. She'll be squashed by an oncoming vehicle."

"Rose," Katie said, "I think she is already a road kill."

There's been no traffic, but frequently long-distance truck drivers use this road to travel between Rapid and Minneapolis. So Katie screeched to a stop by the side of the two-lane interstate. We got out of the van and there she was, slowly moving west across the road. We wished that turtle across the road, but she didn't move. Vulnerable but innocent, protected at her own pace and hopelessly slow, the turtle ignored me.

I walked back to the van for my tobacco bag and then I offered bits of the tobacco and a prayer that she would get across the road safely. Inside my mind, something shifted and I realized my foolishness. "A powerful spirit is crossing our path, and we stop because we think we can help her."

I dropped tobacco down on the ground where I stood. "Here walks the Keeper of Turtle Island, the spirit chosen to stand at the gates of land and sea, inhabiting both realms, a Great Balancer to some, the spirit of fertility to others, the one we sometimes ride to journey to the other side. I don't think she needs our help."

I started to walk back to Katie's van, my head dropping. When I turned back to look at the turtle, I realized she had stopped to look back at me, frozen in her tracks. I wondered if I should just pick her up and put her safely at the shoulder of the road.

"The next semi traveling by will definitely smash her." I said, feeling regret that we had even stopped.

Feeling awkward, like a hare in a foolish race against time with the land tortoise that has no concept of time, I concluded, "Then he'll become a reptile pancake."

"A speed bump," according to Katie, my accomplice in irreverence. I turned back one more time to walk toward the turtle. This time I startled her. She began to move across the road away from me. Then it is almost as though she caught herself in retreat and stopped, resembling the wolf who stops one last time to look at his perpetrators in the midst of the chase for life.

The turtle turned her head back over her right shoulder and hissed a warning at me, "Don't come any closer!"

I walked back to the van and climbed inside, feeling I had interfered.

"You could pick her up and move her, Rose." Katie suggested.

"I couldn't touch her. She told me not to." I said.

Sitting back down into the passenger seat, and leaning over to rest my forehead on the open window frame, I glanced down to see a clock on the ground along the side of the road. It was black and white in color, around twelve inches in diameter. The clock was broken, its covering gone, and the hands read twenty-three minutes after four. Katie's front tire almost hit it as we drove back onto the highway.

I asked her, "Did you see that clock?!"

"I didn't see anything." She looked back at the side of the road as we drove off, "No, there's nothing there."

As we drove off, I looked back a second time to see the clock lying broken on the ground and the motionless turtle.

Katie was concerned about catching up with the RV, miles down the highway and out of sight. She reached for the CB radio to signal Robert. Martin later scolded her for pushing her old van so hard in an effort to catch up.

"Your van's an *"elder"* now. You have to treat it with respect," he reminded Katie in his characteristic gentle voice. "Your van is 17 years old."

His thoughts were very powerful. Her van slowed down later at Green Grass when its axle sank into the gumbo, or "South Dakota mud," outside Stanley Looking Horse's house.

The broken clock was a sign for my eyes only. The Grandfathers heard my cries as I prayed and hung flags on the west-facing tree at Bear Butte. Just a few miles down the road from Bear Butte, they showed me a broken clock at the same time they offered the turtle. I reflected on that. When I told Martin about the turtle and the broken clock, he looked at me.

"You know, Rose," Martin hesitated looking closer, "in all the years I've driven from Sturgis to Eagle Butte, I've never seen a turtle on the road." Martin had been born in South Dakota and lived there most of the years of his life. This was his way of telling me to think about what had happened. He rarely interpreted others' spiritual experiences, preferring they discover the meaning themselves.

I would continue to discover the significance. The power of the turtle is special in its capacity to transcend time, bridge heart and soul, and bring balance to chaos. Turtles live in the Spirit World where there is no sense of time. It would take a while, but I would gradually discover the gift I'd been praying for.

During the seven years I'd traveled with Martin, it was not uncommon for him to become impatient, especially when I took so long leaving town on a trip. There was much to do with his increasingly fragile health. Picking up extra portable oxygen tanks and pharmaceuticals, backing up half-finished work onto diskettes, and calling a family being left behind again. Sometimes I didn't have enough help to get everything done. Packing things into the car top carrier, I had wished for just one afternoon nap before heading off.

As he spiritually advised people to slow down and take time to do things, he would rush me. Maybe the Turtle Medicine will help me stay balanced. Maybe I could say, "I'm sorry, honey, I can't rush. That turtle broke my clock."

THE PIPE BLESSING

Fifteen hundred miles into our journey, we turned onto Green Grass Road. The Moreau River cut an evergreen passage through the rolling plains that had already turned golden from summer heat, but it was always green at Green Grass. This spot resonates with relevance, created by Great Spirit for the purpose of harboring the White Buffalo Calf Pipe Bundle in its little log cabin on the hill above Arvol's house. In the last four days, we had stopped at Elkhorn Butte and Bear Butte, and now we were approaching the White Buffalo Calf Pipe house.

We drove in silence, past the small community, the International Sun Dance arbor, the churches, the grazing herd of horses. Winding our way down the sloping road past fields of sage, toward the river bank, and past the old Looking Horse Sun Dance arbor. We pulled up in front of Arvol's house. Stanley Looking Horse was talking with a couple. Arvol was gone, so he was the man we needed to talk to.

I sat down with Martin. "Honey, we want to have your Pipe blessed with the Sacred Bundle." "No," he said, "bring out your *Čhaŋnúŋpa*, Rose. I want to have your Pipe blessed instead."

I looked to the floor where Chief lied napping, stunned that he would think of me at a time that we were seeking help for him. This is Martin's way to think of others and not think of himself. I stood up, feeling like I could cry, knowing I could not. The Lakȟóta believe we only cry when we have lost a loved one, or if we think we are going to. I walked back to the cabinet above my bed and reached for my *Čhaŋnúŋpa*, enclosed in its deer robe bag, wrapped in red cloth and tucked among fresh sage. He had it made for me several years earlier and placed it into my hands for caretaking. She has become my caretaker and protector, my spiritual advisor, the companion I follow.

There, in the open door of the RV, at the base of the hill where the Sacred Calf Pipe is housed, the smoke from the burning sage swirled its path to the spirits, as he filled my Pipe. Raising his fingers to the western skies where the sun prepares to set, he held bits of kinnikinnik toward the direction of the White Buffalo Calf Maiden, praying soft, gentle prayer words in his Lakȟóta language. Infusing the afternoon air with softness, he asked Her blessings upon us all and upon this little L-shaped Pipe. Reaching out to all directions where the Grandfathers of the Four Directions wait, he offered the tobacco of the red willow bark. Continuing, he raised his hand to the spirits of the sky and earth, filling the pipestone bowl with the circle of prayer blessings.

I suggested to stay behind, "Martin, there are mosquitoes all over in here now that the door has been opened. I don't want to leave you here alone."

"It's okay," he urged. "I'll be fine. Just go on."

Robert said, "I'm saying here with Martin, Rose. Don't worry about him."

I walked up the hill toward Stanley who was helping the family prepare to pray inside the Calf Pipe house. I heard sobs rising from Jan's throat as she followed us up the grassy slope.

My feet touched the soil, moccasins placing themselves among the red earth, the buffalo grass, the little herbs cushioning the earth from the impact of our weight, as they prepared us with every step toward the one they surround. I whispered to the White Buffalo Maiden Bundle. "I humble myself before you, uŋčí, grateful that you allow me to come this close, and that I am so far."

Stanley Looking Horse walked up to us, as miniature streams of sweetgrass smoke curled up into the air. He smudged us with the sweetgrass smoke. I looked to the ground and to the bundle encircled by my thin brown arms as he said, "You can go ahead and go inside to pray when the other family comes back out."

I have always prayed outside the Calf Pipe house on the grassy slope. I have never been inside with the Bundle. I took deep breaths, squinting, looking down, knowing Martin's longing to pray with the Bundle, yet knowing he was there, inside already.

Before we stepped inside, Robert walked up to us, taking long slow strides. He said "Uncle Martin asked me to come up to pray. He said he's fine."

We stepped inside the little Calf Pipe house. Following them, I circled around and dropped to my knees, with my forehead to the earth. I prayed to her, the female prophet, the White Buffalo Calf Maiden, "Oh, Uŋčí ... " The earth reached up to touch me as everything vibrated within reach of the cradle of Lakȟóta spiritual origin. My feet and legs lost all sensation.

We completed prayers and walked out into the light to smoke the Pipe. Standing in indescribable surroundings, we become silent witnesses to the dusky skies that had begun the night's sun setting ceremony. Grandmother Moon was climbing from the east horizon, her fullness painted the valley with luminescent orange. She crossed the watercolor sky to mingle with the streaking salmon-colored light that began to settle in the west. Thunderclouds, dwelling place of the Thunder Beings, circled the sky surrounding Sanz Arc Valley. Rumbling and crashing their distinctive, honoring drumbeat upon the earth, a myriad of flashes kissed the earth from the four directions.

The eager persistence of the mosquito nation also surrounded us, attacking us through our clothing and on our faces and arms. They distracted me for a moment and I wondered why they'd come. We gathered in a circle and smoked the Pipe, ignoring the mosquito buzzes. Wafts of smoke swirled through the air to bless them and us.

"Did the small battalion of attack mosquitoes find you too?" we asked Martin as we stepped back inside the RV. Martin had managed fine without us. He smiled and chuckled, the way he always did and listened to our stories. Then he asked, "Can you drive over to Stanley's? I need to talk to him."

Martin was more interested in getting some of the medicine that he'd always gathered nearby. He didn't see it growing this year and wanted to ask Stanley if he had some stored away.

SEEING MIRACLE

Dave Heider had gone outside early that August morning of 1994 to feed his small herds of buffalo and horses before going on to work for Rock County. When he looked toward the field, he saw what looked to be a small sheep or lamb among the buffalo. He wondered to himself how that sheep could have gotten into the buffalo's field. Looking closer at her outline, he suddenly realized a white buffalo calf had been born.

The Heiders had been blessed beyond their comprehension. As the weeks unfolded, a richer meaning behind this rare birth would emerge and the family would begin to realize they had taken on a role much like Joseph and Mary who'd birthed the Christ Child, Jesus. Awed by this miracle, it would take them a while to realize their

Miracle, the white buffalo calf born at the Heider Ranch, Wisconsin, (1994).

lives would never be the same. As the news broke around the world, and especially in the Great Plains, people began to flock to their little forty-five acre spread just outside Janesville, in southern Wisconsin.

They'd been awaiting our small caravan at the Heider Ranch, the home of the now-famous white buffalo calf, Miracle. As we drove onto the mowed cornfield converted into a parking lot, an elder, a pleasant, easy-going neighbor of the Heider's, greeted us. Cherokee by descent, he helped provide hospitality to a steady stream of visitors who come daily to witness the long-awaited fulfillment of Lakȟóta prophecy.

When we gifted him a braid of sweetgrass, his eyes welled up with tears. He shared that recent guests had not been so kind. Recently, they'd been enduring a variety of conflicts from people, some as serious as death threats called on Miracle's and the caretaker's lives. Minor harassment had included complaints about Miracle's winter coat from those who wanted to see a pure white buffalo and caustic remarks over their requests for volunteer donations.

We mounted the portable oxygen tank on the back of Martin's electric cart and he maneuvered himself out of the RV on his wheelchair lift into the pleasant afternoon air. This was Martin's moment, his gift after having endured twelve days of searing heat and hours of wearying road travel.

The evening before, as we had traveled past Madison, Wisconsin, Martin felt it had cooled enough for him to leave the safety of the RV and have dinner at a truck stop. Walking past the newspaper stand, the headlines startled me. "50 People Die from Heat Wave in Madison."

"Oh, my God! That name, Madison, sounds familiar!" I said to Jan, "Did you see the headlines in the newspaper back there? Where's Madison?"

"It was that last exit." Jan said. "We just passed Madison, Rose."

The next day, we heard the radio report stating that 500 people had died from the unprecedented heat wave in Chicago. Our destination, Janesville, Wisconsin, was just three hours north of Chicago.

I remembered Momaday's phrase, *"Sacred ground is in some way earned. It is consecrated, made holy with joy and sorrow, offerings of life and death."*

Moving slowly down the Heiders' gravel driveway toward the shade trees in back of the property, we noticed how pleasant the air was that morning. It was the first day since we've left Portland that it hadn't been miserably hot. There was even a light, cooling breeze.

We read later in the paper how, in the midst of this killing heat wave, a strong north wind came, as an interlude, to cool the Midwest for a day in July. That was the day we spent at the now-famous Heider Ranch. The next day, the sweltering heat was with us again.

It didn't take long to recognize Miracle behind the Heider's farmhouse. Like a hidden treasure, she stood looking our way among the four yearling buffalo in the field. We stood motionless, trying not to interfere with the moment Martin had waited for. Only those two wondrous spirits were needed at this reunion.

As we stood and watched, the cocoon opened once again and the butterfly flew up into the air, leaving the oxygen tank and all other heaviness behind. He drifted like a song around the meadow. Miracle awaited his presence, motionless.

For the balance of the afternoon, Miracle consumed our complete attention as we lingered at the edge of the pasture, immersed in her feminine countenance, gazing at the exquisitely distinctive way she moved.

I remarked to Katie, "I've never seen a buffalo with such gentle mannerisms."

This journey had made it possible for Martin to connect with the object of his vision, the White Buffalo Calf, the Lakȟóta "Christ Child," the White Buffalo Calf Woman returned.

Miracle, the white buffalo calf born at the Heider Ranch, Wisconsin, (1994).

Katie whispered to me, "Rose, that Calf Pipe energy is like Christ energy. When Martin looks at the calf, his face turns totally soft and childlike. A grace circles him and then everything is okay."

Katie also described a grace around the two of us. "People sometimes bombard you and Martin with conflicts and hatreds," she perceived, "but this same gentle power keeps the balance between you. You remember the teachings the Calf Pipe Woman brought thousands of years ago," referring to the return of the Seven Commandments just two decades ago in Martin's vision. We had partnered together to preserve it and share it with all peoples, even when it was not well received.

"Now," Katie finishes, "the White Buffalo Calf Maiden has returned, and Miracle and her caretakers are sharing it."

We walked farther onto the property and stopped in front of the Heiders' new gate. It had become as heavily laden with gifts and prayer offerings as the original one they had moved inside the barn.

I was in awe. I had felt the same way earlier in the day when we first arrived, stopping at their new barn where they asked us to sign their guest book. I looked at t-shirts and photographs of Miracle for sale to help with expenses in their new public life as caretakers of Miracle. Inside also were memorabilia of Miracle's earliest days and their old gate, completely covered with colorful prayer flags, tobacco ties, sweet grass, sage bundles, beaded leather bags, dream catchers, medicine wheels, feathers and other sacred items gifted to Miracle the past year.

My eyes had been magnetized by the beauty of the prayer offerings and yet they seemed too private for me to stare. After a long moment, I looked away, feeling like an eavesdropper. The Heiders had removed that gate from the fence line when it had become so heavily loaded with offerings. With their Medicine Man's blessing, they had chosen to save it as a testament to her.

Four Colors of Miracle

We realized she wasn't as pure white as the day she was born, with the brown fur from her winter coat still intermingling with her whiteness. We weren't surprised, remembering recent comments floating around the community from doubters the previous fall when her winter coat began to turn black-brown.

"She's turned brown now! What does that mean?" some ask.

Martin reminded us, "She will turn the four sacred colors before she turns white again: black, red, yellow, and then white. This is the way the White Buffalo Calf Maiden turned as she walked away from the people, rising above the buffalo grass a different color each time until she disappeared out of sight."

Then, as spring sunshine came, her coat reddened. Now we saw how the summer sun was bleaching it yellow, like the fur of the grizzly bear bleaches from the Alaskan summer sun.

"This couldn't be the white buffalo everyone was waiting for!"

"This is nothing special. There are always white buffalo being born. How about the white buffalo born in Western Montana in the '50's?"

When prophecy is fulfilled, those who doubt obscure their own perspective with confusion and negativity. Perhaps this color change is meant to test the people who lack faith.

We didn't say too much to the doubters, knowing that in its own time, Miracle's whiteness would return. If their ears weren't open, they wouldn't hear anyway. Sadly, they would miss the opportunity for the renewal of spirit that this discovery had brought into our lives.

But spiritual discovery comes as a gift from the Great Spirit. We don't earn it. We are given it unconditionally, sometimes in return for a prayer or sacrifice we'd made years ago, or perhaps, for a sacrifice from an ancestor, generations ago.

Those understanding that it is time for this Lakȟóta prophesy to be fulfilled have no doubt about Miracle's authenticity. She represents the return of the White Buffalo Calf Maiden. She returned in August – the Moon when the Chokecherries turn Black – the same moon the original maiden had come to the people.

The day Miracle was born was also the fifth day at Green Grass Sun Dance – the day after the four-day ceremony. This was the only day during the entire year that the keeper brings the Sacred Bundle out of its little log house that protects it up on the hill. Wrapped in its buffalo robe, it is placed on its tripod over a bed of sage between prayer flags honoring the Grandfathers of the Four Directions. There the people walk up the hill and humble themselves before Her presence, praying with the Sacred Bundle to have their sacred Pipes blessed.

We knew the timing was right for a miracle. Several years before, the people had commemorated the one hundred-year centenary of the Wounded Knee Massacre. In December 29, 1890, the U.S. Cavalry nearly annihilated Chief Bigfoot's and Sitting Bull's fleeing bands as they sought protection at Pine Ridge Agency.

In December of 1990, descendants huddled together in arctic freezing conditions to complete the Wiping of the Tears ceremony for those ancestors, and to acknowledge the few remaining descendants. They also honored the Bigfoot Riders who, sacrificing health and horses, had just completed the 154-mile horseback ride in -70-degree F. weather. Retracing the frozen steps of those who had fled south after the 1890 murder of Sitting Bull, they huddled in their blankets against the blizzard (that had warmed to -40 degrees) and remembered.

It was during that ride and ceremony that the people realized Black Elk's prophecy had become fulfilled. The seven generations Black Elk had seen in his vision had already suffered severe decline. Some had endured. The next seven generations of Lakȟóta people would now begin to rebuild the culture. A life of harmony and unity would prevail, as this was the time prophesied.

The White Buffalo Calf Maiden returned so the old ways of respect and harmony could be rebuilt among the people in a new way, this time with all races and nations of mankind participating, following the example of the humbled people.

Another sign: Pendleton completed the first White Buffalo Calf blanket at their woolen mill on the day of Miracle's birth. The blanket design included buffalo warriors on horseback on a hunt following the buffalo herd. At the center stands the White Buffalo Calf Maiden and a white buffalo calf.

Lakȟóta ceremonial colors of black, red, yellow and white were used in this legendary blanket. The timing of this prototype was a clear sign. We felt honored to have developed a warm friendship with Bill Nance, the head of Pendleton's Blanket Division. Bill had always brought a natural warmth to his surroundings and Martin felt proud in 1994 when Bill asked him to bless their new Medicine Keeper blanket, a new Pendleton Legendary Blanket design.

No doubts clouded Martin's mind that afternoon. It was as though his life had become fulfilled the moment he came into the presence of the one he had awaited. Mesmerized by her feminine charm, he remembered the Calf Pipe Woman first coming to the people, bringing her gifts, the *Čaŋnúŋpa* – the Sacred Pipe, the seven sacred ceremonies of the people, and a rich, spiritual way of life. Every day during the winter months, he'd waited to see her, prayed for fulfillment of her prophecy, and spoke to our community of the unity she brought to today's world for his people and all peoples.

We spent the balance of the afternoon sitting in the shade under the grove of trees that divided the pastures to the west. On the hillside above us was the rest of their buffalo herd, nineteen in total. On the south side of the path, a small herd of horses grazed, also nineteen in number. They lazily looked our way, seemingly accustomed to daily crowds walking past their fields.

"There are a few of everything here. It's like McDonald's farm!" Martin chuckled. He delighted in the Canadian geese, mallard ducks, white peacocks and other critters that roamed the Heiders' yard. We sat down at the wooden picnic table set out in back of the new pole barn.

Miracle and her three companions spent most of the time in the center of that rectangular field which measured about the size of a football field. A Sweat Lodge fire pit had been dug the previous fall, where Medicine Man Floyd Hand burned prayer flags that had been made to honor Miracle's birth. The fire pit is sacred, as is the ash. She seemed to know this instinctively, as she spent most of her time laying in the ash of that fire pit. For hours on end, she sauntered back to that spot and sat down, facing south, the direction of healing, birth and renewal in the Lakȟóta Medicine Wheel. The color of that direction is white.

We moved down the gravel driveway and followed the fence to the grassy meadow beneath the shade trees. The four buffalo yearlings moved in our direction. They seemed to hover where Martin was sitting in his cart, becoming a society of mutual admiration.

We watched them travel in procession, crossing in front of him. First the three yearling buffalo come in front of him, as if testing the waters like a security team. Miracle then sauntered past him, turning around at the water trough and then stepped up to stop in front of him. Nudged away by the others, she moved on back to her spot in the fire pit. The afternoon passed that way, enriching its meaning as it progressed.

We carried the prayer flags and various gifts from the family that would soon be hanging in thanks from the tree branches west of the field. We prepared the *Čhaŋnúŋpa* for the Pipe ceremony later that afternoon. The four buffalo hovered as I passed the abalone shell around to our small group – Martin, Robert, Katie, Jan, the Heiders – to smudge with sage. We prepared ourselves for the prayer ceremony by purifying body, mind, and spirit with the smoke from the sage. Wafts of smoke drifted into the trees, over the fence toward the buffalo and upward. Our prayers were sent skyward, as though blessed by the buffalo.

Martin put the bowl and stem of his Čhaŋnúŋpa together. He began to fill his Čhaŋnúŋpa with the kinnikinnik – the "tobacco" – the inner bark of the red willow, which he'd always used in his Pipe. Praying in his Lakȟóta language, he thanked the Grandfathers for this day and called upon them to bless the people, especially these caretakers of Miracle. He honored the *Tȟatȟáŋka Oyáte* – the buffalo nation, and asked for blessings for this small herd and for Miracle. He asked that her family be protected from disaster and that his people be blessed.

The buffalo and our small group stood entranced as he continued his prayer, blessing the coming of Miracle and the hope that she brought to the people. He asked help from the Grandfathers, that they would live with health for all the generations, observe silence, help one another, be happy, live with power and respect and honor all of God's creation.

We all offered prayers of thanks in that circle and then we smoked the Pipe. The buffalo seemed to have grown accustomed to ceremony by now. It had become common practice for Indian people to come and pray with the White Buffalo Calf.

Jan said afterwards, "We prayed with the buffalo. They participated with us in ceremony."

Dave Heider had just returned from a long day at work, and joined us in prayer before he set about feeding the herds. He and his wife, Valerie, spoke with Martin for a few minutes as they lingered by the fence. The day was complete.

The Heiders invited us to park our RV by the barn for the night. A waning moon still shone, almost full. I didn't pull the window shade down, instinctively feeling I needed "her" strength to saturate me. I dropped into immediate sleep holding a piece of Mira-

307

cle's fur, feeling "If I hold onto that fur and pray, Martin will have a restful night, free of emergencies."

Just after midnight, the intensity inside the rumpled white fur clutched in my hand awakened me. I prayed again for Martin, moving Miracle's Medicine to a spot underneath my pillow, and immediately fell back to sleep.

Martin woke up at 3:30 A.M. and had a hard time breathing when he returned to bed. The shrill call of the white peacock cut through the silence of the night, and a dog barked in response. It mystified me and yet it made sense that Martin had a harder time breathing when he was close to the sacred. It happened at Devil's Tower and now it was happening at the Heider Ranch. I remembered Momaday again, commemorating the offerings of life and death. *The word sacred and sacrifice are related, and acts of sacrifice make sacred the earth.*

I could not face the truth that his lungs were rapidly depleting. Whenever fear struck, I repeated to myself or others, the reassurance we'd received in ceremony ... that Martin would be able to complete his four-year Sun Dance commitment next year.

The next morning, after coffee, orange juice and a slice of his favorite Home Pride bread with a couple of boiled eggs, Martin took his breathing treatment and prescription medicine and headed back out into the morning sunshine for another visit with Miracle and her family.

The regular breathing treatments were becoming essential. If he didn't take his pharmaceutical remedy of Albuterol every four hours, he became dangerously short of breath.

Our morning routine was becoming a carefully calculated, time-consuming process of thyroid medication, breathing treatment, and herbs to strengthen his immune system, along with a light, low fat breakfast. He could no longer stomach substantial breakfasts even though he still loved to go to IHOP, the "Indian House of Pancakes" for the International Passport breakfast with buttermilk pancakes and strawberry syrup, two eggs over medium and sausage links!

The steroids and other medications he ingested every day seemed to have affected his ability to digest fatty foods. We were unaware that he was developing Transitional Diabetes and that he couldn't eat fat anymore without suffering a breathing attack.

In the mid-morning, Martin came out of the RV. The air was as pleasant as the day before, with a light breeze still blowing from the north. He slowly drove his electric cart along the Heider's driveway to the buffalo yearlings' pasture where, shedding his heavy cocoon, the butterfly once again delighted in fluttering like a breeze around Miracle.

That day, our feminine "Gandhi" had lessons for us in non-aggression. One of the other buffalo seemed more aggressive that day. He walked past her several times so closely that she had to jump up suddenly to avoid being stepped on.

Miracle didn't return the aggression. She jumped up, stepped backwards, and circled her space in clockwise motion. She stood hesitating, then looked toward the south and dropped down into the ash fire pit again. She had avoided conflict by stepping away from it.

It was like Martin had been instructing us to do with the third commandment of quietness. If we could accept her example as a standard in response to others' aggressions, maybe our world, our community, and our family could become more harmonious.

While Martin kept company with Miracle, I took time for Pipe prayers at the fence line among the trees. Sage smudge drifted from my abalone shell, purifying, protecting, as I sent prayers skyward. Sitting in the cool grass, I softly sang the Pipe Loading Song, raising fingerfuls of kinnikinnik in each direction. The stem pointed

Miracle, the white buffalo calf born at the Heider Ranch, Wisconsin, (1994).

West toward the Maiden and this little Miracle as she communed with the elder, the man whose name would soon be shared with her big brother. I sang a song to the Great Spirit, to the Grandfathers and to the four-leggeds. I prayed long and full, not needing to rush. The red willow smoke swirled through the air toward the south. I know they will answer in their own way, in their own time.

We gave Valerie a 25-pound sack of Walla Walla Sweet Onions we'd picked up in Eastern Washington on the first day of our trip. They laughed, amazed at the extra-large size and cut one to taste its famous sweetness. Later, they shared them among the families that were helping care for Miracle.

Before we left, Valerie invited us into their home to view some of the video footage of Miracle taken just after her birth. The family shared that they lived in Rock Township, which was located in Rock County, along the Rock River.

I commented, "How amazing that this buffalo would be born in an area named after *Íŋyaŋ* – the ancient grandfatherm – the rock. That's Martin's spirit name." Katie and I gave tobacco at the Rock River before we left, picking up a few stones to take home as gifts for friends.

As we departed, my mouth dropped open, hearing Martin say to Valerie. "I'll probably be back to see you again in September."

HOME TO THE GRANDMOTHERS

A series of frightening and exhausting night scenes began on the trip home from Wisconsin. Several days out of Wisconsin, we pulled into a Wyoming rest area to sleep for the night. Around 2:30 AM, Martin had another breathing attack returning from the bathroom. His forehead creased from the stress and he began to gasp.

I encouraged him to slow his breathing. The nurse had taught me how to coach him so his lungs could relax and take in fresh air. Our eyes fixed upon each other while I breathed in deeply and slowly through my mouth as though I was breathing for him. Then, pursing my lips, I let the air out slowly, as if slowing his breathing with the force of my own will.

"Blow out slowly between your lips, honey!"

I knelt in front of him to fan and encourage him as oxygen shock began to set in and his legs and arms began to shake uncontrollably from lack of oxygen to the muscles. I fortified my prayers and reassured him again. "Don't be frightened, honey. You'll be alright."

Slowly, painfully slowly, his chest began to relax and his breathing started to recover. When he took over his little red paper fan, I put my hands on his chest to soothe his sore lungs. Moving to the sofa to sit next to him, I put my hands on his back and closed my eyes. After a while, he lied down again. We slept for several more hours before dawn woke us.

At breakfast, I told Katie what had happened. Martin spoke, "Rose, I don't know how much longer I can hold on."

Catching the meaning of his words, Katie says, "Rose, did you hear Martin?" I looked blankly at them and then my eyes dropped to the ground. Katie had struggled through the loss of her son, Mikey, just nine months prior. She had supported her young son until the time came that he was ready to make his transition and she was able to compassionately let him go. She understood Martin and that the time was coming soon when he would no longer endure in his struggle to live.

We drove through Wyoming and onto Crow Reservation where we stopped for a break at Custer's Battlefield Trading Post. I'd planned to call his adopted nephew, Oliver Half, but Martin said, "No, he's busy at work. I don't want to bother him."

One of the Sun Dancers was working at the Trading Post. She let us know Sun Dance had just ended at Crow Agency the day before. Martin was their Medicine Man, but this year he'd advised them to run it without him. They knew his altar and dance movements and how to pierce the warrior to the tree. They had worked with Martin and helped him run that Dance six times since 1989 and had danced in his altar at Mt. Hood Sun Dance.

This helped explain Martin's struggles the past five days. His spirit had been traveling to the Crow Sun Dance. I'd seen it so many times during his sunsetting years. Martin would weaken physically when his spirit handled ceremonial responsibilities.

He'd been cautioned months earlier by Don Alejandro, the Peruvian Shaman, who'd warned Martin to slow down from his spiritual work and not push himself beyond his physical abilities.

The Sun Dancer shared that it had been a good dance and added that a Medicine Man from Sisseton-Wahpeton Oyáte had come from South Dakota to doctor Martin. Since Martin was not there, he'd said prayers for him at the sacred tree and then left. No one knew his name. I immediately flashed back to Martin's brothers at Sisseton.

Traveling east through Watertown on our way to Wisconsin, Martin had suggested we stop at Sisseton to rest up for the night. It was only mid-afternoon and we usually traveled past the dinner hour before we stopped. I wondered if this stop had anything to do with the glittery sign we'd seen a mile back that read "Dakota Prairie Casino" promoting Sisseton Reservation's new gambling casino.

"No," I thought, "it couldn't be." Sure enough, within an hour, we'd headed out to the Dakota Prairie Casino to relax a while and have lunch. Later on, Martin had told me he thought he had seen his adopted brother from the Thompson family. He hadn't seen them for years and I knew he'd missed them. On the way back from Wisconsin, I'd wanted to call them so they could visit, but he said, "No, I don't want them to see me like this."

It was a nice break after miles of driving and everyone was hungry. They were serving potato soup in the cool dining room. The Soup of the Day seemed like such an insignificant thing, but it was a welcome relief to find something he could eat that he enjoyed. His diet had become so limited, compounded by health and his preference for traditional foods. We sat and relaxed and enjoyed the quietness of the dining room. Everything was *wašté* (good) and we were grateful for a peaceful moment and easy breathing.

After eating, he bought me a pair of turquoise earrings, long thin slabs of fragile, cool stone with veins of silver in a natural elongated teardrop.

We then traveled westward through Montana toward Oregon. Martin grew quiet. I knew anxiety was creeping in and that he wondered about nightfall approaching. We made scant progress in miles, winding up in Bozeman. Robert didn't want to risk stopping in the high altitude of the Rocky Mountains up ahead where the air was too thin and dangerous for Martin's lungs. We stopped at an RV park for the night and bought some takeout dinner.

Before she went to bed, Jan said her goodbyes. She was getting up at five in the morning to ride the remainder of the way with friends who were caravanning with us, headed to *Hanbleceya* (Vision Quest) at Four Nations Sun Dance camp. They needed to get to Southern Oregon in time to start their fast that weekend.

This trip had been her gift to Martin and had fulfilled her prayers. Not just the honor of traveling with Uncle Martin to see Miracle, but a family secret had also been revealed to her. Taking a detour to visit her mother in Chicago for a weekend while we visited in Minneapolis, her mother revealed to her that she had Indian ancestry on both sides of her family. (She would later reconnect with her Yanktonai Sioux ancestry and make her pledge as a Sun Dancer).

Around three in the morning, Martin woke me. I turned up his oxygen, and held the oxygen hose so he could back his electric cart into the bathroom. I fanned him until his breathing slowed. He took the fan and I laid back down on the bed to rest a few minutes. When he was ready to get back on his cart, he called me and I got up to help him. He maneuvered his cart back over to his bed on the sofa when another breathing attack began.

As he struggled to breathe, the sense of urgency heightened. Silent prayers and the moving air from his little red paper fan helped a little. We struggled together for what seemed like an eternity as oxygen shock hit, shaking his arms and legs out of control. Careful not to reflect his concern, I reminded him of the nurse's instructions to slow and deepen his breathing.

It was time to call for help. Silently, I said a prayer to his great grandmother, *Hiŋháŋ Makȟóthila*, calling upon her to help us.

How many times over the past two years had I honored her in my prayers-yet did not call upon her to come to his aid, because she had said she would only come three times to save his life. Then the fourth time she would come to take him home. I'd always reminded her in my prayers that we didn't need her right now.

This night, however, was different. Her box with the rattle was nearby and silently, with all her compassion for her special great grandson, she came to help him as she'd said she would.

We laid down to rest, realizing I had now called her twice.

I'd first used her rattle of owl feathers twenty months previously, early January of 1994. Following a Yuwipi ceremony for him in our living room, Martin had given me his piece of raw buffalo kidney to eat and they'd wheeled him back into his bedroom. I was sitting eating it when I heard him call my name. His lungs had shut down and he'd gone into a full-blown breathing attack. I grabbed his favorite red paper fan and started fanning him.

His struggle to breath accelerated. Jeff Walker, a friend who was also a medical doctor, began checking the oxygen in his fingertips and cautioned me.

"Rose, you need to consider Martin's options and call 911."

When Jeff left the room to call 911, I told Martin, "Don't pay attention to that."

I reached into the closet and found the cedar box that held the owl rattle. It had just been blessed in an *Inípi* Sweat Lodge ceremony, waking the spirit of the great grandmother who had been guiding me to care for him. Unwrapping her from the red flannel covering and a protective home on a bed of sage, I took the rattle in my hand and circled his head four times with it. The rattling power of this great grandmother restored his breath.

By the time the ambulance crew rushed into the room a few minutes later, he was breathing again and we knew he would be okay. He was able to stay and rest at home without having to rush to the hospital.

We knew that his great grandmother had now come to his rescue two times to help him. We realized that she would come two more times, the third time to doctor him and the fourth time to take him home.

Martin sitting outside with Chief (1994)..

CHAPTER 15

HOME TO THE GRANDFATHERS

DEATH WAS CREEPING UP ON LIFE

My thoughts lingered upon a coyote I'd seen outside Bozeman the day before. In broad daylight, it was stalking a small herd of deer grazing on the grassy hillside. We drove past them just a mile from the hospital where, the next day, Martin would have another chance at life. They were safe at the moment, but death was creeping up on life.

Martin was so depleted when he woke up that I suggested we drive to the local hospital to ask for something to assist him.

Fear darted through his eyes as he asked, "You aren't going to put me in the hospital, are you?"

I said, "No, honey, but this has been too hard on you. We need to talk to the doctor to see what he can do to help you."

It was fairly early on that warm sunny July morning as we made our way toward Bozeman Deaconess Hospital. I walked inside to the emergency room where it was quiet, empty of emergencies. I asked to speak to the emergency room nurse, explaining to her about his breathing attacks, and that he was asking for help but didn't want to be admitted.

She seemed to understand. She and a second nurse walked outside with me to the door of the RV where Martin was sitting looking drained. The nurse looked up at the weary cowboy, moccasins on his feet, black Wrangler jeans and pale blue striped cowboy shirt buttoned nearly to the top. He acknowledged the nurses, wary of their monstrous White Man's brick building. Chief wagged his upturned tail at them.

She spoke to him with the gentle and patient voice of an angel, undoubtedly accustomed to tough cowboy types who had trouble admitting they needed help. She said "I heard you've been having a hard time breathing these past few days."

"*Ohán!*" he said in Lakȟóta, agreeing with what she was saying. "I'm awfully short of breath."

She told him, "If you would come inside, we would have a better idea of how we can help you."

Slowly considering, he thought of how Dr. Morganroth had helped him back in Portland. He couldn't breathe on his own anymore, so the doctor approved an oxygen prescription, plus pharmaceuticals he now used regularly. This had helped to keep his lung passages open and the White Man's antibiotics cleared up lung infections that had grown so serious. He remembered further back to the early 1970's when he'd been admitted to the Minneapolis VA Hospital to have surgery and recover from cancer in his jaw. He then consented to go inside.

He'd been to the hospital many times over the years to doctor and pray for other people, but he hadn't needed this kind of help for himself. Even when his life was threatened in late 1993 when he'd developed hyperthyroid and they'd diagnosed his progressive emphysema, we nursed him back to health at home on Flavel Drive, where familiar surroundings, the love and the protection of his family, sacred possessions and his Grandfathers were close by.

The hydraulic wheelchair-lift on the passenger side of the RV interrupted the stillness of the morning with a grinding squeak. He rode his cart to the edge of the lift and it slowly lowered him to the ground, leaving cowboy hat and boots by the sofa-bed. The two nurses helped him off the lift, careful not to rush him. They hooked him up to their oxygen tank and wheeled him along the sidewalk through the warm Montana morning air, through the sliding glass doors and into the emergency admitting room.

Robert and Katie parked his RV and waited outside with Chief while I went to the office to complete paperwork and quietly accept their "living will" forms, the first of three times I would receive this for him in the coming months. He never filled out a "living will."

When I walked into the emergency room, Martin was struggling from the strangeness of the surroundings and the extra movements he'd had to make to accommodate hospital personnel. My heart sank when I saw the heavily creased lines on his forehead. I sat down where I wouldn't be in the way of the nurses and covered his hands with mine.

He was hooked onto IV tubing with the intravenous solution of multi-antibiotics and steroids. His arms were taped where they'd drawn blood samples. They had also covered his thin body with warm blankets. We had just traveled through *"a heat wave of heat waves"* that had taken lives all across the Great Plains, so he was chilled from the sterile cold of the cool hospital air.

The respiratory therapist was administering breathing therapy into the air in front of his nose and his mouth. Martin had told the nurses he didn't want a mask on his face, so they held the steam vent in front of his nose. The mixture of liquid and air made a healing steam that he slowly breathed into his lungs, similar to the ventilator he used several times every day.

Looking around the room, the harsh reality of hospital equipment surrounded us. There was IV tubing attached to his slender wrist, oxygen to his nose, beeping sounds that accelerated when his heart rate climbed, red electronic numbers flashing his oxygen reading and heart rate, bright fluorescent lights, shining chrome and that hospital "smell." The monitors unmistakably displayed his heart rate hovering between 135 and 142. Ordinarily his heartbeat registered well below 90, so it frightened me until I remembered that the Grandfathers had said he had a strong heart so I tried not to think about the numbers.

For the next hour, his breath recovered and his heart rate dropped. His expression changed from anxiety into relief and thankfulness. I sat with him through the morning, feeling life might return to the way it was.

After he fell asleep, I walked back outside in the noonday sun to bring the good news to Katie and Robert, that he was breathing easier and resting, unaware that the sight of hospitals would become a familiar sight for the next month.

The doctor arrived and conducted a full exam, asking questions about his condition. For three days they treated him for an acute bronchial infection, exhaustion from travel in the heat and the effects of high altitude. (Montana rises as much as a mile higher than Oregon's sea level altitude so we were grateful for their experience working with high altitude sickness).

The doctor confided in us that they'd planned to transfer him to the Intensive Care Unit, but he had responded so quickly to the inhalation therapy of Albuterol and Ventolin. "...like a sixteen-year-old!" the nurse added. This was not just because he'd rarely used pharmaceuticals, but also because of his spiritual strength and the support of his ancestors.

They transferred him to a regular hospital room and rolled in a cot for me. During his afternoon naps, Katie and I began a ritual of feasting on homemade sticky buns in the hospital cafeteria. Katie, still in her year of grieving since her son Mikey's passing, had endured similar crises, nurturing her boy through twenty-one years of medical emergencies.

Martin missed Chief. Our second evening at the hospital, Katie and Robert smuggled him in to see him, with help from the swing shift nurse. She knew it was against hospital regulations, but said the best time to try was in the calmness of the evening right after dinner.

Chief seemed withdrawn despite attention and lots of walks with Robert and Katie. For three years, Martin and his dog had been inseparable. Chief loved to run off and explore, but always rushed at top speed back to Martin's feet where he would lay for long periods of time. When Martin put his feet up on the bed, Chief would jump up to sleep at his feet. That was their daily way of life at home or on the road. Today, in the hospital, Chief couldn't master the jump up onto the high hospital bed without a lift. Once there, he wiggled his eleven pounds of fur and swung his white tail all over himself.

After three days, they released Martin to return home. Buying expensive medicine in the pharmacy as we departed, we realized it was a small price to pay. Jubilant over our freedom, we headed home, grateful that the American medical system had allowed him to recover in Bozeman and return home to Portland. We looked forward to a good night's rest and a few peaceful days of summer remaining.

THE SECOND HOSPITAL STAY

The exhaustion from the trip and the deterioration of his lungs made it hard for him to have a lot of company, but we never turned friends away. Someone came asking for a spirit name, not knowing the game of life and death he was playing. His house guests that had known him for years, found out he'd been in the hospital and came to visit. He had watched their children and grandchildren grow up and been their Medicine Man since the 1970's.

A few weeks later, two brothers made some medicine for Martin and brought it to the house for him to drink. On their second visit, after drinking the golden-colored tea, he buzzed me on the intercom. I came into the room and felt a sense of urgency in the air. Martin was showing signs of confusion.

"Fan me!" he said, his eyes weary. It was unusual for him to have a breathing attack in the daytime. They usually came in the middle of the night. I began to fan him.

The brothers leaned forward, staring intensely. I ignored their stares, working with Martin to recover his breath while I called for Jerry. When he came into the room, I asked him to turn up the oxygen. Crawling behind Martin, he put his hands on his back and began to move the mucus from his lungs. His hands eventually removed the blockage, but that day it would be a while before his breathing eased.

Martin turned to the men, and said "*Tókšta!*" ("see you later"). He knew they were on their way out of town and that there wasn't much they could do to help him.

They took the buffalo horn half full of medicine, emptied it back into the Mason jar of golden brown liquid. They left the buffalo horn and the medicine with us and departed for South Dakota.

After they left, Martin was still not recovering. He looked at me with a deeply furrowed forehead and heavy concern in his eyes. His attacks were going on much longer than usual and I could tell his lungs were weary of breathing. His heart rate would go so high during these attacks, escalating his need for oxygen. I softly told him everything was going to be alright.

I asked Jerry to go get my little cedar box wrapped in red flannel and sage in the back of the bedroom closet. He knew about the box and brought it into the room.

Martin's breath recovered. I didn't even have to take the rattle out of the box. She came to his aid, the third of three times she said she would come to save his life before the fourth time when she said she would take him home.

Relieved, we looked out the south window to see a ruby-throated hummingbird, dressed in the spirit colors of the Grandfathers with its glowing fiery-red throat and iridescent green robe. He hovered around the bird feeders hanging from the branches outside, as if searching for the *Wóphila*, the thanksgiving feast to celebrate the healing. Then he darted away toward the south, the direction of healing. Thankful that Martin had recovered, Jerry drove to the store and returned with two hummingbird feeders to hang outside the window.

His lungs were sore after his breathing attack, requiring rest and more antibiotics. Later that day, a fever developed. I called the doctor on call who asked us to wait for our own doctor to return the following morning. For the remainder of that evening, we kept his fever under control using Tylenol.

If his inhalation therapy was late, he would be short of breath, so I purchased a timer to keep his treatments on schedule and check his temperature. I gave him Tylenol again and rechecked his temperature as I headed to bed around 11 P.M. At 1 A.M., I got up to take his temperature. It was normal so I went back to bed, setting the alarm for three hours ahead.

Around 4 A.M., the buzzer sounded. I turned it off quickly so it wouldn't disturb his sleep. I found the digital thermometer and gently slipped it between his lips, then beneath his tongue.

I whispered to him, "It's just me, honey. I'm checking your temperature again." He lay there, half-asleep, quiet, his breathing slightly labored. While I waited for the thermometer beep, I touched his hand, silently telling him he was being watched out over and protected by the Grandfathers.

Horror struck my heart as I saw his fever had climbed to 102 degrees. Soon he would be struggling to breathe. I had to ask, "Honey, you need to take more Tylenol." I prayed to the Grandfathers that those two little Tylenol would keep his fever under control until the doctor returned.

He was taught that people never complain, and they never cry unless they have lost a loved one. He would sometimes express concern, but usually he was quiet, having been taught not to disappoint others with his own disappointment.

His Third Hospital Stay

By dawn the next morning, with his doctor's approval, and with his temperature climbing past 104 degrees, I asked Jerry, our housemate, to call 911 again. Within minutes, the ambulance arrived. We traveled to the hospital's emergency room and on to Intensive Care. The doctor arrived immediately. He didn't expect Martin to survive the day and he wanted me to be prepared.

In the Intensive Care Unit, Martin responded to the IV medications. His fever subsided and his breathing improved. Dr. Morganroth examined the x-rays and told me it was pneumonia. It had lodged in a new spot on the left side of his lungs.

Once again, he tried to prepare me that Martin was not going to make it much longer. I listened politely.

During the evening while I was sitting with Martin, they paged us to say that a friend had come by and was in the ICU waiting room. I went out to see Greg standing there with some tobacco ties and two small eagle feathers in his hand. He said something had told him to bring them to Uncle. I gratefully accepted his prayers and his offerings of love and took them in to Martin.

This time, Martin asked me to remove them from his room, that he didn't want feathers and tobacco ties close by, as nurses could be in their moon time (menstrual cycle) and that could make him even more seriously ill. When Maja came by, I asked her to take them home.

That was the only night in all our hospital stays that I slept away from him, since hospital policy did not permit cots in ICU. I slept on the sofa in the waiting room, waiting for daylight to come.

During the night, a young woman came in. She sat there, brooding, sad. Pretty soon, a doctor came out to talk to her about her father. He'd had a stroke in the night and had been admitted to ICU. It didn't sound encouraging, but the doctors were still exploring his options, and invited the woman to come in to sit with him.

I got up, washed my face in the restroom and, after grabbing a cup of coffee, I headed back into Martin's hospital room. He had just sent someone out looking for me and I wasn't in the waiting room, so he had grown anxious. When I came in, I was so happy to see him. I sat close, holding his hand. He was breathing good. Pretty soon, they brought breakfast in for him. He ate a small bit of his meal and some juice.

Life support equipment in the room totally surrounded us and the monitors overhead occupied our complete attention. His signs were stable. We seemed hypnotized by the monitors showing his heart rate and rhythm; his blood pressure; his temperature. It was all over his bed, flashing information in bright red and green colors.

Doctor Morganroth came in and told us Martin's immune system was very low. The bloodwork showed that his white and his red counts were the lowest he'd seen in Martin's records. He recommended a blood transfusion, and ordered two units to be administered that afternoon, trusting it would build his red blood count and allow him to fight this ugly disease that the x-rays had uncovered.

Pretty soon, bells were sounding and alarms were going off and nurses rushed into our room. Martin's signs were stable, but something was setting off the alarm system, making a lot of racket. Whenever the alarm sounded, the printer in the office was programmed to print vital information for the doctors.

The nurse brought a computer programmer in the room to reprogram the equipment so it wouldn't keep setting off the alarm and kicking in the printer. We heard her complain to the programmer, "His signs are stable, but it keeps going off and the printer is using up all our paper in the office." The programmer worked for a while before she was able to get the diagnostic equipment under control.

I looked at Martin, and teased him. "Honey, are your Grandfathers playing with the electronics?" He looked at me and chuckled, appreciating the reminder that his spirit helpers were around and protecting him.

More warnings were delivered by the doctors who would call me into the hallway where they'd say, "Rose, Martin has very little time to be with us."

"Well," I would say, "the Grandfathers have told us that Martin will be here to fulfill his four-year Sun Dance commitment next year."

Martin stabilized and they moved him back to the Respiratory Unit that afternoon. Room 2R40 was a remote, out-of-the-way room around the corner at the end of the hallway. I wondered why they had placed us out of the way, as though they'd expected him to die there out of the way from the others.

From then on, he didn't want me to leave his room, fearing something would happen. I would go out for a cup of coffee or to take a shower down the hallway, and invariably something would happen. X-ray personnel would come for x-rays, moving him and causing a breathing attack, or the doctors would come to discuss his condition, but he wanted me to talk to them and make decisions for him about the medicines.

Technicians came in to get chest x-rays. Martin had large and deep lungs and several times they didn't get his entire lung area, so they had to come in and repeat the entire procedure. Martin pleaded with the doctor who'd come in not to rush him. They agreed to hold off the x-rays for a few minutes until Martin could catch his breath and get into position.

IV injections of morphine helped him endure the x-rays and breathing attacks. Dr. Morganroth had administered morphine to him in the emergency room a few days earlier when his breathing attack intensified. Relief came to him almost immediately and he was able to slow his breathing and heart rate and relax a little.

Peaceful moments would come in the afternoons at the hospital after morning lab tests, x-rays and doctor visits were completed. Then he would rest. One afternoon, as I sat quietly by his bedside, he looked up past my shoulder. I watched his expression soften. I looked over my right shoulder in the corner but saw nothing. He'd seen a spirit behind me.

Chuckling, he said to me, "She must be a nurse."

Later that day, I heard Indian drumming in 2R41, across the hall. I remarked to Martin how beautiful it sounded and he smiled radiantly at me. An older woman had just been transferred into the room. We'd seen the sweetness in her grandmotherly expression as they wheeled her in the hospital bed to and from the x-ray facility.

I'd heard the family telling her they weren't going to allow her to go into a nursing home. They were going to take care of her at home but within 24 hours, she had passed away. Pain bolted through my heart hearing her family sobbing while they removed her possessions from the empty room. They had headed home briefly to complete some errands and she passed away while they were gone. I remember seeing the Respiratory Therapist standing at the nurse's station later, discouraged, shaking his head. He'd tried to save her, but it was too late.

Late the next night, I heard a frightened nurse call out a "Code 99" emergency alert in room 2R49, across the hall and down one room. Personnel came running down our hallway at top speed to the room. It turned out to be a false alarm.

The latest lab tests showed Martin had developed a deadly strain of pneumonia, Xanthomonas Maltophilia. It had no cure except a sulfa product that Martin had shown allergic reactions to while serving in World War II. In response, Dr. Morganroth called in an infectious disease team to custom formulate a special antibiotic that his system might tolerate.

Hearing this diagnosis, I began to make phone calls to his family to consult with them. I spoke to his sister Melda and Eddie, his son. Eddie immediately made plans to head west to Oregon with his wife Midge, their granddaughter Vanessa, and Leonard, Martin's youngest son.

I began to have night frights over his fevers and night sweats. I would wake up startled, fearing that a new fever was developing and that the personnel couldn't respond in time. A weekend relief nurse from Nicaragua working the night shift then showed me how to bring down his temperature using iced water on a washcloth which she put on his forehead and under his armpits. It would help while waiting for the Tylenol to reduce his fever. The night sweats soaked his bed sheets and his gown, so I would help the nurse change his hospital gown and bedding.

The day we'd left the Heider Ranch where Miracle lived, Valerie Heider, with tears in her eyes, had told us of the man whose life had been saved because his sister had put the picture of Miracle under his pillow and prayed. In a state of wonder at Miracle's power, she'd handed me the letter from the Cherokee woman. I read it to Martin.

The letter said that she'd been to see Miracle earlier in the summer and had gotten a postcard with Miracle's picture on it. Her brother was in the hospital for open-heart surgery, but in the operating room, they'd accidentally nicked his heart muscle and he started hemorrhaging. The surgeon felt they couldn't complete the open-heart surgery, so they patched him back up and advised the family. They told the family he would probably die in the night. The sister took Miracle's picture postcard and put it under her brother's pillow. She prayed all night to the Buffalo Calf that her brother's life would be spared. When he woke up in the morning, they realized he had survived. He didn't bleed to death. His cut healed and within a few days they successfully finished the open-heart surgery.

Valerie said they were starting to get letters like that from people all over the country. She was astounded at the power of this little one. After hearing the story, Martin told her, "If you take good care of that animal and treat it right, millions of people will be healed by it." He went on to say, "People will come from all over the world to be healed by this animal, if you treat it right."

As they began to administer the custom intravenous sulfa product, I took the photograph of Miracle, the white buffalo calf, from Martin's bulletin board in the hospital and tucked it under his pillow, along with the little piece of her white fur. I wrapped the rock in the red cloth gifted to Martin by the Heider's that Miracle had nudged with his nose, and put it in a box with sage and put it underneath Martin's bed.

When hospital personnel started administering intravenous sulfa, I asked friends to start a community phone tree to advise the community of his condition. Visitors began to stream to the hospital and we began to get phone calls, not only at the house but at the hospital. Family and friends began to arrive from all over the country, including Martin's sons. We started all-night vigils in his room to detect any early sign of allergic reaction.

No allergic reaction developed. He was able to tolerate the sulfa formulation, and his last chest x-ray showed 30% recovery from the pneumonia deep inside his left lung.

The nurses had grown fond of Martin and decided that he could rest more comfortably and breathe easier if they moved us across the hall from our south-facing room where the summer sun was heating his room. The northern exposure made his room cooler. Then to ease his discomfort, they moved a special bed into his room that had become available. It was programmed to adjust positions slightly and take pressure off of different spots on his left side, the only side he was able to lay on.

Back at our home, Martin's family was staying. His granddaughter, Vanessa, told us that the spirits began playing with the electronics in his room. She'd seen the television go off or on several times and it had frightened her.

Maja was also at home, cleaning our bedroom when the television turned on by itself showing a promotion for the Mike Tyson fight. Martin, who had learned to box during military service in World War II, spoke of that boxing match a few times. It was Tyson's first scheduled fight in 1995 after being released from prison. The boxing match was that night, but the chance of him seeing the match seemed remote.

Maja heard Martin speak of it and after the television aired the Tyson promo, she thought, "OK, I can take a hint."

She ordered the fight and recorded it on a VCR. She and Jerry brought the video down to the hospital later that evening and he was able to watch Tyson knock out his opponent in the first round. Martin chuckled that he had just gotten out of prison and apparently wasn't wasting time getting back in the ring.

The next afternoon, Martin had just recovered from a persistent nosebleed. Since his oxygen counts were dropping, they had turned up his oxygen which caused his nose to dry out and he would get the nosebleeds.

I was sitting holding his hand while he slept. I could see he was dreaming. When he awakened, he looked up at me and said, "I'm so glad to be back!"

I realized he'd been on the edge of the Spirit World close to his loved ones. Despite all his suffering, he seemed to be attached to being here. He had a strong will to live. All the ancestors he loved were greeting him from the other side, yet he came back.

I thought, "Oh, my God! That's the most beautiful thing you could say to me."

Peruvian Shaman Don Alejandro had taught us about Martin's will to live. He said that the spirit yearns for the Father, the Great Spirit, and the body yearns for the Mother, Mother Earth. It is from this attachment to both the Mother and the Father, that we derive our spiritual balance. He explained that Martin was especially attached to the Mother and to being with us.

They also put a mask on his face to increase the flow of incoming oxygen. Later the nurse began to advise us that nothing was coming from his lungs, that they could no longer hear air moving through his lungs. Frustrated with my sense of hope, she then said, "Rose, why won't you let him go?"

I had to tell her that as long as I could see him struggling to stay with us, I needed to support him in his struggle.

The respiration therapy sessions began to provoke breathing attacks, so they began to administer morphine. An occasional overdose of extra morphine administered during a breathing treatment caused him to have daytime terrors. He would be laying there with so little energy left when suddenly he would look over my right shoulder and scream out, perhaps seeing a spirit in the room.

Katie was sitting with him, holding his hand, when he had his last terror. I grabbed a branch of cedar we had hanging from the four directions on the hospital wall. A Crow Medicine Man had taught me how to smudge him without smoke using cedar branches. I put the wand of cedar up to the four directions and then brushed him with it head to toe. Katie saw something shutter all the way down his body, sweep over the bottom of his feet, and leave him, exiting through the west wall.

The night of the fourth Pipe ceremony outside Martin's window, I walked out in the hall and slumped down onto a chair, bewildered and confused. I had lost my strength to support his fight. Realizing he was no longer able to breath and that he was ready to depart, I began to accept the inevitable.

We had been asked not to drum outside the hospital window that night, because it was a little later in the evening than the other nights so they held the Pipe ceremony farther away from the hospital. "A large circle formed that night, encircling a tree on the lawn," Katie said. She went on to share: "It almost seemed as though we were at Sun Dance circling the Sun Dance Tree." As Katie looked around, she saw someone cry. Almost as a wave flowing around the circle, each individual, one after the other, began crying. When it came to Katie, she cried. It was hard to sing the Sun Dance songs because everyone was grieving.

When the Čaŋnúŋpa came around the circle, everyone could see it was Martin's Čaŋnúŋp. It was almost like Martin's spirit had come out to them and consoled every soul in the circle, and that his spirit came to say, "Don't be sad. I will be alright." As they smoked his Pipe, they regained their strength and the Sun Dance songs started strong again. All the way around the circle, from friend to friend, strength came back to the people to sing for him.

I had always stayed up in the hospital room with him during the Pipe ceremonies, but this time I realized it was time to come down to thank the friends. I asked if everyone could come upstairs into his room and pay their respects, so everyone came upstairs to see him one last time.

It was almost 4:30 am, nearly dawn, when Martin's great grandmother came into the room. She moved overhead like a moth flying, hitting the ceiling several times and then she disappeared. Martin stirred and I felt him slip away. Stunned, I looked up at the clock and remembered the broken clock on the side of the highway outside of Bear Butte, frozen in time at 4:23. Later, the nurse came into the room and confirmed he had begun his journey. The hospital would register the time of his passing as 4:40 am.

IN RETROSPECT

After his passing, the Heider's eulogized Martin in a letter to me, a rare surprise. They sent good news, that they had purchased Miracle's older brother from a rancher in January. This special opportunity would never come again since Miracle's father had died in 1994, just one day before the birth of Miracle. The father's death seemed to symbolize the sacrifice or gift needed for the miracle to occur.

They continued to state in their letter regarding the older brother of Miracle, "In trying to come up with a name and keeping with the M's, a family decision was made to give him the name Martin High Bear, in honor of Martin. We felt that was the greatest honor we could give them both."

They went on to speak about meeting Martin, "This was such a privilege and honor, it's hard to put into words. His wisdom gave us so much information and his powerful energy made us all feel more in touch with our Creator. He talked and we listened to his words of wisdom."

They continued, "We knew when he left the farm that we would see him again, if not on this side, then on the other side. His spirit is in our prayers. We think and talk about his great knowledge often."